JUSTICE IN PRIVATE LAW

This book discusses the dominant corrective justice and distributive justice approaches to private law and identifies their strengths and weaknesses. It goes on to propose a general approach to private law, including contract, tort and private property, and explains how this approach can provide solutions to some longstanding problems.

Two general ideas inform this approach: the 'standpoint limitation' and 'remedial consistency'. The standpoint limitation explains the distinctive character of private law, that is to say why it is focused mainly, though not exclusively, on particular individual interests rather than the common welfare. Remedial consistency explains the way in which remedies depend on and give effect to primary rights.

The book also discusses the nature of common law legal reasoning and its relationship to the suggested understanding of private law.

Volume 43 in the series Hart Studies in Private Law

Justice in Private Law

Peter Jaffey

• HART •
OXFORD • LONDON • NEW YORK • NEW DELHI • SYDNEY

HART PUBLISHING

Bloomsbury Publishing Plc

Kemp House, Chawley Park, Cumnor Hill, Oxford, OX2 9PH, UK

1385 Broadway, New York, NY 10018, USA

29 Earlsfort Terrace, Dublin 2, Ireland

First published in Great Britain 2023

A catalogue record for this book is available from the British Library.

A catalogue record for this book is available from the Library of Congress.

ISBN: HB: 978-1-50995-388-2
ePDF: 978-1-50995-390-5
ePub: 978-1-50995-389-9

Typeset by Compuscript Ltd, Shannon

ACKNOWLEDGEMENTS

I am grateful to the Leverhulme Trust for the award of a Major Research Fellowship 2020–22, which enabled me to write this book (and to avoid online teaching through the Covid lockdown).

Some of the ideas and arguments in the book are drawn from earlier work (as cited). Some paragraphs from 'Policy and Principle and the Character of Private Law' (2020) 11 *Jurisprudence* 387, available at https://www.tandfonline.com/, are reproduced in Chapter 6, for which I acknowledge permission from the publishers Taylor & Francis.

I presented some material from the book to the Private Law Research Cluster at Leicester Law School in October 2022, and at a Law School Research Seminar at Bristol Law School in November 2022. I am grateful to the participants for their comments. I am also grateful to Francois Du Bois, Greg Allan, Alison Slade, Patrick Masiyakurima, Paula Giliker and John Murphy for reading and commenting on parts of the book.

I would like to thank the staff of Hart Publishing for their work in bringing the book to publication.

Finally, as ever I would like to thank my family.

CONTENTS

ABBREVIATIONS

EAL	economic analysis of law
MTL	moral theory of law
STL	socio-legal theory of law

1

Introduction

Private Law

Private law is the law applicable as between individuals, by which one person enforces a legal right against another through civil proceedings. The main areas are contract, tort and private property: in contract, rights arising from agreements for the exchange of goods or services for payment; in tort, rights with respect to harm to or interference with person or property, including inadvertent harm in negligence; and, in private property, rights with respect to things, including land, personal property, and, it is widely thought, intangible property, including intellectual property and money. By virtue of these bilateral legal rights, an 'interaction' between individuals, such as a contract or the failure to perform a contract, or an accident, or a transfer of property, can have the legal effect of creating a new bilateral right, including a remedial right or claim, usually a claim for compensation. Thus one can also say that private law is the law of interactions between individuals.

There are two rival schools of thought in the literature on private law, which I shall refer to as the corrective justice and distributive justice approaches. On the corrective justice approach, the bilateral legal relations of private law are based exclusively on the bilateral or interpersonal moral rights of the parties to an interaction: the claimant (C) and the defendant (D). On the distributive justice approach, the justification of private law is in the contribution it makes to justice with respect to benefits and harms of people across society. The standard though not the only version of the distributive justice approach is the 'economic analysis of law' (EAL), which holds that private law should serve to maximise the aggregate welfare or net benefit associated with interactions. In this book, I assess the strengths and weaknesses of the corrective justice and distributive justice approaches, and then I suggest a new approach.

The Characteristic Features of Traditional Private Law

It is helpful to begin with the distinctive features of what one might describe as 'traditional private law'. It may be open to question whether these features continue to characterise private law and whether they ought to, but describing them is a good way to outline the subject matter and the issues that divide the opposing theoretical approaches. The corrective justice approach appears to provide a better account of these characteristic features than the distributive justice approach, though as considered further in chapter two this is not necessarily the crucial issue in evaluating them.

Bilateral Relations

Private law establishes bilateral legal relations between two parties, C and D. As conventionally understood, these bilateral relations consist of a right of C against D and a correlative duty owed by D to C. The relation is correlative in the sense that C's right and D's duty are the same thing expressed from opposite viewpoints: one can describe the law equivalently in terms of C's right and D's duty. In contract, C's right to performance of the contract by D is correlated with a duty on D's part to provide the performance, and in negligence C has a right to a certain standard of care by D, and D has a correlative duty to meet the standard for C's benefit. In property law, the owner C has a right against interference with C's use and possession of the property and D has a correlative duty not to commit such interference.

On the traditional understanding associated with the corrective justice approach, the bilateral rights of private law are apt because they represent 'justice as between the parties' or interpersonal justice. The bilateral relations are a natural feature of private law in the sense that they reflect and give effect to underlying interpersonal moral rights of the parties to the dispute. For some commentators at least, on the corrective justice approach private law is a manifestation or extension of the ordinary personal morality that governs personal and social interactions between individuals.[1] For example, the rationale of the law of negligence is to give effect to the moral right of C against D not to be harmed by D's negligent conduct.

By contrast, on the distributive justice approach, private law is concerned with justice with respect to benefits and harms across society as a whole. The rationale of the law of negligence is to reduce the damage or injury caused by accidents in society, or to spread losses across society to reduce the burden imposed on particular individuals (or some such public or societal purpose). The bilateral legal rights of the parties do not represent justice as between the parties or interpersonal moral rights. Rather than being a necessary and intrinsic feature of private law, they are a device for promoting a societal purpose to which the parties' own interests may be incidental. It would seem that bilateral legal rights have come to be recognised only because the law developed through civil proceedings between the parties to an interaction. This approach is at odds with the traditional understanding of private law and may favour departures from traditional private law. Indeed the implication is that the objectives of private law might often be better achieved through a different sort of legal regime that does not take the form of bilateral relations enforced through civil proceedings, for example a regime that provides

[1] See J Gardner, *From Personal Life to Private Law* (Oxford University Press, 2018).

for compensation for accidents through a compensation fund or even government allocation of goods and services rather than private exchange by contract.

Conventionally the bilateral relation is understood to consist of C's right correlated with a duty on the part of D, and accordingly C's claim arises from a breach of duty or wrong by D (I equate 'wrong' and 'breach of duty'). However, the law does not always seem to reflect the idea that C's claim arises from a wrong by D. For example, sometimes D's supposed primary duty requires D to do something that it is impossible for D to do, or in committing the wrong D's action is something that he is entitled to do. That C's claim can arise without a breach by D of a duty to C, if this is the case, is taken to support the distributive justice approach, since it is taken to imply that the justification for the claim is not a matter of interpersonal justice between C and D.

Primary and Remedial Relations

C's claim is a right to a remedy. The remedy is what the court requires from D for the benefit of C at the conclusion of the proceedings (if C is successful), typically an order for compensation, but sometimes an order to perform or not to perform an action, ie an injunction or order of specific performance.

It is convenient to distinguish between the primary relation and the remedial relation. The primary relation subsists before the claim arises, and it determines the circumstances in which a claim will arise. In negligence, the primary relation is the duty of care and the correlative right, and in contract it is the duty of performance and the correlative right. The remedial relation is the claim – the right to a remedy – correlated with a remedial duty or liability, which arises when D commits a breach of duty.

The relationship between primary and remedial relations is unclear: do the right to a remedy, and the type of remedy to which C is entitled, follow directly and logically from the primary right, so that they are in effect already implicit in the primary right, or are they independent of the primary right and dependent on a new set of considerations, which form the basis for a distinct body of remedial rules? These are the rival positions sometimes described as remedial monism and dualism. One can find support for both approaches in the case law and literature. The claim for compensation is generally understood to follow automatically in the event of a breach of duty, but the availability of specific performance or an injunction is often taken to depend on a new set of considerations, and is sometimes understood to be a matter for judicial discretion.

This issue is related to another contentious issue: why does a right to compensation arise at all? It is often said that the justification is the principle of moral responsibility that a wrongdoer should correct the wrong, but this seems unsatisfactory because it is implausible to think that D is generally morally responsible for the harm for which D is legally liable in private law. Indeed, as mentioned already, it is open to question whether a claim generally arises from a wrong by D at all.

The uncertainty over how remedies, and in particular the right to compensation, arise from primary rights, and about whether, or in what sense, claims arise from wrongs, raises doubts about the traditional understanding of private law and difficulties for the corrective justice approach.

Remedies not Sanctions (or Other Non-remedial Responses)

Any measure ordered by the court at the conclusion of proceedings may be described as a remedy, but it is helpful to distinguish between remedies in the strict sense, and non-remedial responses, including sanctions. A remedy in the strict sense is a measure that serves to protect C's primary right by mitigating or reversing so far as possible the effects of the infringement of C's right, typically by compensating C for the harm C has suffered. By contrast, a sanction serves the public interest by protecting not C's primary right but the rights of others in the same position as C in the future, through the effect of the sanction on D in deterring other people in a comparable position to D from committing a similar wrong, and possibly also by incentivising people in a comparable position to C to take proceedings to secure a sanction.

The traditional position is that private law provides remedies in this strict sense rather than sanctions. In particular, compensation is understood as a remedy in this sense. It seems natural to understand civil proceedings as designed in this way to enable C to protect C's own primary right by securing a remedy. This reflects the corrective justice idea that the legal relations of private law reflect underlying interpersonal moral rights, since a remedy simply serves to protect C's right against D. On the corrective justice approach, there is thus a close connection between the bilateral character and the remedial character of private law. This is why the expression 'corrective justice' is apt for what it might seem preferable to refer to as the 'interpersonal justice' approach. This is not to say that remedies do not actually operate to influence people's behaviour in the future, but on this view that is not their rationale. This understanding is consistent with the fact that punitive damages as a response to a wrong are not normally available. Punitive damages are clearly not a remedy: what C receives through a punitive measure is merely incidental so far as its rationale is concerned, and it is a windfall to C.

On the distributive justice approach, under which private law is justified in terms of its effect on society at large and not in terms of bilateral moral rights, it would seem that the measures dispensed by courts should be understood in terms of their effect as sanctions in influencing the behaviour of people generally, rather than as remedies in the strict sense. On this understanding, even compensation may be understood as a sanction rather than a remedy.[2]

[2] A measure can be non-remedial without being a sanction, eg a measure intended to provide compensation through loss spreading, as considered in ch 4.

Objectivity

Traditional private law is 'objective' or impersonal in its characterisation of individuals. It judges each person under a 'reasonable person' standard with respect to what that person is expected to do or know or how that person will be affected by harms or benefits, regardless of individual strengths and weaknesses. The law of negligence turns on whether D reached a 'reasonable person' standard, which does not depend on what D is personally capable of or knows or intends. Similarly, in contract, the test of agreement is whether the parties would be understood by a reasonable observer to have reached agreement and the contract terms are generally understood as a reasonable observer would have understood them, irrespective of the parties' true intentions or actual knowledge or understanding.

This may be thought justified because it treats people, at least in a sense, as equals – this is the position taken on the corrective justice approach – but, at the same time, for private law not to differentiate between people according to their actual intentions or knowledge or their actual strengths or weaknesses may seem to involve a crude approximation, or even a fiction.

Focus on the Particular Parties

On the traditional understanding, which reflects the corrective justice approach, the rules of private law appear to be generally concerned only with the particular interaction and the particular parties' relationship and their interests. They do not generally depend on the wider ramifications of the interaction or on the effects of that type of interaction across society. The standard of care in negligence is traditionally understood to reflect a balance between C's interest against suffering harm and D's interest in freely conducting the activity that gave rise to the harm, rather than on what would be best to reduce accidents and accident costs across society more widely. In contract, it is the interests of the contracting parties in making and performing the contract that are relevant, not the public interest in the practice of contracting. This feature of the law is expressed in various ways. It is sometimes said, particularly in connection with the law of negligence, that the law is concerned with matters of interpersonal justice or rights rather than with matters of community welfare or social goals or the common good or the public interest. Sometimes it is said, apparently to the same effect, that the law is concerned with principle and not policy or with legal policy and not public policy. The implication is that the law does not draw on 'policy analysis', as it is sometimes described, meaning the analysis of the effects of possible rules across society as a whole, drawing on social and economic theory and knowledge, based on empirical evidence.

This restriction again reflects the corrective justice approach that private law simply gives effect to interpersonal moral rights based on personal morality rather than being concerned with harms and benefits across society more widely. Commentators who favour a version of the distributive justice approach are liable to suggest that there is no such restriction in private law, or that if there is it ought to be abandoned. In fact, although there does seem to be a limitation in the law along these lines, it does not seem to be as strict as the corrective justice approach would require, and the law does not seem to reflect either the corrective justice approach or the distributive justice approach.

Private Law as Common Law

Private law in its traditional form developed through the common law, by virtue of the authority of the decisions made by judges in adjudication. It appears to have arisen through common law legal reasoning by precedent and analogy and to be distinctive of the common law. It seems that analogical reasoning, where the court decides a case in the same way as a previous case that is considered equivalent, is supportive of the corrective justice approach because it involves a focus on the interaction and the parties' relationship, and excludes policy analysis. Proponents of EAL and the distributive justice approach are liable to think that traditional common law reasoning is misguided insofar as it hinders the development of the law to give effect to distributive justice.[3] When the legislature legislates to reform private law, it draws on distributive justice. It does not, of course, use common law reasoning to decide on the content of the legislation, and it can certainly use policy analysis. Law created by legislation may not show the characteristic features of traditional private law. In particular, it may not even take the form of bilateral relations – for example, negligence law might be replaced by a form of public compensation fund for accident victims. Even where the legislature retains bilateral relations, it may abandon other features of traditional private law, for example where it introduces a mandatory regime in contract for the benefit of a sector of the population, on the basis of policy analysis.

It is said that on the corrective justice approach private law is autonomous, in the sense that the interpersonal morality concerning interactions that it draws on is distinct from the political morality of legislation, which is a matter of distributive justice. Thus when judges decide how to develop the law they are not engaging in the same sort of exercise as the legislature when it decides how to reform private law. On the distributive justice approach, there is no such distinction in principle between judicial development and legislative reform. It seems to be generally accepted, even by proponents of the corrective justice approach who think that judges should preserve private law in its traditional form in the common law, that it is legitimate and even desirable for the legislature to reform the law to promote distributive justice in this way, but it is not clear that this is a consistent position.

[3] See eg L Kaplow and S Shavell, *Fairness versus Welfare* (Harvard University Press, 2006) ch II.

The Corrective Justice and Distributive Justice Approaches

The main source of theoretical disagreement over private law is between the distributive justice and corrective justice approaches. The corrective justice approach tends to support traditional private law and purports to account, on the whole, for the characteristic features identified above, in particular bilateral relations. It treats the justice of private law as a matter of interpersonal justice or interpersonal moral rights as against each other of the individuals involved in an interaction, and it holds that in consequence a claim arises from a breach of duty or wrong that gives rise to a remedy in the strict sense to protect C's right. It appears to explain the focus on the parties' relationship and the exclusion of other considerations, and it appears to accord with traditional common law legal reasoning. The distributive justice approach by contrast rejects the idea that the bilateral relations of private law are based on interpersonal moral rights and tends to regard the other features of traditional private law as artificial. It accepts the possibility that justice might be better achieved in some other way that does not conform to traditional private law and may not even involve bilateral relations.

The two rival approaches have quite different visions of private law. Although they do not necessarily lead to different outcomes in particular cases, in some cases the differences emerge explicitly. Over time the two approaches would tend to take private law in quite different directions.

In modern times, the theoretical controversy over private law seems to have begun with the emergence of EAL, which prompted the development of modern corrective justice theory by way of response, broadly with the aim of vindicating the traditional understanding of private law. Corrective justice theory was developed principally with respect to tort law and negligence in particular,[4] and the equivalent reaction to EAL in contract was 'contract as promise',[5] which I treat as a version of the corrective justice approach.

Both the corrective justice and the distributive justice approaches are thought by their opponents to have serious if not overwhelming problems. Proponents of the corrective justice approach tend to reject the distributive justice approach on the ground that it fails to account for private law, that is to say it makes prescriptions about what the law should be but these conflict with what we actually find in private law and legal reasoning in private law. Proponents of the distributive justice approach, in particular EAL, seem to be attracted by its arguments about what the law should be, irrespective of whether it provides a good account of traditional private law, or instead implies that reform of private law is required. They may take the view that the characteristic features of traditional private law are indefensible

[4] In particular, EJ Weinrib, *The Idea of Private Law* (Oxford University Press, rev edn 2012).
[5] In particular, C Fried, *Contract as Promise* (Oxford University Press, 2nd edn 2015).

and have arisen out of the development of the law through an artificial form of reasoning without policy analysis. They may also be sceptical about the theoretical foundations of corrective justice as a genuine alternative to the distributive justice account. The difference between the two schools may in part reflect the fact that the proponents of corrective justice tend to be legal scholars and the proponents of EAL are often economists.

Justice in Private Law

The account I give of private law shows that what I have described as traditional private law is largely, in a certain sense, justified. However, my approach is not a version of the corrective justice approach and I argue that traditional private law can be reconciled, in a sense, with the distributive justice approach. I deal in a broad brush way with the main areas of contract, negligence in tort, and private property. The approach I suggest has implications for the character of each area and for certain controversies in each area. The advantage of covering these areas of private law is to bring out what is common to them, and to provide support for my approach by showing its applicability across private law. However, it comes at the cost of giving limited and selective treatment to each area. My objective is to show some of the implications of my suggested approach rather than to cover the law or literature comprehensively.

In chapter two, I consider how the corrective justice and distributive justice approaches and my own approach should be understood as theories of private law. It is helpful to discuss this general question because the two approaches sometimes seem not merely to be at odds with each other but at cross purposes. Some commentators reject both approaches, and some are sceptical about even the possibility of private law theory as exemplified by either approach.

In chapter three, I consider two aspects of the 'structure' of private law, that is to say the nature of the primary relation in private law and how it relates to the remedial relation. I point out the inconsistencies that arise from treating claims in private law as arising from wrongs – that is to say, from primary rights and duties – and suggest an alternative way to understand the bilateral relations of private law. The relationship between primary relations and remedial relations is discussed in terms of what I call the requirement of 'remedial consistency', ie the requirement that in a certain sense the remedy must be consistent with the primary right. I suggest that the structure of private law does not reflect either the corrective justice approach or the distributive justice approach as they are usually understood.

In chapters four and five, I discuss the corrective justice approach and the distributive justice approach. The corrective justice literature focuses mainly on tort law and in particular the law of negligence. In contract, the corrective justice approach as I understand it is essentially the 'will theory', and more particularly 'contract as promise' and the transfer theory. The most prominent version of the distributive justice approach is EAL, but there are other versions, including in negligence the more pragmatic, less theoretical 'policy reasoning' approach. In contract, there are approaches based on the role of contract in markets, and approaches hostile to private exchange. My objective is to identify what seem to me to be the strengths and weaknesses of the corrective justice and distributive justice approaches, with a view to preparing the ground for the approach I suggest in chapter six.

In chapter six, I set out what I call the 'standpoint limitation', and show how it explains the distinctive limitations and characteristics of the common law. This amounts, as I said, to a sort of reconciliation of the distributive justice and corrective justice approaches in the common law.

In chapters seven and eight, I explain how distributive justice applying the standpoint limitation and the requirement of remedial consistency can account for some characteristic features and particular doctrines of the law of negligence and contract. The doctrines touched on include, in negligence, the duty of care and standard of care, strict and vicarious liability, causation, insurance, economic loss and policy reasoning, and public authority liability; and, in contract, specific performance and the remedial regime, substantive fairness, implied terms and the statutory modification of contract law. I focus on the more general aspects of the law rather than the detailed rules.

Chapters nine and ten deal with private property, drawing on the same basic themes of remedial consistency and the standpoint limitation. The main division in the literature on private property is between the 'right of exclusion' or right of control theories on the one hand and the 'bundle of rights' or progressive property theories on the other. This division does not correspond to the division between the corrective justice approach and the distributive justice approach: both sides of this division are versions of the distributive justice approach. In this context, the corrective justice approach amounts to the application of the Lockean labour principle to private property. As before, my aim is to consider whether the approach I suggest can overcome some of the difficulties that have emerged in the literature. The discussion engages with the controversy over the foundation of property rights in the common law and it touches on various aspects of the law, including remedies, proprietary claims, the supposed doctrine of 'unjust enrichment', the trust, tracing, nuisance and possible objects of property, including intangible property. The emphasis is again on general principle rather than the detailed law.

Chapter eleven considers the nature of common law reasoning, including arguments of precedent and analogy, and how this relates to the standpoint limitation and remedial consistency.

Chapter twelve brings together the main conclusions of the book in the form of a brief general account of private law.

2

Private Law Theory

Introduction

The distributive justice approach and the corrective justice approach may appear to be not merely different theories but different types of theory altogether. One reason is that the corrective justice approach is typically understood as an 'internal approach', meaning that it is a theory that accounts for or explains the law as it is, or at least its basic concepts and structure, if not the law in detail. Thus it is apt as a framework for the law and legal reasoning to be used by a judge or by someone adopting the same perspective as a judge to guide decision-making. One might say that such a theory aims to provide a good interpretation of the law.[1] By contrast, the distributive justice approach might be understood as an 'external approach', meaning that it is employed to evaluate the law and recommend reform.

However, where there have been significant departures from the traditional form of private law, under the influence of the distributive justice approach – as appears to have happened in the law of negligence – the corrective justice approach seems to be invoked as an external approach to criticise the law,[2] and the distributive justice approach as an internal approach for determining and developing it. It is not clear whether the contrast between the internal and external approaches (understood in this way) is helpful in explaining what sort of theories the corrective justice approach and the distributive justice approach actually are. There is also scepticism about whether either approach is actually successful as an internal approach, that is to say in accounting for the law.[3] This is considered in chapters four and five.

Another reason why the two approaches might be thought to be different types of theory is that the corrective justice approach tends to be focused on private law as made by the judges in the common law, and excludes private law as made or reformed by statute. On the corrective justice approach, although statutory

[1] As to which see SA Smith, *Contract Theory* (Oxford University Press, 2004) 7–37. The interpretative approach is associated with Ronald Dworkin: R Dworkin, *Law's Empire* (Belknap Press, 1986).

[2] See eg D Priel, 'Land Use Priorities and the Law of Nuisance' (2015) 39 *Melbourne University Law Review* 346, 363. See further ch 4.

[3] See eg J Goudkamp and J Murphy, 'The Failure of Universal Theories of Tort Law' (2015) 21 *Legal Theory* 47 (2015); SA Hershovitz, 'The Search for a Grand Unified Theory of Tort Law' (2017) 130 *Harvard Law Review* 942; S Hedley, 'Is Private Law Meaningless?' (2011) 64 *Current Legal Problems* 89.

provision for private law is regarded as entirely legitimate, at the same time it seems to be understood not to be a part of private law that needs to be accounted for by a theory of private law. Not surprisingly, this understanding of statute has been criticised.[4] It appears not to be part of the distributive justice approach.

Thirdly, the corrective justice approach is often said to be a philosophical or moral approach and the distributive justice approach an economic or social sciences approach.[5] The leading version of the distributive justice approach is derived from economics and its exponents are economists, whereas the exponents of the corrective justice approach are legal academics and theorists. This might suggest that the two approaches are not really comparable, though at the same time they do seem to be in competition with each other.

The purpose of this chapter is to indicate in broad terms how I understand the corrective justice approach and the distributive justice approach, and the approach I adopt.

Moral and Socio-legal Theories of Law

The most fundamental distinction with respect to theories of law is the distinction between social scientific or socio-legal theories of law and moral theories of law. A social scientific theory purports to describe the social world, and to explain and predict the actions of people in society in causal terms, and a social scientific theory of law or socio-legal theory of law (STL) is such a theory concerning the actions of people and courts and other legal institutions in relation to each other. An STL is empirical and causal – the truth of the theory is in principle established by testing it against observation and experiment to establish causal links.[6]

The standard example of an STL is the application of economics to predict the effects of actual and possible legal rules on people's behaviour, and therefore on the welfare of people across society. With respect to contract law, one might draw on such an STL to predict how legal rules affect the likelihood that people will make contracts and perform them. In tort, one might aim to establish the extent to which deterrence through legal sanctions works to reduce harm through accidents caused by dangerous or careless driving. In property law, an STL might show the extent to which limiting the number of different types of property right, and in what way, makes property more productive and marketable. Policy analysis is the application of an STL such as economics to the law to ascertain or predict the effects of actual or possible legal rules. There are other types of STL. For example,

[4] See eg J Murphy, 'The Heterogeneity of Tort Law' (2019) 39 *Oxford Journal of Legal Studies* 455.

[5] See eg Hershovitz (n 3).

[6] In the literature the application of economics involves mathematical models based on the assumption that individuals act rationally with a view to advancing their own welfare, supplemented by empirical evidence where it is available.

psychological theories might help to establish how the risk of bias on the part of judges or juries can be reduced or how best to evaluate the evidence of witnesses. Historical research can indicate how social, political and economic circumstances influenced the development of the law, for example the development of the law of negligence or employment as a result of industrial development or social change.[7]

An STL can be contrasted with a moral theory of law (MTL). An MTL is a theory about what the law ought to be, that is to say a theory of that part of morality or justice that it is justified to require by law. An MTL might be simply a general moral theory, such as that the law should be utilitarian, or a more specific theory about some aspect of law, for example that tort law should give effect to the moral principle that wrongdoers should correct their wrongs or that contract law should give effect to the principle that promises should be kept. MTLs and STLs are distinct but in determining the rules that should be introduced an MTL can draw on an STL to establish the consequences of possible rules.

With respect to private law, a theory about what sort of law should govern interactions is an MTL, and the distributive justice approach and the corrective justice approach are best understood as MTLs (or as types or families of MTL). According to the corrective justice approach, the law governing interactions should give effect to a distinct form of interpersonal justice applicable to interactions, which gives rise to bilateral duties, wrongs and remedies – for example, in tort moral duties owed to other people not to cause harm and in contract moral duties arising from promises. According to the distributive justice approach, the law governing interactions should give effect to justice in the distribution of benefits and harms across society as a whole. Justice in this form may not support the same sort of moral duties or it may not support duties at all. It may support sanctions to promote contractual exchange or accident avoidance for the good of society in general. The law would be expected to have a different character. But the distributive justice approach is nevertheless an MTL.

Because the corrective justice approach is concerned with the particular interaction and the relationship between the parties, it is concerned with the immediate effects of the interaction and not the further consequences of that type of interaction across society, whereas the distributive justice approach does involve the consideration of such further consequences. It appears that corrective justice is in a sense intrinsic to the relationship of the parties to the interaction and has a deontological character, and distributive justice has a consequentialist or instrumentalist character. The distributive justice approach may draw on an STL and on policy analysis, but the corrective justice approach does not, or only to a very limited extent.

It is important to distinguish between the STL consisting of the application of economics to the law, which shows how individual and aggregate welfare can

[7] A famous example is MJ Horwitz, *The Transformation of American Law 1780–1860* (Harvard University Press, 1979).

be maximised, and the MTL that holds that the law should be used as an instrument for maximising aggregate welfare in society. For convenience, I shall refer to the latter as EAL (economic analysis of law). EAL is a version of the distributive justice approach. Although it does not aim for a certain distribution, under EAL the objective of maximising aggregate welfare determines in practice how harms and benefits should be distributed.[8] EAL, as an MTL, is logically distinct from economics as a social science applied to the law, which is an STL, though EAL naturally incorporates the latter by way of policy analysis.

The Internal Approach

The corrective and distributive justice approaches as explained above would seem to be external approaches, since as MTLs they can be employed to evaluate private law or recommend reform. How then should we understand the internal approach? In the common law, a judge accepts the authority of previous decisions and the conventional practices of legal reasoning. Previous decisions establish binding precedents, but the precedents are not always conclusive of the law, and if a court is not bound by precedent it has to exercise moral judgement in formulating a new rule to make the decision. The law has been built up over time by the exercise of moral judgement by judges in deciding cases. Such moral judgements are encapsulated as authoritative precedents, and the law is an authoritative formulation of the morality applicable to interactions, as determined by the judges. The way in which the judges draw on moral considerations in adjudication determines how the law develops. This is a question of how legal reasoning in the common law allows for moral judgement in the development of the law. Insofar as private law has a general structure and character, it is because in exercising moral judgement to develop the law, judges have drawn on an MTL that gives it that structure and character.

The question is whether the courts draw on, or ought to draw on, the corrective justice approach or the distributive justice approach as MTLs (or on some other MTL). On the corrective justice approach, in formulating a rule to develop the law, the judges should take account of the interests of the two parties, C and D, in the way that the corrective justice approach prescribes. On the distributive justice approach they should take account of the interests of people generally with respect to harms and benefits. The character of the law depends on which approach is adopted. Although the corrective justice and distributive justice approaches can be employed as external MTLs to evaluate or reform the law, they can also be brought into the law in this way, to form the internal approach. In trying to establish the right way to understand private law, we should ask whether the corrective

[8] See further ch 4.

justice or distributive justice approach ought to be introduced by the judges into the common law. Which, if either, is apt for this purpose? This would seem to be simply a question of which approach is morally sound, or could there be other issues relevant to the choice of MTL, concerning the development of the law?

An STL cannot play this role in the internal approach. The judge does not draw directly on an STL. Although a lawyer predicting the outcome of a case might act as a social scientist, this approach would not be apt for a judge, or a lawyer arguing before a judge. Determining what the law is by development from the authorities is not a causal-empirical exercise from the judge's point of view.[9] However, if the court can draw on the distributive justice approach, for example, EAL, it can draw on an STL in working out what distributive justice requires.

It is a crucial fact that when the legislature legislates for interactions governed by private law, it takes the distributive justice approach. This is reflected in the statutory reform of contract law to protect consumers or employees or tenants, or the statutory reform of negligence law to introduce compulsory insurance or strict product liability or accident compensation funds. These reforms are understood to be justified in terms of the distribution of harms and benefits across the population, for example to protect a sector of the population, and they may depart from traditional private law, even to the extent of abandoning bilateral relations. Such legislative reform seems to be generally accepted as fully justified, not only by supporters of the distributive justice approach, but also generally by supporters of the corrective justice approach.[10] Why then should the courts not also draw on the distributive justice approach in their development of the common law? There has indeed been some movement in this direction in recent years, particularly in the law of negligence.[11] This is deplored by supporters of the corrective justice approach, who insist that it is illegitimate to apply the distributive justice approach at common law. But what is the argument against it, if it is the right approach for the legislature in reforming the common law?

There are a number of possible arguments. One might take issue, first, with the assumption that judges draw on moral considerations in developing the law. A crude or 'vulgar' version of formalism or 'mechanical jurisprudence' holds that the common law is a comprehensive system of fixed rules that govern every possible situation and can be applied mechanically by way of technical rules and constructions, without the need for any exercise of judgement.[12] Adjudication, on this understanding, is confined to applying rules previously laid down, and is closed to other considerations – it is entirely self-contained or 'autonomous'. In its ordinary day-to-day operation, the law may seem to work like this, and it may be tempting for judges to present it in this way in order to disguise the need for moral

[9] This might be denied by some legal realists; see eg B Leiter, 'American Legal Realism' in D Patterson (ed), *A Companion to Philosophy of Law and Legal Theory* (Blackwell, 2010).

[10] See further ch 5.

[11] See further ch 4.

[12] See B Leiter, 'Legal Formalism and Legal Realism: What is the Issue?' (2010) 16 *Legal Theory* 111; R Pound, 'Mechanical Jurisprudence' (1908) 8 *Columbia Law Review* 605.

judgement. To be useful in practice, the law must work effectively without moral judgement in most ordinary cases. However, it cannot be right to say that in every case the law is fully determined by previous decisions. The courts have built up the law by the exercise of moral judgement in new situations and they continue to do so.

Some commentators would say that although judges exercise moral judgement in developing the law, the way they do this is very much constrained and does not extend to drawing on anything like a moral theory along the lines of the corrective justice approach or the distributive justice approach. Legal reasoning confines the judges to the exercise of moral judgement in a limited way, in particular through traditional analogical reasoning to develop rules from case to case, and legal theorists would do better to engage with the actual reasoning of judges rather than constructing 'grand theories'.[13] On this view, although one can evaluate the law using the corrective justice or distributive justice approach as external theories, they are not relevant to common law development by judges. As has often been pointed out, however, the judges are in practice bound to be influenced by theoretical assumptions even if there is no explicit reference to a theory.[14] Most commentators do recognise a role for 'top-down' reasoning from theory as well as 'bottom-up' reasoning by way of analogy with the facts of cases, and it does seem from the case law that the way the judges develop the law does reflect the influence of the corrective justice or the distributive justice approach. This is a question concerning common law legal reasoning, which I return to in chapter eleven.

It might be said that the corrective justice approach is simply a better account or interpretation of the common law, as it happens to have developed, than the distributive justice approach and should be retained for this reason. The traditional common law focused on the two parties and developed a character involving bilateral duties and wrongs and remedies. Under the influence of the distributive justice approach, the character of the law would be quite different, for example by not being confined to remedies, by responding systematically to the public interest and the wider effects of interactions, and even by abandoning bilateral duties and wrongs. To adopt the distributive justice approach now would be transformative of the common law.[15] Precedent and the conventions of legal reasoning no doubt impose constraints on legal change, certainly over the short term, but this is nevertheless an unconvincing objection to the adoption of the distributive justice approach in the common law. It does not explain why in principle the corrective justice approach rather than the distributive justice approach

[13] Eg Stapleton rejects grand theories in favour of 'reflexive scholarship': J Stapleton, *Three Essays on Torts* (Oxford University Press, 2021) 24–25.

[14] See eg K Mason, 'Do Top-Down and Bottom-Up Reasoning Ever Meet?' in E Bant and M Harding (eds), *Exploring Private Law* (Cambridge University Press, 2010); M Bryan, 'Justice Callinan's Judgements in Private Law: Story Telling, Legal Coherence and Corrective Justice' (2008) 27 *University of Queensland Law Journal* 29, 30.

[15] See eg JL Coleman, *The Practice of Principle* (Clarendon Press, 2001) ch 1.

is the right approach. Is it just by virtue of an accident of history that the corrective justice approach became established in the common law, rather than the distributive justice approach? Some commentators argue that traditional legal reasoning is artificially restrictive and that where it obstructs the introduction of the distributive justice approach it should be discarded.[16]

Weinrib's theory of corrective justice is advanced as a more sophisticated version of formalism. According to Weinrib,[17] the normative considerations that give rise to private law emerge from the structure of the relationship between the parties in civil proceedings. They are a matter of the 'immanent rationality' of the law. This guides the development of the law, along with the authority of previous decisions, to give rise to a coherent body of law structured around the concept of bilateral moral rights. All other considerations are excluded – not only considerations of distributive justice, but moral considerations altogether. Thus private law is a 'self-contained normative practice'. According to Weinrib, 'the purpose of private law is to be private law' and 'private law is like love', in the sense that it is not directed at any objective outside the practice.[18] This might suggest that private law is like a game or sport, with rules that are only of internal significance. It is obscure what sort of normativity it can be that is generated by structure without any basis in morality (if this is how it should be understood). In the light of the discussion above, one might think that there is a feature of legal reasoning that requires courts, in developing the law, to draw on the corrective justice approach as an MTL. In any case, it seems to me that this argument concerning legal reasoning in private law has not made clear why it is that the courts should not follow the distributive justice approach as the legislature does.

The corrective justice approach can also be understood in terms of the distinction between 'intrinsic' and 'extrinsic' considerations. Intrinsic considerations relate to the way the interaction affects the two parties. 'Extrinsic' considerations relate to the interests of other people and the public interest. On the corrective justice approach, only intrinsic considerations are relevant to the development of the law, that is to say, to the internal approach.[19] Extrinsic considerations are relevant only to an external approach. As considered further in chapter five, it is implausible to think that all extrinsic considerations are actually or could in practice be excluded from private law. It remains unclear why considerations of distributive justice should be excluded in the development of the common law if they are relevant to the legislature in making law for the same circumstances.

There are no doubt institutional limitations on how the courts can or should develop the common law. The judges may not be competent to make law in the

[16] Eg Collins attacks the 'self-referential character and closure rules' of the traditional 'discourse' of private law: H Collins, *Regulating Contracts* (Oxford University Press, rev edn, 2004) 53. See also L Kaplow and S Shavell, *Fairness versus Welfare* (Harvard University Press, 2006) ch II.

[17] EJ Weinrib, *The Idea of Private Law* (Oxford University Press, rev edn 2012), especially ch 2 'Legal Formalism'.

[18] Weinrib (ibid) 5–6.

[19] Weinrib (ibid) ch 2 'Legal Formalism'. See further ch 5.

way that the legislature can, because of their lack of executive power or administrative resources, and they may lack the democratic legitimacy to develop the law in certain ways. What these limits are is open to argument, but they surely do not confine the courts to taking account only of 'intrinsic' considerations, and they do not seem to explain the character of traditional private law as compared to what the distributive justice approach would require or what the legislature has done or can do in reforming the law. In any case they seem to be arguments for applying a restricted form of distributive justice rather than applying the corrective justice approach, and the nature of the corrective justice approach does not appear to be determined by these institutional limitations.

It is difficult to explain why the courts do not or should not follow the distributive justice approach as they understand it, so far as they can, if the legislature should do so. This goes to the nature of corrective justice. The same problem is implicit in the work of the 'new private law' school.[20] The new private law school recognises that private law is based on moral considerations that support bilateral rights and wrongs and remedies, in the spirit of the corrective justice approach.[21] It also recognises the legitimacy of policy analysis and policy reasoning drawn from the distributive justice approach. This would appear to accommodate a wide range of theoretical positions. It does not seem, as yet, to have overcome the crucial problem of how to establish which sorts of consideration are relevant to the development of private law and which are excluded.[22] It appears to allow for some considerations that go beyond what the corrective justice approach would allow, without admitting the full range of considerations that the distributive justice approach would require, but it is not clear that this is a coherent position. It might be understood to be attempting to combine the corrective justice and distributive justice approaches, but both are intended as comprehensive theories of private law and on this understanding are mutually exclusive.[23]

Justice in Private Law

The corrective justice and the distributive justice approaches are moral theories of law or MTLs. They can be employed to evaluate private law, on the external approach.

[20] See generally AS Gold et al, *The Oxford Handbook of the New Private Law* (Oxford University Press, 2020). In the US context, the problem is how to negotiate a path between the extremes of classical formalism and legal realism.

[21] It also rejects the scepticism engendered by legal realism over the moral dimension of the law and the moral language of normativity and doctrine: see JCP Goldberg, 'Introduction: Pragmatism and Private Law' (2012) 125 *Harvard Law Review* 1640; EL Sherwin, 'Formalism and Realism in Private Law' in AS Gold (ed) (ibid).

[22] See AS Gold, 'Internal and External Perspectives: On Methodology in the New Private Law' in AS Gold et al (eds) (ibid).

[23] See Weinrib (n 17) ch 8. See further ch 5.

They can also be understood as MTLs that are imported into the common law to guide the development of the law on the internal approach. As discussed further in chapters four and five, the corrective justice approach appears to correspond more closely than the distributive justice approach to the common law, though the corrective justice approach also has problems in accounting for the common law. In any case, even if it were correct to say that the courts have adopted the corrective justice approach rather than the distributive justice approach, the question remains why they should do this. It would seem that it cannot be simply that it is the right moral theory for interactions, because it is accepted that it is legitimate and appropriate for the legislature to adopt the distributive justice approach for the same interactions. As I argue further in chapter five, proponents of the corrective justice approach have not managed to provide a convincing response to this objection, and this highlights the elusive nature of the corrective justice approach.

As I explain in chapter six, the standpoint limitation is a constraint on adjudication that limits the considerations that it is legitimate for the courts to rely on in the development of the common law. It governs the internal approach. It is also an MTL, that is to say it is a moral theory of how the courts ought to develop the common law. In principle, it is to be assessed by moral argument rather than tested against the decisions of the courts. But I also think it has guided the development of the common law, so that it also shows why traditional private law is broadly justified. It seems to me that, as discussed in later chapters, this approach provides, on the whole, a good account of private law as it has developed at common law.

3

Remedial Justice and the Structure of Private Law

Introduction

On the orthodox picture, across private law C has a primary right against D correlated with D's primary duty to C. C acquires a claim for compensation or some other remedy when D commits a breach of the duty, that is to say a wrong against C. In due course, if necessary, the court makes an order for the appropriate remedy for the wrong and authorises enforcement. One problem with this picture is that it is difficult to understand private law as being systematically concerned with wrongs.

Enforcement

It has at times been widely thought that by its very nature a legal duty involves coercion by the state – force or a threat of force – to secure compliance. However, a duty is normative, meaning that it gives guidance or direction to the person subject to the duty. Whether there is a duty is a distinct question from whether there should be a coercive response to a breach of duty. What characterises a legal duty is not that it is coercive but that it has the authority of the law.[1] It is not inconsistent to have a breach of legal duty for which there are no enforcement measures. Nevertheless, cases of breach of duty for which there is no enforcement are exceptional and are regarded as anomalous.[2] In practice, legal duties are enforced by order backed by the use of coercion where necessary. This is because, although a legal duty does not by its nature involve coercion, the law is confined to giving effect to that aspect of morality or justice that it is justified to enforce by coercion.[3] The decision whether to recognise a new legal duty involves assessing whether it would be justified to enforce the duty by coercion. It is a truism that there are

[1] J Raz, *The Authority of Law* (Oxford University Press, 2nd edn 2009).

[2] Eg in connection with the enforcement of a trust with no beneficiary: see *Re Endacott* [1960] Ch 232.

[3] See eg R Dworkin, *Law's Empire* (Fontana, 1986) 93.

moral duties that should not be recognised as legal duties for this reason. The state may issue non-legal official guidance about how people should behave, and it is a crucial difference between such guidance and law that the guidance is not intended to be enforceable by coercion. It makes sense to limit the scope of the law in this way, because, if it were not possible to enforce the law where necessary, disregard of the law would undermine its authority. In any case, I assume for present purposes that legal duties are duties that it is generally justified to enforce by order backed by coercion if necessary.

It follows that, if D has a legal duty to do X, it is justified for D to be ordered to do X, simply because this is implicit in the recognition of the duty. It may nevertheless be the case that, even if D cannot complain that it would be unjust to order him to perform, D should actually be ordered to perform only when this is strictly necessary to maintain respect for the authority of the law.[4] But if D owes C a duty in private law, the justification for the duty, and for compelling D to perform it, must arise from the fact that C is entitled to have the benefit of actual performance of the duty. In private law, C should have the right to an order requiring D to perform the duty to C, secured by coercion if necessary. It does indeed seem clear that an order would be made to secure performance of D's duty not to trespass on C's land, for example. C has a right to the order, which follows directly from the fact that D has a duty not to enter the land. Similarly, no-one would doubt that D's duty not to assault C would be enforced by order if a court were ever in a position to make such an order.

If a court finds that D has a duty on certain facts and these facts still prevail, it should order performance of the duty. However, it does not follow that, where circumstances have changed since the breach, D should still be required to perform the duty. This may now be impossible: for example, where D breached a duty not to interfere with goods and the goods were destroyed by the interference. Here the duty must have lapsed. Even in a case where it is still possible to perform the duty, it may now be unfairly burdensome to order D to perform it. For example, if D trespassed on land by erecting a building, it might be unfair to require D to demolish the building, and D may only have to pay compensation. Again, it would seem that the duty must have lapsed. This would not in my view amount to denying the character of the original duty as a duty that C was entitled to have enforced by order. We can certainly say that, if the circumstances remain the same, the order to perform the duty should be made.

This appears to be at odds with the established remedial position in certain types of case, for example in contract. In contract, D is understood to have a duty to perform the contract and, following a breach, the circumstances may remain exactly or almost exactly as they were before the breach. It would seem that the court should order D to perform the duty, but normally only compensation is available and not an order for specific performance.[5]

[4] See eg G Lamond, 'Coercion and the nature of law' (2001) 7 *Legal Theory* 35.

[5] See generally A Tettenborn. 'Literal Enforcement of Obligations' in R Halson and D Campbell (eds), *Research Handbook on Remedies in Private Law* (Edward Elgar, 2019).

This may appear to be inconsequential, because an order for specific performance will in fact be granted where 'damages are inadequate',[6] and where damages are adequate it would seem that C can have no complaint. But even in such a case the absence of a right to specific performance is significant. If specific performance were generally available, C would have effective control over D, who would have to perform unless released by C. C could make the decision whether damages are adequate and in what measure. Furthermore, with a right to specific performance, C could secure a share of D's profits from an opportunity that is available to D only if D does not perform, simply by making it a condition for releasing D from the contract. In such a case, compensation representing the value of the performance due to C is liable to undervalue the benefit to C of a right corresponding to a duty of performance. Thus the absence of a right to specific performance represents a significant failure in securing C's entitlement if D does indeed owe C a duty to perform the contract. Some commentators have accordingly argued that a general right to specific performance should be recognised. It is said that without such a right the law fails to protect C's primary right fully, or, as it sometimes put, C's contractual 'performance interest'.[7]

However, some commentators defend the established remedial position. It is said that D has a legal duty to perform, but it is a legal duty that D should not necessarily be required to perform. This is of course contrary to the assumption made above about the nature of a legal duty. There may be some exceptional cases, for example where the contract is for the provision of certain types of personal services, where it may be possible to say that the law does not require D to perform, though it still recognises that D has a duty to perform and does not strictly speaking condone the breach. But in an ordinary commercial contract, where no such objection arises, and there is no new impediment to performance, and D is perfectly capable of performing the duty, it would seem that the law simply recognises that D has a duty that D is at liberty not to perform, subject to the payment of compensation. This is surely simply self-contradictory, since the law cannot recognise both a legal duty to perform and a legal liberty not to perform. One might be tempted to say that D has a legal duty whose legal rationale is that it need not be performed,[8] but this still seems self-contradictory.

The established remedial position is explicable only on the assumption that, when C has no right to specific performance, and is required to accept compensation, the reason is that D has no duty to perform. This may appear misconceived on the ground that, if D has no duty to perform, the contract has no legal effect and there can be no basis for the claim for compensation. But logically it is quite possible for the contract to have a legal effect without creating duties to perform. The legal effect of the contract can be to allocate the risk of loss arising from

[6] See eg *Co-operative Insurance Society v Argyll Stores* [1998] AC 1.

[7] D Friedmann, 'The Performance Interest in Contract Damages' (1995) 111 *Law Quarterly Review* 628.

[8] D Campbell, *Contractual Relations* (Oxford University Press, 2022) 252.

non-performance without creating duties to perform, so that the reason why D has to pay compensation is not that D has acted wrongfully by failing to perform D's duty under the contract, but simply that the contract has allocated to D the risk of liability for loss in the circumstances that have arisen. I shall say that in such a case D has a 'primary liability' with respect to loss from non-performance, as opposed to a primary duty to perform. As considered further later, there are other reasons for thinking that private law adopts a primary liability approach.

This understanding in terms of primary liabilities is how we should make sense of the law of specific performance and, as discussed later, the overall remedial regime in contract. I leave open for the moment why it is that contract law normally takes the form of primary liabilities rather than primary duties. There is a longstanding controversy over the availability of specific performance, which on the approach I suggest is about this question (as considered further in later chapters), though it is usually understood as a controversy over the remedy that should be available for the breach of a legal duty to perform.

Compensation for Wrongs

Claims for compensation are invariably understood to arise from a breach of duty. A right to compensation arising from a breach of duty may seem entirely natural and appropriate, but in fact it is not easy to explain the law in this way. The traditional rationale and the natural understanding is that D is liable to pay compensation because D was morally responsible for a wrongful action and its consequences.[9] This implies that D must be blameworthy or morally at fault.[10] In other words, there should be a legal requirement of subjective fault, meaning that D must have been aware of the risk that D might cause harm through the wrongful action. However, a claim for compensation is very rarely subject to such a requirement in any part of private law. It is not a requirement in contract. In negligence, liability arises from D's failure to meet a certain standard of conduct. The standard is uniform and impersonal and does not depend on what D knows or could have found out. There is no requirement that D was, or should have been, aware of the risk to C. Negligence is described as a 'fault-based liability', but this means so-called 'objective fault' – conduct falling short of the prescribed standard – not subjective fault.[11]

[9] I mean the sense of 'responsibility' in which it is associated with agency and choice rather than substantive duty. This is the choice or decision or control theory of responsibility associated with amongst others: HLA Hart, *Punishment and Responsibility* (Oxford University Press, rev edn 1970).

[10] See generally J Goudkamp, 'Moral blameworthiness and liability for negligence' (2004) 28 *Melbourne University Law Review* 343. See also NJ McBride, *The Humanity of Private Law* (Hart, 2019) 3; L Alexander and K Kessler Ferzan, 'Confused Culpability, Contrived Causation, and the Collapse of Tort Theory' in J Oberdiek (ed), *Philosophical Foundations of the Law of Torts* (Oxford University Press, 2014); HM Hurd, 'Finding No Fault with Negligence' in Oberdiek (ibid).

[11] See eg McBride (ibid).

Furthermore, if D's liability depends on personal moral responsibility, it would seem that, as a matter of fairness to D, the measure of liability should reflect the degree of D's moral fault (just as the severity of punishment for a wrong should reflect the degree of moral fault). However, in private law, since subjective fault is generally irrelevant, not only may D be liable to compensate for loss in the absence of any subjective fault, D may incur a liability that is quite out of proportion to the degree of actual subjective fault, such as where a driver's momentary lapse of concentration causes serious injury and gives rise to a very large liability. This also seems difficult to justify on the basis that liability depends on moral responsibility for wrongdoing.[12]

One might object that this line of argument is misconceived in presupposing a personalised or subjective concept of duty, as opposed to an impersonal or objective concept. According to the subjective concept, whether a duty arises and what it requires depend on what the duty-bearer knows,[13] so that a breach of duty involves subjective fault, whereas under the objective concept of duty whether there is a duty and what it requires depend on the actual facts, irrespective of what D knows, so there is no requirement of subjective fault for a breach of duty. The two concepts are best described as duty relative to the actual facts (the objective concept) and duty relative to the evidence (the subjective concept).[14] It is said that in private law, in order to achieve a fair balance between C's interest in protection against harm and D's conflicting interest in being free of the constraint of the duty, the law ought to adopt the objective approach – duty relative to the actual facts – because what D knows is irrelevant to what the balance should be. In addition, particularly with respect to negligence, it is said that C should receive a uniform and impersonal level of protection, which cannot be dependent on what D knows. The subjective concept of duty, by limiting D's liability according to what D knows, would tilt the law unfairly in favour of D and against C and give C uneven protection.[15]

But this argument is beside the point. If liability depends on moral responsibility for a breach of duty, it does not explain how it can be fair, as between C and D, for D to be liable for loss caused by a breach of duty if D did not have the knowledge that could make D morally responsible for the breach. As considered

[12] See J Waldron, 'Moments of Carelessness and Massive Loss' in DG Owen (ed), *Philosophical Foundations of Tort Law* (Clarendon Press, 1997). In addition, although some form of legal response to a legal wrong may be required, it is not clear that it must be a remedial liability, as opposed to punishment. See P Cane, 'Retribution, Proportionality, and Moral Luck in Tort Law' in P Cane and J Stapleton (eds), *The Law of Obligations: Essays in Celebration of John Fleming* (Oxford University Press, 1998).

[13] Including what the duty-bearer ought to have found out, given what the duty-bearer did know (as opposed to what a reasonable person in the same position would have known or found out).

[14] D Parfit, *On What Matters*, Vol 1 (Oxford University Press, 2011) ch 7. Parfit also distinguishes the belief-relative concept of duty, meaning duty relative to the facts D believes. See further ch 6.

[15] See eg EJ Weinrib, *The Idea of Private Law* (Oxford University Press, rev edn 2012) chs 6 and 7; A Ripstein, *Equality, Responsibility and the Law* (Cambridge University Press, 1998) 31; A Beever, *Rediscovering the Law of Negligence* (Hart, 2009) 79–84; J Gardner, 'Obligations and outcomes in the law of tort' in *Torts and Other Wrongs* (Oxford University Press, 2019) ch 5; JCP Goldberg and BC Zipursky, *Recognising Wrongs* (Harvard University Press, 2020) ch 6.

further in chapter six, the two concepts of duty both have a role in the appropriate context. When the issue is whether D should be held liable for the consequences of an action as a wrong, on the ground of D's moral responsibility for it, the evidence-related concept of duty should apply, so that knowledge of the relevant facts would be required. The use of an objective fault standard in private law suggests instead that the basis for liability is not in fact D's moral responsibility for wrongdoing, but an allocation of the risk of harm, that is to say, a primary liability, as I have already suggested for contract.

A further problem in explaining claims for compensation in terms of moral responsibility for a wrong is that D may be incapable of doing what D is supposed to have a legal duty to do, or of avoiding doing what D is supposed to have a legal duty not to do. The problem arises with respect to strict liability. D is sometimes said to have a 'strict liability duty' not to cause harm, where D is liable for harm in specified circumstances irrespective of D's conduct. For example, D's liability for harm caused by the escape of water stored on land under the rule in *Rylands v Fletcher*[16] arises whether or not D could have done anything to prevent the escape. Furthermore, anything that D did that contributed to causing the damage, such as bringing the water onto the land or holding it there, was something D was legally entitled to do.[17] It seems clear that D is simply at risk of liability in these circumstances irrespective of whether D has committed a breach of duty.[18] The same problem that D may be incapable of performing the legal duty arises with respect to objective fault in negligence, because D may be incapable of meeting the standard of care.[19]

It is impossible to explain C's right to compensation in terms of D's moral responsibility for wrongdoing. This problem has been widely acknowledged. Some might argue that the availability of a right to compensation should be cut back drastically to cases where D was subjectively at fault. It would be better to accept that, where D is liable for harm simply because it resulted from a failure to meet a certain standard of conduct, or simply because it occurred in certain circumstances, irrespective of D's responsibility for it, the liability arises from a primary liability, that is to say an allocation of risk with respect to loss.

For a primary liability, there is no reason to require subjective fault in the sense that D must have been aware of the risk of loss to C resulting from D's action at the time when D acted, because the liability is not based on D's moral responsibility for the consequences of the action as a breach of duty. However, for a primary liability with respect to harm arising out of an activity, in principle D should be liable only if he knew or ought to have known that the activity carried the risk of harm.

[16] *Rylands v Fletcher* (1868) LR 3 HL 330.

[17] As in the much discussed *Vincent v Lake Erie* 109 Minn 416, 124 NW 221 (1910) where D was liable for damage caused through the use of C's dock, though D was entitled to use it.

[18] See eg GC Keating, 'Strict Liability Wrongs' in Oberdiek (n 10). GC Keating, 'The Priority of Respect over Repair' (2012) 18 *Legal Theory* 293.

[19] See Alexander and Kessler Ferzan (n 10); Hurd (n 10).

For example, with respect to D's liability arising from an accident whilst driving, D must have known of the risks caused to others by driving. One can express this by saying that we should use an evidence-relative concept of the primary liability. (I shall come back to this point, which is important to the discussion in later chapters.)

It is sometimes argued that the justification for compensation for loss is that, by restoring the prior position, before the loss, compensation annuls the gains and losses resulting from an unjust interaction. Take the case where property is transferred from C to D as a result of D's wrong – for example, a wrongful seizure or fraud. A claim for the return of the property is justified simply to annul the loss and gain by reversing the transfer, and this does not depend on subjective fault. However, in this case a claim arises to recover a transfer from C to D, because the transfer was not authorised by C and was therefore invalid. This claim for restitution (as I shall describe it in chapter nine) does not depend on a wrong. There is also a claim for compensation for loss based on D's seizure as a wrong, and in this sort of case the claim for compensation would also reverse the transfer. But a claim for compensation does not in general reverse a transfer or undo a gain in order to restore a loss.[20] Where D has inflicted injury or damage on C, the loss cannot be understood as a sort of transfer from C to D that should be reversed by compensation. One cannot infer that in general there should be a claim for compensation for a wrong without subjective fault.[21]

One might say, finally, that there is simply a special legal concept of duty, distinct from the moral concept, and that the right to compensation is simply intrinsic to this legal concept of duty,[22] and no further explanation is required. But legal usage cannot provide a moral justification for compensation. It is true, however, that the law adopts a distinctive usage of 'duty' in private law – it is often used to refer to what I have described as a primary liability, as well as a primary duty in the strict sense. It would be better to distinguish explicitly between a primary liability and a primary duty. There is a difference between making D liable to pay compensation because D caused harm by failing to act as D ought to have acted according to law (primary duty), and making D liable to pay compensation because D caused harm

[20] According to Weinrib, one can overcome this problem with the concept of 'normative gains' and 'normative losses': see Weinrib (n 15) ch 5. This is criticised by KW Simons 'Justification in Private Law' (1996) 81 *Cornell Law Review* 698, 727–33 and P Cane 'Corrective Justice and Correlativity in Private Law' (1996) 16 *Oxford Journal of Legal Studies* 483.

[21] Other arguments have been advanced to explain liability for wrongdoing without subjective fault. One suggestion is that D is liable because otherwise C would be motivated to take revenge: see eg S Hershovitz, 'Treating Wrongs as Wrongs: An Expressive Argument for Tort Law' (2017) 10 *Journal of Tort Law* 405; A Robertson, 'On the Function of the Law of Negligence' (2013) 33 *Oxford Journal of Legal Studies* 31; NB Oman, *The Dignity of Commerce* (University of Chicago Press, 2016) ch 6. See also: McBride (n 10) ch 6, 203. Honoré's theory of 'outcome responsibility' was developed to account for liability in the absence of subjective fault: see T Honoré, 'Responsibility and Luck' (1988) 104 *Law Quarterly Review* 530, criticised in Ripstein, *Equality, Responsibility and the Law* (n 15) 74; R Avraham and I Kohler-Hausmann, 'Accident Law for Egalitarians' (2006) 12 *Legal Theory* 181.

[22] See eg JCP Goldberg and BC Zipursky, *Recognising Wrongs* (Belknap Press, 2020) ch 6, criticised in CM Sharkey (2021) 134 *Harvard Law Review* 1423.

in circumstances in which the law allocated to D the risk of the harm (primary liability). Distinguishing between the two may not always be necessary but it is sometimes helpful, as considered below and in later chapters.

Primary Liabilities and Primary Duties

A primary liability relation allocates the risk of loss by specifying an act or event and the particular resulting losses to C for which D is liable if the act or event occurs and the risk materialises.[23] C's claim for compensation for loss arises directly from the primary relation in the sense that it is implicit in the primary relation. It does not arise on the basis of a principle that wrongdoers should correct their wrongs. In negligence, the standard of care does not represent the content of a duty owed by D to C, but a criterion for the allocation of the risk of a certain loss caused to C by D. With respect to strict liability, the law allocates to D the risk of liability for loss caused in the specified circumstances without any requirement that it results from D's having acted in a certain way or fallen below a certain standard. In contract law, the contract allocates the risk of loss resulting from non-performance of the contract. Negligence and contract are pervasively understood to involve an allocation of risk in just this way: there is said to be a duty owed by D to C by virtue of which the risk of loss is allocated between C and D.[24] The primary liability approach implies that the supposed duty is redundant: the legal relation is simply the allocation of risk of certain losses. C's right is not a right to performance of a duty by D; it is a right against D that D bear the risk of loss resulting from D's actions (as specified in the legal relation). This way of understanding compensation claims can clarify various aspects of the law, as discussed in later chapters.

Generally claims for compensation arise from a primary liability, but there can also be a primary duty, arising in conjunction with the primary liability. In contract, as discussed earlier, there is normally only a claim for compensation for loss caused by non-performance, based on a primary liability, but there can be a claim for specific performance, and where this is the case it is because exceptionally a primary duty to perform arises. On the orthodox understanding, there is always a duty to perform a contract, but the duty should be enforced by an order of specific performance only where 'damages are inadequate'. But the 'damages are

[23] See also P Jaffey 'Duties and Liabilities in Private Law' (2006) 12 *Legal Theory* 137–56; 'Liabilities in Private Law' (2008) 14 *Legal Theory* 233–55. See also John Murphy, 'Rights, Reductionism and Tort Law' (2008) 28 *Oxford Journal of Legal Studies* 393, 397–400; J Goudkamp and J Murphy, 'The Failure of Universal Theories of Tort Law' (2015) 21 *Legal Theory* 47, 78–81.

[24] As to negligence, see eg A Ripstein, *Private Wrongs* (Harvard University Press, 2016) 87–88; Ripstein, *Equality, Responsibility and the Law* (n 15) 54; R Merkin and J Steele, *Insurance and the Law of Obligations* (Oxford University Press, 2013) 205–06. As to contract, see eg NB Oman, 'Why There is No Duty to Pay Damages: Powers, Duties, and Private Law' (2012) 39 *Florida State University Law Review* 137.

inadequate' test should be understood not as a test to establish whether the court should enforce a duty to perform, but as a test to determine whether a duty to perform has arisen. C's right is normally that D bear the risk of loss to C from non-performance, but if the circumstances are such that it is not possible for D to compensate C adequately, D incurs a duty to perform. Where a duty has arisen, the court should enforce it by order.

This means that the court always simply determines and enforces the subsisting legal position. This follows from the fact that the law incorporates the condition that it should be enforced by coercion. In the same way, where a primary liability has given rise to a remedial liability for compensation, C has a remedial power, that is to say a right against D to have the payment from D secured by the court, if necessary by the extraction of money out of D's property through the actions of legal officials.[25] The court is bound to enforce D's liability for payment just as it should enforce a duty. In other words, there is no remedial discretion, in the sense of a discretion to depart from the subsisting legal position. The court has a discretion only in the sense that judgement may be required to establish the subsisting legal position, as in the case of the 'damages are inadequate' rule.[26] As the example of specific performance shows, it is the failure to distinguish between primary duties and primary liabilities that has given the impression that the court has a remedial discretion – a discretion to depart from the subsisting legal position.

Compare the law of nuisance. As nuisance is ordinarily understood, a landowner owes his neighbour a duty not to commit a nuisance by interfering with the neighbour's enjoyment of his property, for example by creating a noise or smell or an obstruction to light. If a nuisance is established, it is said that the court has a remedial discretion whether to award an injunction against the activity or instead allow the activity to continue and award damages. When damages are awarded instead of an injunction, the legal effect appears to be, just as for contract, to endorse or ratify the wrong and cancel the duty for the future, in effect allowing the defendant to expropriate the claimant's right by the payment of compensation. As with contract, it seems impossible to accept this account at face value,[27] though it seems to be a standard formulation of the law.[28]

Some commentators infer that it can never really be justified to award damages instead of an injunction, just as some commentators have insisted that specific performance should always be available in contract. However, there do seem to be

[25] D's remedial liability is not a duty to C to pay compensation. D may be incapable of paying or may not know the facts that render D liable to pay. The court could secure the payment by ordering D to pay, thereby subjecting D to a duty, or D might incur a duty through notice. See further the articles by Jaffey (n 23).

[26] And there is no more uncertainty here than in many other contexts where judgement is required to determine the legal position, for example where it depends on reasonableness: see A Burrows, 'We Do This at Common Law but That in Equity' (2002) 22 *Oxford Journal of Legal Studies* 1.

[27] See eg HE Smith, 'Exclusion and Property Rules in the Law of Nuisance' (2004) 90 *Virginia Law Review* 965, 1023; D Rendleman, 'Rehabilitating the nuisance injunction to protect the environment' (2018) 75 *Washington and Lee Law Review* 1859.

[28] See eg *Coventry v Lawrence* [2014] UKSC 13 at [160].

cases in nuisance where it is appropriate to deny an injunction and award damages, for example where it would be very expensive for D to discontinue the activity and the loss to C is relatively small and measurable (like the case in trespass where D constructs a building that inadvertently intrudes into C's land, and an injunction would require D to demolish the building).[29] It is said in such a case that it would be oppressive to award an injunction, or that the right to an injunction unfairly puts C in a position to extort an excessive price from D in return for a waiver from C.[30] But if D is still actually in breach of duty, it is difficult to say that at the same time it would be oppressive to require D to perform the duty, or that C is extorting money from D by threatening to require D to do what D has a duty to do. Again, it makes more sense to say, where it is justified to deny an injunction and award damages, that this is because the circumstances and events have caused the duty to lapse, leaving only a primary liability relation that allocates to D liability for the loss caused to C by the activity. If the matter comes to court, the court's job is not to exercise a remedial discretion to cancel a breach of duty and endorse a wrong, but to determine the subsisting rights of the parties and give effect to them. This is not just a matter of terminology, because, as in the contract case, it reveals the flaw in what would otherwise appear to be a compelling argument for a general right to an injunction or specific performance.

Thus it seems to me important to recognise the distinction between primary liability and primary duty relations. There is some support in the literature for the distinction. It amounts to a version of the famous distinction between property rules and liability rules.[31] It also has something in common with the distinction between rights to compensation and rights to prohibition.[32]

The primary liability approach might be mistaken for a reductionist account of legal duties.[33] A reductionist account defines a duty in terms of the legal consequences of D's act: to say that D has a legal duty not to act in a certain way is just

[29] A standard example is *Shelfer v City of London Electric Lightning Co* [1885] 1 Ch 287.

[30] *Jaggard v Sawyer* [1995] 1 WLR 269 at 287–88, per Millett LJ. The same argument about extortion is made with respect to specific performance in contract: see *Co-operative Insurance Services v Argyll Stores* [1998] AC 1.

[31] G Calabresi and AD Melamed, 'Property Rules, Liability Rules, and Inalienability: One View of the Cathedral' (1972) 85 *Harvard Law Review* 1089. On the analysis suggested here (i) the distinction is not to do with property; (ii) the remedial position cannot be evaluated in isolation from the primary relation, which was described as an 'entitlement'; (iii) the property rules/liability rules distinction does not overcome the problem of remedial inconsistency; (iv) it does not distinguish between rights against loss and rights to benefit (the latter is considered in ch 9); and (v) the property rules/liability rules distinction was based on a distributive justice (EAL) approach, according to which all measures are forms of sanction rather than remedy, and the distinction is between penalty and price.

[32] See BH Fried, 'The Limits of a Nonconsequentialist Approach to Torts' (2012) 18 *Legal Theory* 231; N Jansen, 'The Idea of Legal Responsibility' (2013) *Oxford Journal of Legal Studies* 1; R Stone, 'Private Liability Without Wrongdoing' (2023) 73 *University of Toronto Law Journal* 53.

[33] Associated with the 'bad man' theory: see OW Holmes, 'The Path of the Law' (1897) 10 *Harvard Law Review* 457. For objections to the theory, see HLA Hart, *The Concept of Law* (Oxford University Press, Clarendon Press, 1961); JCP Goldberg and BC Zipursky, 'Seeing Tort Law from the Internal Point of View: Holmes and Hart on Legal Duties' (2006) 75 *Fordham Law Review* 1563; Ripstein, *Private Wrongs* (n 24) ch 1, 238–40.

to say that if D does act in this way D will be liable to pay compensation (or be subject to some other legal consequence). The implication is that a legal duty does not lay down a requirement for how the duty-bearer should act. It is said that such an approach denies the internal or normative dimension of the law. One might think that a primary liability is a reductionist account of a primary duty, but this is not what is intended. On the primary liability approach, there are primary duties as well as primary liabilities. Like a primary duty, a primary liability is normative, but in the sense that it gives guidance or direction concerning the risk of loss to C that D ought to bear according to the law, rather than about what D ought to do according to the law.

Neither does the primary liability approach deny that C has a right against D or that there is a bilateral relation between them. C has a right against D that D bear the risk of harm caused. On the corrective justice approach, there are primary right–duty relations, which reflect underlying moral rights and duties. On the distributive justice approach, it is thought that the legal relations of private law are only nominally bilateral. They are based on underlying public rights and public duties or liabilities enforced through civil proceedings. Although C takes action for C's own benefit, the justification for the claim is that, by enforcing the right against D, C procures the imposition of a sanction on D that promotes distributive justice through its influence on people generally.[34] Again, this is not the implication of the primary liability approach. The primary liability relation is a genuine bilateral relation, like the primary duty relation.

Thus the suggested understanding of primary relations is at odds with both the corrective justice and distributive justice approaches as they are usually understood. But the approach suggested does seem to reflect the law as it is. The problem is to explain how it can be justified for the law to have legal relations of this sort.

Remedial Consistency

Consistency Over Time and Remedial Consistency

Where circumstances remain the same, the legal position should remain the same as well. Where there are new circumstances, the legal position may change but it should do so in a way that is consistent with the justification for the original position. The requirement of consistency applies between primary and remedial relations. This is the requirement of 'remedial consistency'.[35] Where there is a

[34] See further ch 4.

[35] See also P Jaffey, 'Remedial Consistency in Private Law' (2022) 72 *University of Toronto Law Journal* 216. This issue appears in various guises, for example as remedial 'monism' and 'dualism'. See eg EJ Weinrib, *Corrective Justice* (Oxford University Press, 2012) ch 3; EL Sherwin, 'An Essay on Private Remedies' (1983) 6 *Canadian Journal of Law & Jurisprudence* 89; E Voyiakis, *Private Law and the Value of Choice* (Hart, 2017) ch 1.

primary liability relation, a claim for compensation arises simply as a matter of consistency, given the primary relation, not on the basis of a principle of responsibility for wrongdoing, or a duty to repair a wrong. The claim arises directly from the materialisation of a risk of loss to C for which D is responsible.

When a court has to decide whether to order performance of a duty, as argued above the exercise of judgement should be understood to relate to the determination of the subsisting legal position, that is to say whether or not there is a duty. If it determines that there is a duty the court should enforce it. If D has a duty to perform (a genuine duty and not a primary liability) and the court does not order performance, there is remedial inconsistency or remedial 'dualism'.[36] The justification for the remedial position is inconsistent with the justification for the primary relation (given the character of a legal duty as a duty performance of which should be required). The failure to recognise the distinction between primary duties and primary liabilities leads to remedial inconsistency.

In contract, there is said to be always a legal duty to perform, and the court is understood to exercise a remedial discretion under the 'damages are inadequate' test to determine whether to give effect to the duty by ordering performance. This involves remedial inconsistency. This is clear where the reasons given for not ordering performance by D are really reasons why D does not have a duty to perform – for example where it is said that an order should not be made because in the public interest D should be legally free to take up an alternative opportunity instead of performing.[37] The better analysis, as discussed above, is that ordinarily D is subject to a primary liability by which D bears the risk of loss to C. If it becomes impossible for C's risk to be satisfactorily protected by compensation – if compensation becomes inadequate in the circumstances – D incurs a duty to perform. This is a matter of consistency with respect to justification.[38] The 'damages are inadequate' test is a test of whether a duty has arisen. This reflects the requirement of remedial consistency.

Similarly, a duty may lapse as a result of a change of circumstances without remedial inconsistency. Say D encroaches on C's land in breach of a duty against trespass. As a matter of remedial consistency, D should have a duty to leave C's land, which one might say is a variant of the original duty not to encroach on the land. However, to take the case mentioned earlier, where D trespasses on C's land by building on a small part of it, so that it would be very expensive to undo the effects of the trespass, the burden for D in undoing the effect of the trespass is far greater than the insignificant burden of refraining from encroachment in the

[36] Ibid.

[37] See further ch 4.

[38] Remedial discretion has been criticised on various grounds: see eg P Birks, 'Three Kinds of Objections to Discretionary Remedialism' (2000) 29 *University of Western Australia Law Review* 1; D Jensen, 'The Rights and Wrongs of Discretionary Remedialism' (2003) *Singapore Journal of Legal Studies* 178.

first place. Given the hardship to D, it is not inconsistent with the justification for the original duty for D's duty to lapse, so that D is not required to demolish the building.[39]

Some commentators have advanced an argument similar to the remedial consistency argument, as I have described it above, to justify the right to compensation for a wrong. Take the case where, in breach of duty, D destroys C's property. According to Gardner, in such a case, where actual performance of the original duty is no longer possible and the duty has lapsed, the reasons behind the original duty nevertheless continue as 'reasons for conformity', which give D a new duty to provide C with the next-best alternative to the performance of the original duty, that is to say, the payment of compensation. This is Gardner's 'continuity thesis'.[40]

In support of the continuity thesis, Gardner points out that if D has a contractual duty to provide C with a benefit and fails to provide it, and the circumstances remain the same, the duty must continue to subsist; and if the circumstances differ slightly from the circumstances before the breach, a variant of the duty arises, for example a duty to provide the benefit late. This seems to illustrate the requirement of remedial consistency, in the terminology adopted above. By extension, according to Gardner, where no variant of the original duty is any longer possible, as in the case of the destroyed property, the reasons behind the original duty persist to justify the next-best alternative in the new circumstances, that is to say the duty to pay compensation. This may also seem to be the application of the requirement of remedial consistency.

However, the requirement of remedial consistency does not justify compensation for a wrong. The remedial consistency argument applies in the case of a continuing duty in contract because the new circumstances, though not identical to the original circumstances, are analogous, in the sense that the change in circumstances does not affect the position in a morally significant way. The considerations that justify the original duty continue to justify a modified duty in the new circumstances. There would otherwise be an implicit inconsistency with the primary relation. But in a case of compensation for loss, after the loss has occurred the new circumstances are entirely different from the circumstances beforehand. If D had a duty not to cause the loss, before the loss occurred the duty reflected a balance between C's interest against loss and D's interest in acting without constraint. In the new circumstances, C no longer has any interest that D not act in a way that might cause the loss that has already occurred and now has a quite different interest in receiving compensation. At the same time, the burden of paying compensation for loss is likely to be far greater than the burden involved beforehand in avoiding damage, which is likely to have been very slight. The new situation is not analogous to the situation before the wrong in the sense that a right

[39] Thus a mandatory injunction can be denied without inconsistency: see *Shelfer v City of London Electric Lightning Co* [1885] 1 Ch 287.

[40] J Gardner, 'What is Tort Law For? Part 1: The Place of Corrective Justice' (2011) 30 *Law and Philosophy* 1, 28–37; J Gardner, *From Personal Life to Private Law* (Oxford University Press, 2018) 102–24. EJ Weinrib, *Corrective Justice* (Oxford University Press, 2012) ch 3; Ripstein (n 24).

of compensation is required as a matter of consistency with the justification for the primary right. One might argue that the burden imposed on D as a remedy for a wrong might be justified on the basis of D's responsibility for the wrong, but this is not relevant to the continuity thesis.

The remedial consistency argument accounts only for a right to compensation arising from a primary liability. With respect to a primary liability, one might say – echoing the way the continuity thesis is expressed – that the remedial right to compensation is essentially the same right as the primary right, or that there is a continuity in the underlying reasons.

Remedies and Sanctions

The right to a remedy is what C is entitled to from D, as a matter of remedial consistency, given the primary right. The role of the court is to establish the current position, tracing from the primary right in the light of events, and give effect to it. C's remedial right must be enforced at C's instigation, to give due recognition to the primary right. By contrast, C does not, as a matter of remedial consistency, acquire a right to a sanction. C may have a right to a sanction – for example, punitive damages – but its justification is not to protect C's own primary right. If punitive damages are awarded, they are a windfall to C since the response goes beyond what is necessary to protect C's primary right.

If private law typically consists of primary duties, as on the conventional view, there is a systemic problem of underenforcement. D typically commits a wrong for which D pays compensation but D may be left better off and generally D is not punished. As it has been put, this is an embarrassment to the conventional analysis.[41] If private law generally has the form of primary liability relations, this problem is much less significant.[42]

Remedial Consistency and 'Free-standing' Remedies

Sometimes the law is presented as giving the court the power to make a remedial order because this is what justice requires in the light of events, even though C has no right to the remedy derived from a prior right against D – there is a 'free-standing remedy'. Equitable remedies were developed in the equity or Chancery courts, but were available for a primary right recognised at common law – for example, this was the case for specific performance. As a matter of doctrine, the remedy was dissociated from the common law primary right. This is conducive

[41] See J Morgan, *Great Debates in Contract Law* (MacMillan, 3rd edn 2020) 50.

[42] A distinction is drawn between the 'guidance' and 'remedial justice' roles of private law: see GJ Postema, 'Introduction: Search for an Explanatory Theory of Torts' in GJ Postema (ed), *Philosophy and the Law of Torts* (Cambridge University Press, 2001) 2. The tension between them is much reduced on the primary liability approach.

of remedial inconsistency. In some circumstances, an equitable remedy is said to be available where C had no primary right at all, or the primary right is not identified. This may be the case for an injunction where the ground for awarding it is D's unconscionable behaviour.[43] One can see how the law arrived at this position, because equity developed the jurisdiction to award a remedy, for rights that were not recognised in equity, but it seems impossible to defend in principle, because it is contrary to the requirement of remedial consistency. The requirement of remedial consistency implies not only that C is entitled to a remedy based on the primary right, but also that there can be no remedial right or remedy without a prior right from which the remedial right arises.

Take the case of the equitable doctrine of proprietary estoppel. Where D has made a promise to C concerning an interest in D's land, and C has relied on the promise to C's detriment, it may be unconscionable for D to go back on the promise (which is not binding contractually). It is said that the court has a remedial discretion to award a remedy – the 'minimum equity to do justice' – which may, but need not, amount to awarding a property right in the land. This is liable to be formulated without reference to a primary right arising from D's promise and C's detrimental reliance.[44] As considered further below, the law is clearer when the remedial award can be understood to satisfy a primary right and the primary right is recognised explicitly and articulated.

Even with respect to compensation in contract and tort, it has been suggested that the right to compensation is in the nature of a free-standing remedial right, not based on any primary right.[45] It is a matter of doing justice in the circumstances. The appeal of this approach may be in part that it avoids the difficulty of justifying the claim for compensation as a response to a breach of duty, the assumption being that if a claim is based on C's primary right it must arise from the breach of a primary duty. The better explanation is that it arises from a primary liability relation, involving a right of C's against D that D bear the risk of loss to C.

Remedial Consistency and Alternative Remedies

Various remedies can arise out of a contract. The requirement of remedial consistency implies that they should form a coherent regime, in the sense that each should be consistent, in the circumstances in which it arises, with the same primary relation in contract. This is worth discussing at some length, as an illustration of the implications of remedial consistency,[46] and also because the remedial regime in

[43] *South Carolina Insurance v Assurantie Maatschappij de Zeven Provincien* [1987] AC 24.

[44] See *Guest v Guest* [2022] UKSC 27.

[45] See eg A Robertson, 'On the Function of the Law of Negligence' (2013) 33 *Oxford Journal of Legal Studies* 31; SA Smith, *Rights, Wrongs, and Injustices* (Oxford University Press, 2019) ch 7.

[46] For another example, take the case where D makes a mistaken valuation for C. Should C recover the difference in value or the loss incurred in reliance on the valuation? On one view the alternatives are different remedies arising from the same primary relation: see J Stapleton, 'The Normal Expectancies

contract is relevant to the discussion of the corrective justice and distributive justice approaches to contract in later chapters.[47]

As discussed above, the absence of a right to specific performance in the usual case supports the primary liability approach, as does the absence of a requirement of subjective fault. The absence of a duty to perform also follows from the mitigation rule in contract. Where D has declined to perform, but could still do so, C cannot recover for losses incurred by relying on the assumption that D will still perform. This is difficult to understand on the orthodox primary duty approach, because, if C is bound to accept that D's duty has lapsed, the implication is that in breaching this duty D negates or cancels it.[48] It makes more sense with respect to the mitigation rule to say that D did not have a duty to perform, only a primary liability.

On the primary liability approach, the 'damages are inadequate' test is a test for when, exceptionally, a duty to perform arises and C accordingly has a right to actual performance in order to protect C from uncompensable loss. In some other contexts, there is an equivalent test, the 'legitimate interest' test. Say A has commissioned B to provide a service but A then tells B that A is withdrawing from the contract. Is B bound to accept the termination, so that B is confined to a claim in damages, or can B choose to perform the service and recover the contract price, if B can do so without A's assistance? It appears that B must accept A's repudiation of the contract and so is confined to accepting damages unless B has a 'legitimate interest' in keeping the contract alive.[49] If A has a duty to perform and B a right to A's performance, as they do on the orthodox understanding, this is difficult to understand: A must surely be obliged to allow B to perform and be paid for this work. How can it make sense to ask whether a party has a legitimate interest in the continuation of a contract if that party has a right to it? It does make sense if the parties normally have only a right that the other party bear the risk of loss from non-performance, and the 'legitimate interest' test, like the 'damages are inadequate' test, is a test for when a duty to perform and a right to performance have arisen to protect C against uncompensable loss.

The same approach is reflected in the rule on 'disgorgement', that is, the removal of D's profit from a wrong according to the principle that wrongdoers should not profit from their wrongs. Disgorgement is not a remedy in the strict sense – it does not serve to undo the effect of the wrong on C. It is in the nature of a sanction, and the disgorgement is a windfall to C. Thus some argue that disgorgement should not

Measure in Tort Damages' (1997) 113 *Law Quarterly Review* 257. This involves remedial inconsistency or dualism. The better view is that there are two different primary relations. See further P Jaffey, *Private Law and Property Claims* (Hart, 2007) ch 2.

[47] See further P Jaffey, 'Restitutionary Remedies in the Contractual Context' (2013) 76 *Modern Law Review* 429.

[48] See eg PS Atiyah, *Essays on Contract* (Clarendon Press, 1986) 124; D Campbell, 'Market damages in sales of goods and their relationship to the general principles of remedies for breach of contract' in Halson and Campbell (n 5).

[49] *White & Carter v McGregor* [1962] UKHL 5.

be available at all.[50] But, if it is available, it should be available only with respect to the profits of a wrong. Consistently with the primary liability approach, it is not generally available in contract, but it is available exceptionally where damages are inadequate, or, as it is also put, where C has a 'legitimate interest' in preventing D's profit-making activity in breach of contract.[51] This is apt on the suggested approach because it implies that a duty has arisen and so exceptionally it is wrongful not to perform.

A similar issue arises with respect to penalty clauses. The traditional rule was that a contractual clause setting a pecuniary measure of recovery in the event of non-performance is valid if it was intended as a genuine pre-estimate of loss (an agreed remedy of compensation) but not if it was designed to deter non-performance (an agreed sanction). The rule in English law now is that such a clause is valid if it protects a legitimate interest under the contract.[52] Normally C has a legitimate interest only in compensation, but sometimes C has a legitimate interest in actual performance and here a clause that seeks to protect such an interest by deterrence through an agreed sanction can be valid. Again, it is difficult to see how it can make sense to ask whether someone has a legitimate interest in actual performance when that person has a right to it and the other party a duty to provide it, as on the orthodox understanding. It would be better to say, consistently with the primary liability approach, that a provision for deterrence going beyond compensation is justifiable where exceptionally D has become subject to a duty to perform and this is where C has a 'legitimate interest' in performance – that is, a right to performance.[53]

The various aspects of the law referred to above support the primary liability approach rather than the primary duty approach. But what about the measure of compensation? The standard measure of damages in contract is of course the expectation measure. It is conventionally understood to arise from a primary duty to perform the contract, since it represents the loss relative to C's position if the duty had been performed. Can the expectation measure be explained on the primary liability approach, if D has no duty to provide performance and C no right to it?

One way of understanding the basis for the primary liability approach is as follows. The contract is an agreed exchange by which typically C expends work

[50] See eg A Beever, 'The Structure of Aggravated and Exemplary Damages' (2003) 23 *Oxford Journal of Legal Studies* 1; EJ Weinrib, 'Punishment and Disgorgement as Contract Remedies' (2003) 78 *Chicago-Kent Law Review* 55.

[51] *Attorney-General v Blake* [2001] 1 AC 268; K Barnett, *Accounting for Profits for Breach of Contract* (Hart, 2012). Similarly when a contract is fiduciary there is always a duty actually to perform it – this is the duty of good faith or duty of loyalty or duty to advance the interests of the principal – and disgorgement is always available, as illustrated by *Attorney-General v Guardian Newspapers Ltd (No 2)* ('*Spycatcher*') [1988] UKHL 6: see further P Jaffey, *The Nature and Scope of Restitution* (Hart Publishing, 2000) ch 13.

[52] *Cavendish Square Holding v El Makdessi* [2015] UKSC 67.

[53] See generally S Rowan 'The "Legitimate Interest in Performance" in the Law on Penalties' (2018) 78 *Cambridge Law Journal* 148.

and materials in return for payment from D. The contract sets the price and once C has provided the performance C has a right to payment, not because D has a duty to pay, but because the contract allocates this liability to D in the event of performance by C. This is explicable on the basis that the contract protects C's reliance interest, that is to say, C's interest in being paid for the work and materials C has expended in performing the contract. There is, in other words, a primary liability relation allocating liability for loss relative to the reliance interest. On completion of performance by C, this is equivalent to the expectation measure. This is a version of the reliance theory of contract. It explains C's remedy as satisfaction for C's reliance interest, rather than as a remedy for D's breach of duty to perform.[54]

If C has only part performed, the appropriate measure to protect the reliance interest is payment for the work done under the contract, measured relative to the amount due for complete performance. This is indeed usually available, in the form of a quantum meruit.[55] The quantum meruit claim is difficult to explain on the orthodox approach because, as matter of remedial consistency, it is not apt as a remedy for breach of the duty to perform. What C is entitled to under the orthodox approach is simply the performance of D's duty, or compensation for the failure to perform the duty, measured in terms of the value of D's performance to C, not the satisfaction of C's contractual reliance interest. Although the quantum meruit is justified on the reliance approach, it is reasonable to allow the expectation measure generally, even at the risk of overcompensation, because of the difficulty of measuring the reliance interest directly, and taking into account that if C had not made the contract with D, C might well have made a contract with someone else that would have brought a comparable return.[56]

C may also have a claim to recover a payment C has made in advance for work and materials to be supplied by D, if D has not performed, even if the measure of recovery exceeds C's expectation measure. Again it is difficult to see why this claim should be allowed on the orthodox approach: as a matter of remedial consistency, the measure cannot be explained as a remedy for a breach of a duty to perform. It does not represent the loss to C resulting from D's non-performance of the duty. But again it can be understood as a claim to protect C's reliance interest. Whereas the quantum meruit, as payment in satisfaction of part performance, should be measured as a proportion of payment due for full performance, there is no reason why the recovery of a payment in satisfaction of the reliance interest should be limited to the expectation measure.

The quantum meruit and the claim for recovery of a payment made in advance are commonly said to be based on a non-contractual principle of unjust enrichment. This is how remedial inconsistency is avoided on the orthodox understanding

[54] See further ch 4.

[55] See further P Jaffey, 'Restitutionary Remedies in the Contractual Context' (2013) 76 *Modern Law Review* 429.

[56] The opportunity cost argument, derived from LL Fuller and WR Perdue, 'The Reliance Interest in Contract Damages' (Pt 1) (1936) 46 *Yale Law Journal* 52.

of contract. The unjust enrichment explanation of these claims is that the claim does not arise from the agreement as such, but from the failure of the basis on which the payment or work was done, or the failure of a condition on which it was done – from 'failure of basis' or 'failure of condition' as an 'unjust factor' in unjust enrichment, as it is put.[57] The basis that fails is the agreement and the failure of basis is the non-performance, and similarly the failure of condition is the non-performance of the agreement. It is difficult to see how this can be understood as a non-contractual rationale for the claim. For some purposes it may not matter that the claim for recovery of a prepayment and the claim for a quantum meruit are treated as non-contractual claims, but it certainly runs the risk of treating the contract as governed, at the same time, by two different allocations of risk. This leads to remedial inconsistency. It is incoherent and subversive of the contractual allocation of risk, which reflects the terms of the agreement. It may allow for a measure of recovery that is not justified under the contract.[58] The claim for a quantum meruit and the claim to recover a prepayment are more plausibly explained as contractual reliance claims.[59]

In connection with the reliance approach, and as an illustration of remedial consistency, it is worth making a comparison with proprietary estoppel, as analysed in the Supreme Court.[60] As mentioned above, where D has made a promise to C with respect to an interest in land – for example, a promise to leave D's farm to C when D dies if C works on the farm in the meantime for minimal pay – C may have a claim against D (though there is no valid contract) on the ground that it would be unconscionable for D to go back on the promise. The appropriate remedy is the 'minimum equity to do justice'. The law is understood to involve a remedial discretion. The usual issue has been whether, in the exercise of its discretion, the court should aim to compensate C for C's detrimental reliance, or to satisfy C's expectation interest by ordering D to pass on the farm or pay C an equivalent sum.

As pointed out above, the requirement of remedial consistency implies that the primary right should be identified and protected. One possibility is that D has a primary duty to perform the promise and C a correlative legal right to performance of the promise.[61] This would mean that the court has a remedial discretion whether or to what extent to protect C's primary right. This is analogous to the orthodox approach to contract. It involves remedial inconsistency, since the court may depart from the subsisting legal position. Another possibility is that C has a

[57] See eg A Burrows, *A Restatement of the English Law of Unjust Enrichment* (Oxford University Press, 2012) section 15 on 'failure of consideration'.

[58] See further Jaffey (n 55).

[59] Jaffey (ibid). The primary liability approach is also preferable to the idea that contract law protects three distinct 'interests' in contract of equal standing, the expectation, the reliance and the restitution interests, giving rise to three different remedies, the approach due to Fuller and Perdue (n 56). In the light of the remedial consistency argument this would seem to imply three different inconsistent primary rights in contract.

[60] *Guest v Guest* [2022] UKSC 27.

[61] The approach taken by Lord Briggs.

right against D that D bear the risk of loss from C's reliance on the promise, and D has a correlative primary liability.[62] This would mean that normally there is a right to compensation for detrimental reliance, but it may be that C's reliance interest can be satisfactorily protected only by ordering D to fulfil the promise, in which case D incurs a duty to perform the promise and grant the property right or pay an equivalent sum. This analysis involves a primary liability relation with an allocation of risk with respect to the reliance interest, which sometimes generates a primary duty. The court does not have a remedial discretion to depart from the subsisting legal position. It has to determine the subsisting legal position in the light of events, in accordance with the requirement of remedial consistency. This reliance approach is equivalent to the reliance theory of contract. It is a preferable analysis because it avoids remedial inconsistency. It is worth pointing this out because, although it may not be the standard analysis of proprietary estoppel, it has received recognition as a legitimate alternative, and by implication it lends support to the reliance approach as a legitimate understanding of contract.

I have discussed contract remedies to illustrate the implication of the requirement of remedial consistency that remedies should form a coherent regime. The remedial rules in contract taken together form a coherent regime on the assumption that there is a primary liability relation in contract based on the protection of contractual reliance, ie on an allocation of risk with respect to the reliance interest. By contrast, for the law to give full effect to the primary duty approach, a dramatic reform would be required. In particular, specific performance would have to be generally available. I shall come back to the question whether there ought to be a primary duty or primary liability regime in contract, and to the reliance theory, in connection with the discussion of the corrective justice and distributive justice approaches to contract in later chapters.

Summary

On the approach I suggest, the bilateral legal relations of private law are not normally right–duty relations, and a claim for compensation is not based on a breach of duty or a wrong. Claims for compensation arise from primary liability relations consisting of an allocation of the risk of liability for loss. There may also be duties to avoid or prevent loss, which can give rise to claims for specific performance or an injunction, or possibly disgorgement or punitive damages. The justification for the remedy relative to the primary right is remedial consistency, not a principle of moral responsibility for wrongdoing. There is no remedial discretion, in the sense of a discretion to depart from the subsisting legal position – the court's role is to determine the subsisting legal position and give effect to it by

[62] The approach taken by Lord Leggatt.

an order for compensation or other appropriate remedy, not to determine in what way or to what extent it is appropriate to respect or depart from the subsisting legal position. The bilateral relations of private law, understood in this way as primary liability relations, do not reflect the usual understanding on either the corrective justice approach or the distributive justice approach. Why private law has, and whether it ought to have, primary liability relations as defined above is a crucial question to be considered in later chapters.

4

The Distributive Justice Approach

Distributive Justice and Interactions

The Distributive Justice Approach

The corrective justice approach does better than the distributive justice approach in explaining traditional private law, and so it might seem more apt to discuss the corrective justice approach first. However, the nature of corrective justice is more elusive, and part of its appeal is that it is thought to overcome the weaknesses of the distributive justice approach. Thus it may be easier to consider the distributive justice approach and its weaknesses first.

People have interests in having benefits and avoiding harms, and distributive justice is concerned with how these interests should be advanced and accommodated in the way society is organised and how it operates. According to the distributive justice approach, when judges develop private law or the legislature legislates for the interactions of private law, it is distributive justice that they should draw on. Private law is concerned with interactions that generate benefits and harms, and private law stipulates whether the parties ought to engage in the interaction, or what risk of liability they should bear in doing so, and what the legal consequences should be. The rules on these issues contribute to determining the distribution of benefits and harms across society and so do seem to be in principle a matter for distributive justice.

The best developed body of work applying a distributive justice approach to private law is EAL. According to EAL, private law should be understood as an instrument for the promotion of aggregate welfare or net benefit across society.[1] The rationale of the law of negligence is to reduce loss through accidents or other forms of inadvertent harm,[2] and the rationale of the law of contract is to maximise the benefit obtained through the contractual exchange of goods and services for payment. As mentioned in chapter two, EAL (an MTL, which holds that aggregate net benefit should be promoted across society) should be distinguished from economics as a social science (an STL, applied to the law to establish how aggregate

[1] Amongst the influential works are L Kaplow and S Shavell, *Fairness versus Welfare* (Harvard University Press, 2002); G Calabresi, *The Cost of Accidents* (Yale University Press, 1970); RA Posner, *Economic Analysis of Law* (Little Brown, 1973).

[2] I shall use 'accidents' to refer to inadvertent harm generally.

net benefit can be maximised). EAL draws on economics in this sense by way of policy analysis of the effect of possible rules.

EAL amounts to a version of utilitarianism, and an objection to EAL has been that since, like utilitarianism, it is concerned only with aggregate welfare or net benefit, it takes inadequate account of distributive or egalitarian concerns. One might object that for this reason it should not be understood as a theory of distributive justice at all. However, like utilitarianism, EAL can be understood as a theory of distributive justice because, although it does not aim for a certain pattern of distribution across society, it does nevertheless determine the distribution, and in so doing it takes account (on its own terms) of the interests relating to benefit and harm of everyone across society. In any case, it is argued that it is possible to incorporate distributive concerns into EAL by weighting benefits and harms.[3] There are of course other theories of distributive justice that take account of egalitarian considerations in various ways. In particular, Rawls's theory of distributive justice supports the promotion of aggregate net benefit, following utilitarianism, but qualified to protect basic liberties and advance the position of the worst off. One might also object that EAL does not adequately recognise the value of liberties or opportunities as types of benefit.[4]

In any case, it is not necessary for present purposes to pursue these or other controversial questions about distributive justice or EAL in particular. They concern objections to particular ways of understanding distributive justice, not to the distributive justice approach to private law. It is said that private law cannot be a matter of distributive justice, irrespective of the particular theory of distributive justice, because, it is said, distributive justice does not apply to interactions between individuals at all, and it cannot therefore explain private law.

Does Distributive Justice Apply to Interactions?

It is said that distributive justice is concerned purely with distribution or division of the benefits and harms of society amongst its members – it is about what is divisible and how to divide it at the level of society.[5] It therefore has no application to interactions, which are not concerned with distribution or division of benefits and harms across society as a whole, but rather with benefits and harms arising as between the particular parties to an interaction. On this view, benefits

[3] Through a 'social welfare function' that gives weight to inequality or need: see Kaplow and Shavell (n 1) ch 2. Where EAL is understood in terms of wealth maximisation, it is open to the objection that wealth is not the same as welfare and wealth maximisation may undervalue the welfare of poor people: see RM Dworkin, 'Is Wealth A Value?' (1980) 9 *Journal of Legal Studies* 191.

[4] And more generally that it values harms and benefits only in terms of subjective preference: see eg NB Oman, *The Dignity of Commerce* (University of Chicago Press, 2016) ch 4.

[5] EJ Weinrib, *The Idea of Private Law* (Oxford University Press, rev edn 2012) ch 3; J Gardner, 'What is Tort Law For? Part 1. The Place of Corrective Justice' (2011) 30 *Law and Philosophy* 1.

and harms arising from an interaction must be governed by a different form of justice: interpersonal or 'interactional' justice arising as between individuals, that is to say corrective justice. Private law is then a matter of corrective justice, not distributive justice.

This understanding is difficult to accept, simply because the benefits and harms arising from interactions are part of society's benefits and harms. If distributive justice is concerned with interests in benefits and harms, it seems bound to extend to interactions. The challenge, one might think, is really for the corrective justice approach to find a place for corrective justice. There are various ways of trying to identify a place for corrective justice from which distributive justice should be excluded, as considered further in chapter five.

One might say, first, that on the corrective justice approach there are moral rights against others with respect to person and property and moral rights to contract that bind other people directly with respect to interactions and exclude any considerations of distributive justice. This could be understood as in fact a version of the distributive justice approach – a libertarian version that excludes distributive justice in the usual more egalitarian sense that supports risk-sharing and redistribution. A second position, which is a more widely held view, is that interactions are governed by corrective justice in this sense in private law as developed at common law, so that distributive justice in the usual sense is irrelevant at common law, but the legislature can make provision by statute for interactions on the basis of distributive justice, thus reforming or replacing the common law if it considers that this will advance distributive justice. In other words, on this view distributive justice does apply to interactions, though (for some reason) not so far as the courts are concerned with respect to the common law.

A further view is that the prior position of the parties to an interaction is governed by distributive justice, and if the benefits and harms arising from the interaction are unjust it is because they involve a departure from this prior position. Corrective justice is concerned with protecting and restoring the prior position. It would seem that the rationale for protecting and restoring the prior position is to uphold distributive justice, and so corrective justice is actually dependent on and ancillary to distributive justice.[6] It is argued that the courts should assume that the prior position correctly reflects distributive justice. Again, this seems to show that interactions are in principle a matter for distributive justice, though again (for some reason) the courts cannot draw on it directly.

None of these approaches shows that distributive justice does not in principle apply to interactions. The problem raised is really how to find room for the corrective justice approach, as considered in chapter five.[7]

[6] See eg J Gordley, *Foundations of Private Law* (Oxford University Press, 2006); J Gordley, 'Equality in Exchange' (1981) 969 *California Law Review* 1587; H Sheinman 'Tort Law and Corrective Justice' (2005) 22 *Law and Philosophy* 21; H Dagan, 'The Distributive Foundations of Corrective Justice' (1999) 98 *Michigan Law Review* 138.

[7] Cf R Avraham and I Kohler-Hausmann, 'Accident Law for Egalitarians' (2006) 12 *Legal Theory* 181.

A related argument against the distributive justice approach is that distributive justice is concerned only with the operation of the institutions of society, and not individual actions. In particular, according to Rawls, distributive justice is concerned only with the 'basic structure' of society, meaning the main political and social institutions, which include in particular the market system and the means for collecting tax and providing public services and individual state benefits.[8] According to Rawls, the rules applicable directly to individuals should be clear and simple so that it is feasible and practicable to expect individuals to follow them, which means that they cannot be subject to the principles of distributive justice that govern the basic structure. There has to be a 'division of labour' between the institutions forming the basic structure, which are subject to distributive justice, and individuals, who are subject to rules that govern interactions in private law without giving effect to distributive justice.[9] It seems that interactions must be concerned with a different form of justice, presumably again corrective justice.

There are certainly principles of distributive justice that are applicable only to institutions – no doubt the most important principles – and a theory of distributive justice might reasonably be focused on these principles, but this does not imply that the benefits and harms affecting individuals as a result of interactions are not also in principle a matter for distributive justice. If institutions are concerned with distributive justice when they determine how responsibility for harms and entitlement to benefits should be allocated by institutions, it is difficult to see why the allocation of rights with respect to the harms and benefits of interactions is not also a matter for distributive justice. Furthermore, it is part of the function of the basic structure to adjust continuously for any adverse effect that interactions under private law may have on distributive justice across society, for example by way of taxation and social security benefits,[10] and this again seems to imply that the benefits and harms of interactions for which adjustment is made are themselves a matter for distributive justice.

It would seem better to say that there is a division of labour between institutions and individuals with respect to the implementation of distributive justice, in the light of the practical constraints on rules for individuals, and with appropriate adjustment in response to the benefits and harms of interactions, in order to achieve distributive justice overall.[11]

[8] J Rawls, *A Theory of Justice* (Belknap Press, 1971) 6–10; J Rawls, *Justice as Fairness: A Restatement* (Harvard University Press, 2001) 39–40; S Freeman, *Liberalism and Distributive Justice* (Oxford University Press, 2018) ch 5; S Scheffler, 'Distributive Justice, the Basic Structure and the Place of Private Law' (2015) 35 *Oxford Journal of Legal Studies* 213; L Martins Zanitelli, 'Rawls and Private Law' (2019) 22(28) *Revista Juris Poiesis* 59; ZX Tan, 'Where the Action is: Macro and Micro Justice in Contract Law' (2020) 83 *Modern Law Review* 725.

[9] J Rawls, *Political Liberalism* (Columbia University Press, 1993) 267–69.

[10] Rawls (ibid) 267–68. See also A Ripstein, 'The Division of Responsibility and the Law of Tort' (2004) 72 *Fordham Law Review* 1811.

[11] Various writers argue that the harms and benefits of individual actions and interactions are a matter of distributive justice, but it seems unnecessary to argue that they must be within the basic structure for

There are certainly principles of distributive justice that have no application to individuals or interactions and are concerned only with division across society or with the functioning of institutions, but this does not mean that the benefits and harms of interactions are not also a matter of distributive justice. In my view, one should say, as EAL assumes, that distributive justice comprises all the moral considerations arising from the interests relating to benefit and harm of everyone across the society, including the benefits and harms arising from the interactions governed by private law.

Can Distributive Justice Explain Private Law?

If distributive justice applies to interactions, it would seem that the crucial question for private law is simply which theory of distributive justice is the right one and how it applies to interactions. But the puzzle is that private law, as it has developed, often seems to depart from what any plausible theory of distributive justice could possibly prescribe. In particular, private law takes no account of the societal distribution of wealth. A possible explanation for this, already alluded to, is that private law should be understood as a limited part of a wider system under a division of responsibility with respect to distributive justice. The difficulty with this explanation is that on the face of it one would think that such a division of responsibility would have to be introduced and recognised openly, but the understanding of the courts seems to be that they are applying a comprehensive concept of justice that applies to interactions rather than merely a limited aspect of justice. Furthermore, this explanation does not give any indication of how private law should be limited or why it has developed in the law in the way that it has.

One might conclude that private law is indefensible in its traditional form and needs reform in order to give effect properly to distributive justice. Some commentators do take this view.[12] However, private law has been developed over a long period by judges who in various contexts have determined the justice of the case as it seemed to them, and it is these decisions that constitute the law. Can it be entirely an illusion that this largely coherent body of law gives effect to a genuine

this to be the case: cf Scheffler (n 8). See GA Cohen, 'Where the Action is: On the Site of Distributive Justice' (1997) 26 *Philosophy and Public Affairs* 3; Avraham and Kohler-Hausmann (n 7) 210; LB Murphy, 'Institutions and the Demands of Justice' (1998) 27 *Philosophy and Public Affairs* 251; ZX Tan, 'Where the Action Is: Macro and Micro Justice in Contract Law' (2020) 83 *Modern Law Review* 725. Cf Raz's 'dependence thesis' according to which an authority's reasons for its directives are the reasons of the people to whom the directives are directed: J Raz, *The Morality of Freedom* (Clarendon Press, 1986) ch 3.

[12] See eg L Alexander and K Kessler Ferzan, 'Confused Culpability, Contrived Causation, and the Collapse of Tort Theory' in J Oberdiek (ed), *Philosophical Foundations of the Law of Torts* (Oxford University Press, 2014); LA Alexander, 'Causation and Corrective Justice, Does Tort Law Make Sense?' (1987) 6 *Law and Philosophy*; S Hedley, 'The Unacknowledged Revolution in Liability for Negligence' in S Worthington, A Robertson and G Virgo (eds), *Revolution and Evolution in Private Law* (Hart, 2018).

form of justice? The modern development of the corrective justice approach has been based on the conviction that this is the case.

In this chapter, I shall consider the problems that arise in explaining private law in terms of distributive justice. Distributive justice is concerned with how the interests of individuals across society with respect to benefits and harms should be advanced and accommodated in the way that society is organised and operates. Each person's entitlement in distributive justice depends on that person's circumstances relative to everyone else's across society, all considered together because of their interdependence. It would seem that one cannot feasibly understand distributive justice in terms of the moral rights of each person against every other person. In practice, distributive justice depends on the operation of societal institutions to mediate between individuals, and so it has to be understood in terms of individual rights against and duties to the state, given effect in law as public rights and duties, most obviously in the form of rights to public services and benefits and duties to pay tax. The moral rights and duties arising from interactions as a matter of distributive justice are, it would seem, fundamentally moral rights against and duties to the state. In private law, these moral rights are given effect through bilateral legal relations, but these legal relations are, it would seem, an artificial device to give effect to moral rights and duties vis-à-vis the state. C acts on behalf of the state and D suffers the imposition of a sanction or other measure as a means of promoting distributive justice across society.

Thus it is an illusion, on the distributive justice approach, that the bilateral relations of private law reflect and give effect to underlying bilateral moral rights as a matter of interpersonal justice, as the corrective justice approach assumes. Of course, from the point of view of the corrective justice approach, it is the fundamental weakness of the distributive justice approach that it cannot account satisfactorily for the bilateral relations of private law. This objection has been developed in particular by Weinrib and Coleman in their critiques of the EAL approach to the law of negligence.[13]

Negligence

EAL

As conventionally understood, the law of negligence imposes a duty on D owed to C to take reasonable care to avoid causing harm to C, and requires D to pay compensation if D commits a wrong by breaching the duty. The traditional

[13] See EJ Weinrib, *The Idea of Private Law* (Oxford University Press, rev edn 2012) ch 1; EJ Weinrib, 'Corrective Justice' (1992) 77 *Iowa Law Review* 403, 407; J Coleman, *The Practice of Principle* (Oxford University Press, 2003) 13–24; JL Coleman, 'The Cost of The Cost of Accidents' (2005) 64 *Maryland Law Review* 337.

understanding (reflecting the corrective justice approach) is that the law is based on what is fair and just as between the two parties; compensation is understood as a remedy, not a sanction, and the relevant facts are about the two parties and their relationship, not about society as a whole.

On the EAL approach, negligence is understood to have the rationale of minimising the aggregate costs of accidents and accident prevention measures across society. The justification for compensation is that it is an incentive for people in D's position in the future to take appropriate precautions against harming people in C's position. C's power to take proceedings is not to enable C to protect C's own interest, but to empower C to promote the public interest in harm reduction, in effect as an agent acting for the state.[14] C just happens to be a convenient person to play this role. This implies that the bilateralism of the law of negligence is artificial, in the sense that the justification for C's claim against D is not a moral right of C against D. This is the 'bilateralism objection'. Similarly, the payment of compensation from D to C is intended not as a remedy to compensate C for C's loss, but as a sanction. Whether C is compensated for C's own loss is entirely incidental. This is the 'remedial justice objection'. On this understanding, it would seem that negligence should really be understood as a sort of public regulation imposing penalties, operating in conjunction with the criminal law to reduce the incidence of infliction of harm.[15]

This understanding would lead the law to diverge from its traditional form. A measure imposed on D as a sanction might be quite different from what would be appropriate as a remedy to compensate C. Furthermore, pursuing the EAL rationale, the law might go so far as to allow someone to act as a claimant who has not actually suffered harm at all, merely because it is convenient for that person to take proceedings. Similarly, the law might allow an action against someone who has not yet inflicted harm but has acted in a way that might cause harm and is liable to do so again, as a way of providing an appropriate deterrent.

This approach seems liable to cause injustice. Although the distributive justice objective of reduction of loss from accidents is no doubt justified, its implementation through private law may impose an excessive burden on D and give C an unjustified windfall exceeding C's loss. In addition, it is arbitrary in the sense that people who unreasonably create a risk of harm – for example by driving dangerously or carelessly – but are lucky in not causing loss are unaffected. It might seem that the objective would be better pursued through a system of penalties that focuses, like the criminal law or health and safety legislation, on conduct unreasonably creating a risk of harm rather than on providing compensation for loss.

[14] See n 11 above. See also R Posner, 'A Theory of Negligence' (1972) 1 *Journal of Legal Studies* 29.

[15] See n 11 above. See also RW Wright, 'Substantive Corrective Justice' (1992) 77 *Iowa Law Review* 625, 702–10; A Ripstein, *Private Wrongs* (Harvard University Press, 2016); P Cane, 'General and Special Tort Law: Uses and Abuses of Theory' in J Nyers et al (eds), *Emerging Issues in Tort Law* (Hart, 2007) 20; BC Zipursky, 'Rights, Wrongs and Recourse in the Law of Torts' (1998) 51 *Vanderbilt Law Review* 55–69.

Alleviation of Hardship

Some commentators reject EAL in favour of a different understanding of what distributive justice requires for negligence,[16] which may have been more influential in the UK than in the US. On this approach, the role of distributive justice in private law is not to reduce overall loss associated with accidents, but to alleviate need or hardship arising from accidents by providing compensation for loss. Again, negligence on its traditional understanding would seem inapt for this purpose. Alleviating hardship, as such, is a public purpose and the same objections apply as for aggregate loss reduction. With respect to the bilateralism objection, C's interest in alleviation of hardship supports a right against the state rather than against D, and D is used as a means of providing compensation to D to fulfil the state's public purpose of alleviating hardship. With respect to the remedial justice objection, the rationale of D's payment to C is not to satisfy C's moral right against D, but to alleviate hardship which for convenience is made the responsibility of D. Just as C is an instrument for imposing a sanction on D under EAL, so here D is merely an instrument for alleviating C's hardship.

Again, the law of negligence looks inapt to secure this public purpose. As a matter of distributive justice, one would think that the right to a payment for the alleviation of hardship should depend simply on hardship, not on whether the hardship was due to an accident or resulted from a failure to meet a standard of care. Just as negligence under EAL seems to be in the nature of an extension of the criminal law, so here it seems that negligence is a way of doing what would be more fairly and effectively achieved through workers' compensation schemes or no fault accident schemes or through the public benefits system or mandatory or social insurance.

If the law of negligence is developed to reflect this rationale it will again tend to move away from traditional private law. There will be pressure to extend the availability of compensation as widely as possible, simply according to whether D has or might acquire the means to pay compensation without undue hardship by absorbing the loss or passing it on and spreading the loss or recovering through insurance. This does not reflect the idea of interpersonal justice and again, as for sanctions to prevent future losses, there is a risk that this is unfair to D in the sense that D bears an excessive burden for the sake of advancing the public interest.

[16] See eg Hedley (n 12); S Hedley, 'Making Sense of Negligence' (2016) 36 *Legal Studies* 491; J Conaghan and W Mansell, *The Wrongs of Tort* (Pluto Press, 2nd edn 1999) chs 3 and 4; T Keren-Paz, *Torts, Egalitarianism and Distributive Justice* (Ashgate, 2007); P Cane, *Atiyah's Accidents, Compensation and the Law* (Cambridge University Press, 7th edn 2006); J Goudkamp and J Murphy, 'The Failure of Universal Theories of Tort Law' (2015) 21 *Legal Theory* 47, 78–81.

Policy Reasoning Over the Duty of Care

The traditional core cases of negligence concern personal injury and property damage caused by positive action by private individuals. The more controversial types of case arise when the law moves beyond this core, for example with respect to claims for 'pure economic loss' and claims against a public authority for failure to carry out its duty to provide a benefit. The availability of a claim is addressed in terms of whether there is a 'duty of care' in the circumstances. The duty of care concerns not the standard of conduct required of D but whether a claim against D is available at all in the circumstances. If there is no duty of care, D cannot be liable even if D's behaviour shows a complete disregard for C's interests. Whether a duty of care arises depends, at least in some circumstances, on whether the balance of 'policy factors' favours liability.[17] Policy factors are considerations that count for or against a possible rule of liability in the circumstances on the ground that the rule is likely to increase or decrease benefits or losses across society. The duty of care is said to be a 'control device' that limits the scope of the law of negligence according to the balance of policy factors.[18] Policy reasoning in this sense is an application of the distributive justice approach.

Consider the case of pure economic loss. The general rule is that there is no duty of care and no claim. For example, if C's factory is damaged by D, C can recover compensation only for the physical damage and associated economic loss, and not for pure economic loss in the form of the loss of profits resulting from disruption to the business. Similarly, where C suffers disruption to business because a bridge that C ordinarily uses to transport goods to C's factory has been damaged by D, or where the business is disrupted because the roads are blocked by the breakdown of a car due to a maintenance failure by D, C cannot recover for loss of profits.[19] The rule is usually thought to reflect the balance of policy factors.[20] Pure economic loss is taken to be a less serious type of harm than personal injury or property damage, so that with respect to pure economic loss the policy favouring compensation is outweighed by other policy factors. These other policy factors include the risk that allowing too many claims will clog up the courts with litigation, and the risk of indeterminate liability that could overwhelm defendants. These are usually understood as versions of the 'floodgates' argument.

[17] On one view, in English law policy factors come into play only once it is established that as a matter of interpersonal justice a claim is prima facie justified: A Robertson, 'On the Function of the Law of Negligence' (2013) 33 *Oxford Journal of Legal Studies* 31.

[18] See JG Fleming, 'Remoteness and Duty: The Control Devices in Liability for Negligence' (1953) 31 *Canadian Bar Review* 471. See also T Weir, 'The Staggering March of Negligence' in P Cane and J Stapleton (eds), *The Law of Obligations: Essays in Celebration of John Fleming* (Oxford University Press, 1998) 98–101; J Stapleton, 'Duty of Care Factors: A Selection from the Judicial Menu' in Cane and Stapleton (eds) (ibid); J Plunkett, *Duty of Care in Negligence* (Hart, 2020) 148–49.

[19] *Spartan Steel v Martin* [1973] QB 27.

[20] The argument is attributed to F James, 'Limitations on Liability for Economic Loss Caused by Negligence: A Pragmatic Appraisal' (1972) 25 *Vanderbilt Law Review* 43.

These policy factors, along with promoting certainty as a policy factor, are said to support the pure economic loss rule, as a convenient bright-line rule.

Pure economic loss may, however, be recoverable in a claim based on a negligent misstatement, for example a credit reference, as in the famous case of *Hedley Byrne v Heller*.[21] On one view, this also depends on the balance of policy factors. The following policy factors have been said to be relevant for negligent misstatements: unduly inhibiting freedom of expression; contradicting a contractual allocation of risk or regulatory regime; swamping courts with evidentially complex cases and unmanageable workloads; imposing liability disproportionate to fault; imposing liability so great as to distort the market for information; imposing uninsurable liability on advisers; imposing liability where C could have taken protective measures against loss, for example by taking out insurance.[22]

Another type of case where the balance of policy factors has been thought to determine liability is where the claim is against a public authority in connection with the provision of a service to C as a member of the public. The issue has arisen, for example, as to whether the police have a duty of care to a victim of a criminal who the police might have apprehended, or whether a local authority social services department has a duty of care to a child to take the child into care to prevent abuse, or whether a local authority in enforcing building regulations has a duty of care to a house purchaser to save the purchaser from buying a defective building.[23] The policy factors are considerations such as whether liability would incentivise the authority to perform its duty; or whether it would incentivise it to act defensively and apply excessive resources to avoid liability; or whether it would divert public funds into compensation that would be better spent on the normal functions of the authority; or whether it would lead to an excessive bureaucracy of oversight and the investigation of the authority's officials in connection with complaints.

The Supreme Court has recently held that in general in English law public authorities can be liable only in the way that a private individual would be liable, that is to say for causing harm, and not for a failure to provide a benefit under a public duty.[24] This is understood to reflect the longstanding common law rule excluding liability for omissions, or for failing to provide a benefit. However, it does not seem to amount to a general exclusion of policy reasoning. It could be understood as an assertion of the traditional legal position, or as a policy exclusion

[21] *Hedley Byrne v Heller* [1964] AC 465.

[22] K Barker, 'Hedley Byrne v Heller: Issues at the Beginning of the Twenty-First Century' in K Barker, R Grantham and S Swain (eds), *The Law of Misstatements: 50 Years on from* Hedley Byrne v Heller (Hart, 2015), 3.

[23] See eg *Hill v Chief Constable of West Yorkshire* [1989] AC 53; *Murphy v Brentwood BC*; *CN & CN v Poole BC* [2019] UKSC 25.

[24] Including taking action to prevent C suffering harm at the hands of a third party: *Robinson v Chief Constable of West Yorkshire* [2018] UKSC 4; *CN & CN v Poole BC* [2019] UKSC 25.

of public authority liability. There remains support for the position that the balance of policy factors must ultimately lie behind the determination of whether there is a duty of care.

Policy reasoning in these types of case seems very unsatisfactory for various reasons. On the face of it, the pure economic loss rule is an artificial limitation on liability. If C has a claim for compensation when D's careless action has caused personal injury or property loss to C, why should there not equally be liability for pure economic loss in comparable circumstances, if the loss is equally foreseeable? By contrast, a policy favouring compensation for alleviation of harm or loss spreading would seem to be an artificial extension of liability. The legal position as between C and D is merely the incidental outcome of the balance of policy factors concerned with distributive justice across society. C recovers because policies favouring recovery, including the policy of providing compensation, outweigh policies against recovery, including the policy of avoiding imposing an excessive burden on D. This may be what justice requires on the distributive justice approach, but the outcome may not seem just as between the parties.[25] Proponents of the corrective justice approach would say that it is a problem of incoherence that liability depends on issues incidental to and only contingently related to the relationship between the parties.[26]

The problems are exacerbated by the fact that it is very difficult to weigh up policy factors. It is difficult to say how a decision for or against liability would contribute to the promotion of a policy, or how one policy can be weighed against another, for example a policy of securing compensation against a policy of avoiding an excessive burden of liability. The weighing up exercise involves policy analysis, involving finding and evaluating evidence, which should require the assistance of expert policymakers, and the courts may not have the necessary resources and competence. Furthermore, the weighing up of policies in the interests of distributive justice may amount to an essentially political exercise that raises a problem of political legitimacy for the courts.

The law is liable to be excessively uncertain.[27] It is said that, once the judgement is made and a rule is established for the future, the problem of uncertainty is overcome.[28] However, the balance of policy factors is likely to be very context-specific. It may also be time-sensitive, as circumstances across society change, for example as to the organisation of public authority or the state of the public

[25] See R Stevens, *Tort and Rights* (Oxford University Press, 2007) especially at 1–3, criticising the 'loss model' of negligence, ie negligence understood to be aimed at reducing losses or alleviating hardship from accidents; A Beever, *Rediscovering the Law of Negligence* (Hart, 2009) ch 5; NJ McBride, 'Rights and the Basis of Tort Law' in D Nolan and A Robertson (eds), *Rights and Private Law* (Hart, 2012); A Botterell, 'Rights, Loss and Compensation in the Law of Torts' (2015) 69 SCLR 2d 135.

[26] EJ Weinrib, 'The Disintegration of Duty' in S Madden (ed), *Exploring Tort Law* (Cambridge University Press, 2005).

[27] Stevens (n 25) 310.

[28] This is an aspect of the incrementalist approach: *Robinson v Chief Constable of West Yorkshire* [2018] UKSC 4; *CN & CN v Poole BC* [2019] UKSC 25; Barker (n 22).

finances. Thus a rule arrived at in this way on the basis of policy factors is likely to be applicable only in a narrow range of circumstances.

These seem strong objections to the distributive justice approach. It would seem that, once the law moves away from the core cases of liability for positive actions causing physical harm, the ramifications of careless behaviour are liable to become so far reaching and so many considerations are likely to be relevant that the distributive justice approach is bound to become unmanageable. As discussed in the next chapter, according to the corrective justice approach, the law should be confined to the core cases, and this will mean that there is no need to weigh up policy factors.[29]

But it is understandable that proponents of the distributive justice approach may not be persuaded that there is any good reason to confine the law to the core cases or to exclude policy considerations. This would seem to involve arbitrarily limiting the scope of the law and arbitrarily disregarding relevant considerations.[30] They may accept that private law is not an ideal way or even a very appropriate way to promote distributive justice for accidents for some or all of these reasons. It might be better promoted by way of public rights and duties, for example through an accident compensation fund and health and safety regulation introduced by statute. But given that private law is in place, the judges have to address the issues that arise in adjudication and it would seem that they should make the decision that they think best promotes distributive justice. After all, this means simply taking into account everyone's interests with respect to harm and benefit.

One might say that, because it draws on policy reasoning and policy analysis instead of focusing on the particular interaction and the particular parties, and because it treats bilateralism as artificial and denies that the law is based on underlying bilateral moral rights, the distributive justice approach requires a complete transformation of the traditional common law and is illegitimate for this reason. It also abandons the traditional autonomy of private law and assimilates it with politics.[31] But, as pointed out previously, in the absence of an argument for excluding policy or distributive justice arguments, beyond simply the objection that it clashes with traditional private law, proponents of the distributive justice approach may well think that the real problem is historical error and the inadequacy of traditional legal reasoning.[32]

[29] There is a large literature on the exclusion of policy and what counts as policy: RM Dworkin, *Taking Rights Seriously* (Duckworth, 1977) 22–28, 90–100, 294–330; Weinrib (n 26); Stevens (n 25) ch 14; J Bell, *Policy Arguments in Judicial Decisions* (Clarendon Press, 1983); J Coleman, *The Practice of Principle* (Oxford University Press, 2001) 13–24; A Beever, *Rediscovering the Law of Negligence* (Hart, 2009) ch 1; R Grantham and D Jensen, 'The Proper Role of Policy in Private Law Adjudication' (2018) 68 *University of Toronto Law Journal* 187; J Plunkett, 'Principle and Policy in Private Law Reasoning' (2016) 75 *Cambridge Law Journal* 366.

[30] See eg J Stapleton (n 18); J Stapleton, 'The Golden Thread at the Heart of Tort Law: Protection for the Vulnerable' (2003) 24 *Australian Bar Review* 135; J Steele, 'Scepticism and the Law of Negligence' [1993] CLJ 437.

[31] Weinrib (n 5) ch 8; Stevens (n 25) ch 14.

[32] See eg L Kaplow and S Shavell (n 1); CM Sharkey, 'Preventing Harm, Not Recognising Wrongs' (2021) 134 *Harvard Law Review* 1423.

Contract

As with respect to negligence, difficulties arise in explaining the traditional law of contract in terms of distributive justice.

The Power to Make an Agreement

On the conventional view, a contract arises from an agreement in the form of an exchange of promises between C and D. A promise is the exercise of a 'moral power' by the promisor by which the promisor incurs a moral duty to perform as promised. The moral duty is recognised in the law as a legal duty to perform the contract and a correlative right to performance. This conventional understanding I equate with the 'will theory' of contract, according to which the contract consists of duties that arise through an 'exercise of will' on the part of the contracting parties.[33]

On the distributive justice approach, the justification for the parties' moral powers to make an agreement lies not simply in an 'exercise of will' but in the fact that the agreement facilitates the voluntary exchange of goods and services for money, and thereby advances distributive justice. It advances distributive justice on the assumption that the exchange is likely to be mutually beneficial because people are competent to assess the likely value of the benefit and the cost to them of the exchange (including the risks involved). The contract overcomes the practical problem for voluntary exchange: the problem that one party has to perform first and in so doing runs the risk that the other party, having received a benefit, will not reciprocate. With a contract, a contracting party can act first with confidence that this performance will not be wasted. The contract is, in other words, a means of enabling social co-ordination.[34]

By contrast, on the will theory as conventionally understood, the exchange of goods and services for payment may be the purpose of the contract so far as the parties are concerned, but the contractual duties arise purely by virtue of the parties' promises, that is to say through their exercise of will, and quite independently of their interests in receiving or supplying goods and services. Thus contract law is independent of distributive justice. The will theory is a version of the corrective justice approach, which I shall come back to in the next chapter.

Although the distributive justice approach can explain why agreements should be binding, the way in which one would expect contract law to give effect to agreement on the distributive justice approach appears to be at odds with contract law as it has developed in the common law.

[33] C Fried, *Contract as Promise* (Oxford University Press, 2nd edn 2015).
[34] See generally Oman (n 4); D Campbell, *Contractual Relations* (Oxford University Press, 2022).

Bilateral Rights and Remedies

The corrective justice approach seems able to account for the bilateral relations of contract law, since the promise is made by one contractor to the other and gives rise to a right against the promisor to performance of the promise.[35] On the distributive justice approach, there would seem to be a difficulty in accounting for bilateral relations and remedies: as for negligence, the issue is whether the bilateralism objection and the remedial justice objection can be overcome. The problem is that, although the promise may have been given to the promisee, because the justification is a matter of distributive justice it is said that the moral duty to fulfil it is not a duty owed to the promisee, but a public duty. The interest protected is not the promisee's interest in performance of the promise, but the public interest in the performance of contracts in general, to facilitate exchange across society. More particularly, there is a public interest in the maintenance of an established social practice of promising, which people participate in when they make a contract. The duty to perform in contract is really a duty to support the social practice of contracting. By reneging on their contractual promises, contractors harm the social practice, by undermining confidence in it. Just as for negligence, it would seem that, although proceedings may advance the claimant's own interest, their justification lies in the public interest rather than the claimant's interest. It would seem to follow that there is no justification for C to have a remedy from D; only sanctions are justified, to promote contractual performance in the public interest.[36] This is broadly the position under EAL. According to EAL, an agreement is binding because by facilitating exchange it contributes to promoting aggregate welfare.[37]

According to Murphy, although bilateral legal rights do not reflect underlying bilateral moral rights, they may nevertheless be justified because they support the illusion that there are such moral rights, and the illusion may be effective in maintaining the social practice of contracting.[38] But even if this could justify the remedial regime in contract, it would presumably be a legitimate alternative for the law to operate more transparently as an aspect of public law with public duties enforced by sanctions. In any case, it is difficult to accept that there are no bilateral moral rights arising from promising or agreement. It would seem to preclude the possibility of 'substantive fairness' in contract – the idea that an exchange can be fair as between the parties in the light of its terms. Is it really impossible for a distributive justice approach to explain bilateral moral rights in contract?

[35] See ch 5.

[36] See eg L Murphy, 'The Artificial Morality of Private Law: the Persistence of an Illusion' (2020) 70 *University of Toronto Law Journal* 453. Personal losses to contractors may sometimes justify a remedy but cannot explain bilateral moral rights in general: ibid 459–60. See also Oman (n 4).

[37] According to EAL, the optimal measure of recovery for C is not typically the same as the optimal measure of liability for D, since each is determined as an individual incentive rather than as a right or liability to a remedy: see Oman (n 4).

[38] Murphy (n 36) 484–85.

The starting point for distributive justice as discussed earlier is that it involves rights and duties or liabilities to and from the state. In practice, distributive justice has to be implemented through particular arrangements. It is helpful to say that there is an abstract right against the state to distributive justice in the abstract, and in particular circumstances there is a concrete or 'fully specified' right, which takes account of the way in which distributive justice is to be implemented in the circumstances in question.[39] There might, for example, be a right to welfare in the abstract and a concrete right to the support offered under a particular welfare scheme. The concrete right is a derivative right in distributive justice. It protects the right-holder's interest, but it also reflects the balance of relevant interests across the society as a matter of distributive justice.

With respect to an interaction in private law, can there not be bilateral derivative rights, at least in contract?[40] The objection to the distributive justice account of negligence considered above was that it could not explain bilateral relations. This may be true in negligence, but it is not obviously true in contract. In contract, the contribution that an agreement makes to distributive justice is mainly, and sometimes exclusively, through the mutual benefit of the exchange, and this takes place in accordance with and by virtue of the mutual commitments that the parties make to each other under the agreement.[41] One would think that derivative bilateral moral rights based on the principle of agreement might be possible if the principle is justified by virtue of its contribution to distributive justice, through its facilitation of mutually beneficial exchange. If so, the contractual regime should recognise bilateral rights, and the legal treatment of contracting parties would be inadequate without remedies.

Limited Recognition of Distributive Justice

Even if it is possible in theory (as I think it is) for bilateral moral rights to arise as a matter of distributive justice, there is an objection that this would not actually be the case in practice in contract because, at least in the circumstances of our society, private exchange does not actually advance distributive justice. According to the 'administrative approach' to contract, an exchange that is ostensibly voluntary is invariably tainted by coerciveness arising from disparities of wealth and power

[39] See the discussion of 'rights as individuated claims' as opposed to 'rights as trumps' in DH Regan, 'Glosses on Dworkin: Rights, Principles, and Policies' (1978) 76 *Michigan Law Review* 1213, 1228–34.

[40] See Avraham and Kohler-Hausmann (n 7) 212. For a discussion of the range of usages and understandings of rights in private law, see eg R Stevens, discussing 'instrumental rights' in D Nolan and A Robertson, *Rights and Private Law* (Hart, 2011) 138–43; N McBride, 'Rights and the Basis of Tort Law' in Nolan and Robertson (ibid) 339–40; F du Bois, 'Social Purposes, Fundamental Rights and the Judicial Development of Private Law' in Nolan and Robertson (ibid).

[41] As Murphy (n 36) discusses, contract rights are widely understood to arise independently of distributive justice but subject to modification by it. See also A Bagchi, 'Distributive Justice and Contract' in G Klass, G Letsas and P Saprai (eds), *Philosophical Foundations of Contract Law* (Oxford University Press, 2014).

between contractual parties.[42] On this view, there may well be no genuine moral rights in contract law, and contracts should be heavily regulated to ensure that an exchange is fair, or even replaced with a system for the allocation of goods and services by a public authority.

The administrative approach may seem an extreme position, but even if contractual agreements are not generally coercive, it seems undeniable that a system of private exchange may sometimes conflict with distributive justice. Given the way that wealth is distributed across the society, the effect of contracting may be to unfairly exclude some people from certain types of valuable and expensive benefit – for example health and education – by pricing them out of the market, and its cumulative effect may be that some people acquire a disproportionate share of the societal benefits of exchange, and this may lead to an unjust distribution of wealth. A more balanced position might then be that there should be voluntary exchange through contract law for a certain range of cases, with regulation of other types of contract, and for some goods and services a centralised system of allocation not based on contract at all, with taxation and public benefits in the background to adjust for unjust distribution of wealth. The extent to which contract should be available and in what form has to be determined as a matter of distributive justice.

This general approach is reflected in the legislative reform of contract (in addition to provision for taxation and public benefits). Contract has sometimes been reformed by statute by the introduction of mandatory regimes, for example for consumer contracts, employment and tenancies.[43] These regimes are understood to promote distributive justice by enabling particular categories of contractor to contract for benefits that they would not otherwise be able to obtain or on terms that they would not otherwise be able to agree. In developing the common law, the courts have not taken account of distributive justice in this way. The main reason why the courts have not done this is taken to be that they have assumed a corrective justice approach – the traditional will theory approach – according to which the contract should be based purely on the intentions of the parties to the contract. Some commentators have argued that the courts ought to promote distributive justice in the way that the legislature has done, so far as they can. This has given rise to a debate over the extent to which distributive justice should be implemented through mandatory regimes in contract law,[44] as opposed to leaving contract in its traditional form and giving effect to distributive justice only outside contract through taxation to fund redistribution and public services.[45]

[42] RL Hale, 'Coercion and Distribution in a Supposedly Non-coercive State' (1923) 38 *Political Science Quarterly* 470. See C Fried, 'Contract as Promise in the Light of Subsequent Scholarship' in *Contract as Promise* (Oxford University Press, 2nd edn 2015).

[43] See eg J Adams and R Brownsword, 'The Ideologies of Contract' (1987) 7 *Legal Studies* 205.

[44] AT Kronman, 'Contract Law and Distributive Justice' (1980) 89 *Yale Law Journal* 472; Bagchi (n 41).

[45] L Kaplow and S Shavell, 'Why the Legal System Is Less Efficient than the Income Tax in Redistributing Income' (1994) 23 *Journal of Legal Studies* 667.

In fact, under the doctrine of public policy at common law, contract law does take account, to a limited extent, of considerations going beyond the agreement of the parties to invalidate a contract. Some of the recognised categories of contract falling under the doctrine are contracts to break the law, contracts for prostitution, gambling contracts, contracts of insurance against criminal penalties, contracts to evade tax, and contracts in restraint of trade.[46] Unsurprisingly, the doctrine has been controversial, because it overrides the parties' agreement, contrary to the will theory, and, furthermore, it is not clear what its rationale is or its limits in principle. One might think that the concept of public policy could encompass any aspect of distributive justice that a legislature might legislate for. Why then have the courts not applied the doctrine to invalidate contracts, in the way that the legislature has done by statute for unfair consumer or employment or tenancy contracts? One might make a comparison with negligence, where, as discussed above, policy factors, very broadly understood, can be taken into account to determine liability. In fact, public policy for the purposes of the doctrine is understood far more narrowly than policy in the broad legislative sense, which amounts to distributive justice in general. It is applied, I suggest, only to conduct that is open to objection without any need for careful calculation or investigation of its effects.[47] In any case, if the doctrine is a matter of distributive justice, as it would seem to be, the question remains why, unlike the legislature, the judges at common law can take account of distributive justice to this extent and no further.

Consider how these issues are addressed in the 'joint maximisation' theory of contract law,[48] which is a version of EAL and a distributive justice approach. On this approach, contract law has as its rationale the maximisation of the joint welfare of the contracting parties, which is taken to reflect the parties' intentions. This is behind the ordinary rules of common law contract. Considerations relating to this objective are internal to contract law. By contrast, considerations of the public interest or the interests of third parties are external. They are taken into account in statutes on, for example, employment law, competition law, and environment law, which override the common law of contract. Both internal and external considerations are concerned with maximising aggregate welfare across society. Internal considerations are concerned with the parties' welfare, on which their intentions are taken to be determinative, and external considerations are concerned with adjusting for the adverse effects of the contract that the parties' intentions will not take into account, that is to say 'externalities'. It makes sense to keep these different types of consideration apart in legal reasoning. But why should the judges not take account of the external considerations in developing the common law, as the legislature does in reforming it? All these considerations are relevant in the end

[46] See eg S Judd, 'The Unruly Horse Put out to Pasture: The Doctrine of Public Policy in the Modern Law of Contract' (1998) 8 *Auckland University Law Review* 686, 692.

[47] See further ch 8.

[48] RE Scott, 'A joint maximization theory of contract and regulation' in H Dagan and BC Zipursky (eds), *Research Handbook on Private Law Theory* (Edward Elgar, 2020).

because they are considerations of distributive justice. Furthermore, the doctrine of public policy, though it is to do with externalities, is recognised and applied in the common law. Why do the courts not take account of considerations of distributive justice going beyond the doctrine of public policy?

In my view, the main problem for the distributive justice approach to contract is that the common law does not take account of the interests of third parties or the public interest in the development of contract law in the way that one would expect on the distributive approach, rather than the problem of explaining bilateral rights and remedies.

The Remedial Regime

I suggested in chapter three that contract law adopts what I described as a 'primary liability' not a 'primary duty' approach. The parties do not have duties to perform but merely bear the risk of liability for compensation for non-performance. As discussed in chapter five, it is not easy to see how the primary liability regime can be reconciled with the corrective justice approach. The corrective justice approach would seem to imply that contract law should give effect to the parties' promises by way of legal duties of performance. But the distributive justice approach does seem quite apt to explain the remedial regime in contract.

On the distributive justice approach, the justification for enforcing agreements through contract law is to facilitate a mutually beneficial exchange. If the contract is not completed, a mutually beneficial exchange may not be possible. If one considers distributive justice with respect to the allocation of the harms and benefits of the particular contract, disregarding other considerations of distributive justice, it is plausible that the law should aim to protect the parties' reliance interests, that is to say the interest in a return on work done and expenses incurred in reliance on the contract, valued in terms of the payment due in return, whether by payment for work done in reliance on the agreement or recovery of a payment made in reliance on the agreement, also taking account of any benefit received. As suggested in chapter three, a reliance approach to contract can explain the primary liability relation in contract. The contract allocates the risk of loss relative to the reliance interest. If D does not perform, C's claim is for the satisfaction of C's reliance interest. It is not a claim to secure the performance of D's duty to perform (unless this is the only way to protect the reliance interest), or a claim based on a wrongful failure to perform.

There are various versions of the reliance theory. The approach suggested is consistent with Raz's version of the reliance theory, which holds that the contract recognises moral duties to perform arising from the agreement, but only to the extent necessary to protect the reliance interest.[49] Raz relied on the

[49] J Raz, 'Promises in Morality and Law' (1982) 95 *Harvard Law Review* 916. See also Murphy (n 36).

'harm principle': the principle that no-one should be restricted in what they are free to do except as necessary to protect others from harm. He argued that the harm principle precluded recovery in contract except to the extent necessary to protect the reliance interest. To allow specific performance as a general rule would be an unjustified imposition on D because it would go further than necessary to protect C against harm. The argument might be open to the objection that the non-performance of a promise does necessarily cause harm because the promise confers a right to receive the promised performance, and so non-performance denies C what C is entitled to and so necessarily causes harm.[50] One could say instead that a promise should be enforced only insofar as justified in the light of the justification for enforcing it, which can be taken to be the value of the exchange as a contribution to distributive justice.[51]

Another version of the reliance theory is that a primary liability relation protecting the reliance interest directly reflects what was agreed.[52] The parties specify the terms of the exchange, and agree that each party is to accept responsibility for the other's reliance interest with respect to performance of the agreement, by implication measured in accordance with the value placed on the performance by the terms of exchange. Neither party undertakes a duty to perform by the agreement, but each is subject to a primary liability, by which that party bears the risk of a liability to satisfy the other party's reliance interest. With respect to sophisticated commercial contractors, who can be taken to be aware of the remedial regime in contract, it seems plausible to think that they intend their agreement to reflect their legal position.

It is often assumed that the reliance theory refers to the theory of 'death of contract' or 'contract as tort'.[53] On this understanding, the agreement itself is legally inert – it has no direct effect on the legal position of the parties. It may be understood to have the effect of a tortious misstatement by D, leading to detrimental reliance by C, which can give C a claim for compensation, in tort rather than contract. This has something in common with the administrative approach mentioned above.[54] The death of contract theory is implausible as an account of contract law because it denies that the agreement has any direct legal effect. A claim in tort takes no account of the value placed on performance by the parties

[50] D Kimel, *From Promise to Contract* (Hart, 2003) ch 4.

[51] This is consistent with Raz's discussion of promising: see Raz (n 49); J Raz, 'Is There a Reason to Keep Promises?' Columbia Public Law Research Paper 12-320 (2012).

[52] See P Jaffey, *The Nature and Scope of Restitution* (Hart, 2000) ch 2. The agreement governs the terms of exchange rather than simply the conduct of the parties as under the will theory. Cf Atiyah's theory of promises as 'conclusive admissions': PS Atiyah, *Promises, Morals, and Law* (Clarendon Press, 1981) 184ff.

[53] A theory associated with G Gilmore, *Death of Contract* (Ohio State University Press, 1974); PS Atiyah, *The Rise and Fall of Freedom of Contract* (Clarendon Press, 1979) and *Promises, Morals and Law* (Clarendon Press, 1981).

[54] But the death of contract theory understood as a matter of tort law presumably does not involve imposing fair terms of exchange.

through the contract, including the value placed on the work itself, which is paid for through a quantum meruit or the expectation measure. The reliance theory can take account of this through the protection of the reliance interest, which encompasses an interest in being paid for work done, and through the valuation of performance by the parties in the contract. There is no reason to equate the reliance theory with the death of contract theory.

However, there do appear to be strong objections to the reliance theory explanation of the remedial regime as a distributive justice approach. It is supposed to be based on the distributive justice approach, but it is concerned only with the harms and benefits of the particular contract treated in isolation. It disregards the prior position of the parties, which may not be in accord with distributive justice. In addition, one would think that the distributive justice approach should take account of distributive justice with respect to contracts in general, across the whole society rather than the particular contract in isolation. By contrast, for EAL, the issue is whether aggregate welfare or net benefit through contractual exchange in general is more likely to be maximised if the contractual regime has primary duties or primary liabilities. Famously, EAL has another explanation for the absence in the usual case of a right to specific performance, namely the efficient breach theory.[55] It is said that allowing D not to perform the contract normally promotes aggregate welfare. It provides an incentive to D to abandon the contract with C in order to take up an alternative opportunity, when D can make a profit large enough to pay compensation to C and still have a surplus, or alternatively in order to escape from the burden of performance when its cost exceeds the cost of compensating C. In either case, this represents an increase in aggregate welfare relative to the position if D had performed the contract. By adopting a primary liability regime, the law can secure this increase in aggregate welfare. Only where C's loss cannot be compensated for by D is it justified for D to have a duty to perform because here non-performance may not lead to an increase in aggregate welfare.[56]

However, in practice, it may not be easy to say when requiring actual performance is more welfare-maximising than allowing non-performance subject to compensation. C's loss may be difficult to establish, and it may be that by requiring D to perform, unless released by D, the law can ensure that C does not actually lose out. Possibly this would better promote aggregate welfare overall, even if it means that D will not be able to take advantage of an alternative opportunity or escape from a burdensome performance when this would actually advance the

[55] Attributed to R Birmingham, 'Breach of Contract, Damage Measures, and Economic Efficiency' (1970) 24 *Rutgers Law Review* 273 and R Posner, *Economic Analysis of Law* (Little Brown, 1st edn 1972). See also D Campbell, *Contractual Relations* (Oxford University Press, 2022) 272.

[56] The efficient breach theory, as usually formulated, faces the immediate objection that it involves condoning a legal wrong (remedial inconsistency, in the terms of ch 3): see eg D Friedmann, 'The Efficient Breach Fallacy' (1989) 18 *Journal of Legal Studies* 1. The theory of efficient breach can be understood instead to hold that there is a primary liability relation that allows D to choose not to perform and pay compensation.

aggregate welfare. Whether a primary liability or a primary duty arrangement would better promote aggregate welfare is a matter of policy analysis and is not easy to establish.[57]

Although there is some reason to think that the distributive justice approach can account for the primary liability regime in contract, on the reliance theory approach or the EAL approach of efficient breach, there also seem to be problems with both of these approaches.

Conclusion

The objection to the distributive justice approach, with respect to both negligence and contract, is not that distributive justice does not in principle apply to interactions. The objection is that private law, as it has actually developed, does not seem to have dealt with interactions in a way that is explicable in terms of distributive justice.

With respect to negligence, the distributive justice objectives of loss reduction or hardship alleviation cannot account satisfactorily for bilateral relations, or for the fact that the law traditionally focuses on facts concerning the parties and their relationship rather than on the effects of liability or non-liability across society through policy reasoning. The influence of policy reasoning in negligence seems to have been to marginalise the issue of justice between the parties and increase uncertainty and this seems to confirm the inaptness of the distributive justice approach for private law.

With respect to contract, I suggested that the distributive justice approach could in principle account for bilateral relations arising from agreement, and that it can possibly also account for the primary liability approach in contract. But again it seems unable to account for the fact that the law focuses almost exclusively on the parties and their relationship, excluding the wider effects of contracting across society. In developing the law the courts have focused on what, according to the distributive justice approach, is an unduly limited perspective.

Supporters of the distributive justice approach are unlikely to be perturbed by these objections. They are more likely to be fortified in their view that private law should be reformed or in part abolished in order to give effect to the distributive justice approach. However, as pointed out earlier, judges have built up the common law over many years, exercising moral judgement in individual cases

[57] The efficient breach theory is criticised in MA Eisenberg, *Foundational Principles of Contract Law* (Oxford University Press, 2018) ch 6. There seems to be something paradoxical for EAL in even addressing this question. According to EAL, the justification for enforcing an agreement presupposes that individual contractors can be taken to know what serves their interest, so voluntary exchanges can be assumed to be mutually beneficial. Presumably this means that the law should leave it to the parties to determine whether they should make an agreement that establishes primary duties or primary liabilities and enforce the agreement that they make.

where necessary, and private law represents the accumulation of these exercises of moral judgement in combination with precedent. Looking at cases individually, they do not seem to be, on the whole, unjustly decided, and indeed they seem to form a largely coherent body of law. Thus it may not be surprising that critics of the distributive justice approach insist that there is a 'form of justice' entirely distinct from distributive justice, namely corrective justice, which can provide a justification for private law as it is traditionally understood, including features such as bilateral relations, remedies rather than sanctions, and the focus on the immediate parties to an interaction at the expense of broader society.

5

The Corrective Justice Approach

Introduction

On the corrective justice approach, private law is based on individual moral rights against other people. On the standard view,[1] these are moral rights protecting personal liberty, encompassing not only freedom of action with respect to the body and property, but also the power to acquire property and to make contracts. The bilateral legal relations of private law are based directly on these moral rights of one person against another. This is why private law is intrinsically a matter of interpersonal justice. In negligence, the law reflects a balance between C's security, in the sense of a right to be free from interference, and D's liberty to pursue D's purposes, and when D breaches the duty of care, D infringes C's basic right with respect to person or property. Contract is based on the intentions of the parties, which give effect to their moral powers to make an agreement by exchanging promises, and a breach of duty is the infringement of a right of C's to the benefit of a promise made by D.

Only these basic liberty rights are relevant to private law. The interests with respect to harm and benefit of the parties to the interaction or other people are irrelevant. Private law does not give effect to distributive justice or to public purposes such as loss reduction, or alleviation of hardship or need, or promoting the exchange of benefits. Private law rights are not based on what were referred to in the previous chapter as derivative rights against the state or against the other party, reflecting a balance of interests in harm and benefit aggregated across society. This is the basis for the exclusion (as it is variously put) of policy or public policy or community or social welfare or the public interest from private law. In other words, the law takes account only of 'intrinsic factors', that is to say considerations relating to the balance of the liberty rights of C and D, as the parties to the interaction, and not 'extrinsic factors'.[2] It also follows that policy analysis of the

[1] EJ Weinrib, *The Idea of Private Law* (Oxford University Press, rev edn 2012); EJ Weinrib, *Reciprocal Freedom* (Oxford University Press, 2022); A Ripstein, *Private Wrongs* (Harvard University Press, 2016); P Benson, *Justice in Transactions* (Harvard University Press, 2019); A Beever, *Rediscovering the Law of Negligence* (Hart, 2009); RW Wright, 'Substantive Corrective Justice' (1992) 77 *Iowa Law Review* 625; A Brudner with JM Nadler, *The Unity of the Common Law* (Oxford University Press, 2nd edn 2013). See also n 8.

[2] Weinrib, *The Idea of Private Law* (n 1) 32–38.

effects of possible rules governing the interaction on harms and benefits across the society is not relevant to private law. Only facts concerning the two parties and the interaction between them are relevant.

Because they protect C's liberties, D's duties are negative duties against interference. There is no positive duty to assist or to provide a benefit, or, as it is put, there is liability only for misfeasance (interference), not nonfeasance (failure to assist). This is why there is no duty of rescue in tort, and, as considered below, this is thought to explain other important features of private law. Even in contract, D's duty may be understood as a negative duty not to interfere with C's right to the performance of the promise. It is said that this provides a better account of the law, and that, by contrast, on the distributive justice approach the balance of interests in benefit and harm would sometimes generate duties to provide a benefit.[3]

In corrective justice, everyone is treated equally in the sense that each should have the same basic rights – a sphere of liberty – securing for each person the same level of protection from others. This is achieved by treating people impersonally and uniformly, and disregarding an individual's particular strengths and weaknesses. This is why people are characterised as 'reasonable' and why private law has its distinctive objective character.[4]

Claims in private law arise from a breach of duty or wrong owed by D to C. D's liability arises from a failure to act as D ought to have acted according to D's legal duty, and this suggests that private law is also concerned in principle with holding D personally responsible for a wrong to C. Thus, at least on one view of the corrective justice approach, liability is based on a principle that, by virtue of D's responsibility for the wrong, D should provide C with a remedy (or some other principle of compensation for wrongs).

It is said that, on the corrective justice approach, because there are only bilateral rights based on interpersonal justice, private law should provide only remedies in the strict sense, that is to say measures that serve to rectify an injustice by D to C, by undoing its effects on C. There is no justification for sanctions, which are measures that are intended to create incentives or disincentives for others with respect to the same sort of behaviour. Sanctions are not a matter of justice as between C and D, since their purpose is to promote the public interest and the interests of others for the future.

The corrective justice approach is thought to show why private law has the characteristic features of traditional private law identified earlier: why it has bilateral relations, why it is wrong-based, remedial and objective, and why private law is focused on the parties' relationship and not on the wider consequences for society. However, as I argue below, although the corrective justice approach may do better than the distributive justice approach, it also has difficulty in providing an adequate account of traditional private law.

[3] Weinrib, *The Idea of Private Law* (n 1) 153ff; Ripstein (n 1) ch 3.

[4] By virtue of this feature, individuals are treated as abstract purposive agents. Weinrib, *The Idea of Private Law* (n 1) 80–83. EJ Weinrib, *Corrective Justice* (Oxford University Press, 2012) 21–29.

Corrective justice is sometimes understood in a purely remedial sense, for example to refer only to the principle that a wrongdoer D should rectify the wrong to C, or that the gains and losses arising from a wrong should be undone or annulled.[5] In this sense, corrective justice is concerned not with primary relations, but only with how a right to a remedy arises from a primary relation. In chapter three, I argued that the claim for compensation arises not from a wrong but from the materialisation of a risk under a primary liability relation, as a matter of remedial consistency. The operation of remedial consistency might also be understood as a matter of corrective justice in a remedial sense. Corrective justice in the remedial sense does not amount to a full theory of private law in the sense of a theory of the justice of interactions, including primary relations. This chapter is concerned with corrective justice in the latter sense, rather than corrective justice in the purely remedial sense. The expression 'corrective justice' might seem more apt for the remedial-only version, and some commentators prefer an alternative expression, such as 'substantive corrective justice' or 'interpersonal justice' or 'interactional justice' for the full theory of the justice of interactions.[6] However, I shall continue using the conventional expression to refer to a full theory of private law.

Some proponents of the corrective justice approach, or a version of it, do not rely on the idea that private law is based on liberty rights. It does seem difficult to accept that private law is confined to protecting liberty rights, and takes no account of the interests of the parties to an interaction with respect to harms and benefits more generally.[7] For example, surely tort law protects interests against harm when it protects physical integrity or privacy rather than only a liberty right, and similarly, is contract not concerned with interests in acquiring or supplying goods and services rather than just the creation of duties? And if private law is not concerned with protecting interests with respect to harms and benefits, it is surprising that remedies seem to be so carefully tailored as a response to harm and benefit as such, by way or compensation or restitution. Indeed, if the law were concerned to protect individual liberties, it might seem more effective to protect those liberties through sanctions.

On the alternative version, private law is based on the balance of the interests of C and D with respect to harm and benefit (understood to include liberties and opportunities to benefit).[8] In negligence, it would be concerned with an

[5] See eg JL Coleman, *The Practice of Principle* (Oxford University Press, 2001); J Gardner, 'What is Tort Law For? Part 1. The Place of Corrective Justice' 30 *Law and Philosophy* 1 (2011). The practical difference between the purely remedial sense and the substantive sense of corrective justice may be slight because in the remedial sense corrective justice presupposes primary bilateral moral rights: see Coleman (ibid) 32.

[6] W Wright, 'Substantive Corrective Justice' (1992) 77 *Iowa Law Review* 625.

[7] See eg N Jansen, 'The Idea of Legal Responsibility' (2014) 34 *Oxford Journal of Legal Studies* 221; V Tadros, 'Independence Without Interests?' (2011) 31 *Oxford Journal of Legal Studies* 193; S Hershovitz, 'The Search for a Grand Unified Theory of Tort Law' (2017) 130 *Harvard Law Review* 942.

[8] Ie 'welfare rights'. Possible examples are JCP Goldberg and BC Zipursky, *Recognising Wrongs* (Belknap Press, 2020); H Dagan and A Dorfman, 'Just Relationships' (2016) 116 *Columbia Law Review* 1395; R Stevens, *Torts and Rights* (Oxford University Press, 2007); N Sage, 'Relational Wrongs and Agency in Tort Theory' (2021) 41 *Oxford Journal of Legal Studies* 1012.

interest against injury and damage, including lost benefits and opportunities, and in contract it would be concerned with interests in the benefits and costs involved in contracting for goods and services, including the interest in being paid for work done. The problem on this understanding is that, whereas liberty rights are necessarily bilateral rights, rights protecting interests with respect to benefit and harm must presumably reflect a balance of the interests of people generally with respect to benefit and harm, aggregated across society, and as discussed in the previous chapter this would not necessarily give rise to bilateral rights. Indeed, it might seem that this approach is really a version of the distributive justice approach. In any case, as discussed further below, in either form the corrective justice approach has a difficulty in explaining its relationship with distributive justice.

Some Problems with the Corrective Justice Account of Negligence

Negligence as Wrongdoing

On the corrective justice approach, a claim for compensation is understood to be based on a wrong, in the form of the breach of a primary duty, and, as discussed in chapter three, it is difficult to accept that this is reflected in the law, in particular because of the absence of a requirement of subjective fault. Objective fault in negligence is said to be appropriate in order to secure a fair balance between the rights or interests of the two parties,[9] but this does not explain the absence of a subjective fault requirement if the claim arises from D's moral responsibility for a breach of duty. Strict liability is even more of a problem for the corrective justice approach. Proponents of the corrective justice approach may regard strict liability as anomalous because it does not involve a genuine breach of duty,[10] but the problem of justifying liability for compensation applies equally for objective fault.

A number of other difficulties arise with respect to the duty in negligence. A natural understanding of D's duty is that D has a duty to take reasonable care – that is to say, a duty to meet the standard of care – and accordingly D's wrong is the failure to meet the standard of care,[11] but this understanding is at odds with certain features of the law, as some commentators have pointed out.[12]

One problem is that D can be liable for a certain type of loss to C and not another type of loss arising from the same action by D, even though they were

[9] Weinrib, *The Idea of Private Law* (n 1) chs 6 and 7; Beever (n 1) 79–84; Goldberg and Zipursky (n 8) ch 6; see also R Avraham and I Kohler-Hausmann, 'Accident Law for Egalitarians' (2006) 12 *Legal Theory* 181.

[10] Weinrib rationalises strict liability duties under his theory for example as involving a hidden wrong: see Weinrib, *The Idea of Private Law* (n 1) ch 7.

[11] J Oberdiek, 'The Wrong in Negligence' (2021) 41 *Oxford Journal of Legal Studies* 1174.

[12] D Nolan 'Deconstructing the Duty of Care' (2013) 129 *Law Quarterly Review* 559.

equally foreseeable consequences. For example, compensation for pure economic loss may be irrecoverable in circumstances where it would be available for personal injury or property damage. Similarly, D can be liable to C1 but not C2, even though the loss caused to C2 is just as much a foreseeable consequence of D's action as the loss caused to C1. An example is where a company auditor prepares the company's accounts negligently, and only an existing shareholder and not a prospective shareholder who buys overvalued shares can have a claim.[13] It is said that there is a duty owed to C1 and no duty owed to C2, but if the liability arises because loss is caused by the wrongfulness of D's action, it is not easy to see why C2 and C1 should be treated differently, if the loss is in each case the foreseeable consequence of the same wrongful action.

Another problem is that harm to C is an element of the cause of action in negligence – no claim arises until harm has been suffered. If the duty is a duty to take reasonable care, the occurrence of harm is separate in principle from the wrong, and one would expect harm to be relevant only to the measure of compensation and not to the existence of the cause of action.[14]

One might say that nevertheless harm should be a condition for a claim, because private law is concerned with providing remedies, and in the absence of harm to C no remedy is required. But, if harm is required, there is still the problem that there are often legal wrongs that have no legal consequences at all, or even any possibility of legal consequences, where D breaches the duty to meet the standard but by good fortune no harm results. This is an example of the problem mentioned previously of underenforcement in private law where it is understood in terms of wrongdoing.[15] It has been suggested that the harm requirement in negligence is anomalous and should be abandoned.[16] This would mean that C could take action if D's conduct fell below the standard of care and thereby subjected C (and others) to a risk of harm, even without actual harm.[17] This might be understood as in the nature of a public interest action, treating D's action as a public wrong. Putting aside the harm requirement, it is not easy to see why the wrongful action should be understood as bilateral.[18] It might seem logical for the law to move in this direction,[19] but it is not what the law traditionally allows and of course it does not help to explain how the corrective justice approach can account for the law.

[13] *Caparo v Dickman* [1990] 2 AC 605, HL.

[14] Oberdiek (n 11).

[15] See ch 3 at n 41 and n 42.

[16] See eg Y Adar and R Perry, 'Negligence Without Harm' (2022) *Georgetown Law Journal*. See also Avraham and Kohler-Hausmann (n 9).

[17] It is already possible where harm to C personally is likely and imminent for C to seek an injunction, but not where the risk is not to C in particular.

[18] Cf Oberdiek (n 11).

[19] The view that negligence is a public wrong has strong support and is consistent with EAL. See generally J Stapleton, 'Controlling the Future of the Common Law by Restatement' in M Stuart Madden (ed), *Exploring Tort Law* (Cambridge University Press, 2005) 273; HM Hurd and MS Moore, 'Negligence in the Air' (2002) 3 *Theoretical Inquiries in the Law* 333.

In the light of these difficulties, some commentators argue that D's duty in negligence is best understood not as a duty to take reasonable care, but as a duty not to cause harm to C by falling below the standard of care. This appears to be the usual understanding amongst proponents of corrective justice.[20] It is said to explain the fact that harm to C is an element of the claim in negligence: the claim arises only once C has suffered harm, because only then has the breach of duty been completed. Also, on this understanding, it would seem that the duty is necessarily bilateral and owed to a certain claimant and not others, and it can be limited to a certain type of loss. But does it make sense to recognise such a duty? A duty is ordinarily understood in terms of an action of the duty-holder, D, that D is required to perform or not to perform.[21] The action is what D has actual direct control over, and D can be responsible with respect to the action itself and its foreseeable consequences. The consequences of the breach of duty should be kept separate from the breach of duty itself.[22] Having the element of harm in the definition of the duty is like having an objective fault standard, or strict liability, in that it means that the duty can no longer be a duty for the breach of which D can be held responsible.

It is said that the legal duty in negligence is simply a distinctive type of duty, a duty that is by nature bilateral, objective and inclusive of harm.[23] But although this may be true as a matter of legal usage, it does not overcome the problems considered above. If D is to be made liable on the ground of moral responsibility for wrongdoing, liability should depend only on what D can be blamed for, namely actions under D's control. Similarly, legal usage cannot provide an explanation of bilateralism or harm-inclusivity.

It would make more sense to say that this legal usage disguises the fact that there is actually a primary liability relation in negligence involving an allocation of risk of loss. Such a relation is intrinsically bilateral, objective and inclusive of harm. There is no need for a condition of subjective fault. Harm is necessarily an element of the cause of action. There is nothing conceptually anomalous or problematic about a primary liability relation that allocates to D the risk of a certain type of loss to C, without extending to any other loss or a loss to any other claimant. As discussed in chapter three, it is also possible for a distinct duty to arise to avoid or prevent the loss for which D is liable under the allocation of risk, and this can explain the occasional cases where an injunction or a punitive response is appropriate.

[20] Discussed in D Nolan 'Deconstructing the Duty of Care' (2013) 129 *Law Quarterly Review* 559; Goldberg and Zipursky (n 8) 183–88; Ripstein (n 1) ch 1; Weinrib, *The Idea of Private Law* (n 1) ch 5.

[21] D Nolan, 'Rights, Damage and Loss' (2017) 37 *Oxford Journal of Legal Services* 255.

[22] Oberdiek (n 11). Oberdiek's focus is on whether the duty is capable of providing guidance. See also Y Adar and R Perry, 'Negligence Without Harm' (2022) *Georgetown Law Journal*. See also Avraham and Kohler-Hausmann (n 9).

[23] Goldberg and Zipursky (n 8).

The primary liability approach is more apt in another way. D is understood to have a duty with respect to the risks of certain types of loss to certain people. It is these risks that are taken into account in determining the standard of care. This is understood to be an established principle of the law of negligence – the 'risk principle': liability is limited to harm that results from the materialisation of a risk that contributed to making D's conduct negligent.[24] However, the risk principle is not easy to reconcile with the conventional understanding that a claim arises from a breach of duty or wrong. If liability arises from a breach of duty, it should in principle arise with respect to losses that are the foreseeable consequences of the breach of duty, and these losses do not necessarily correspond to the losses the risk of which go to determining the standard of care. They do correspond, however, on the primary liability approach. In other words, as pointed out in chapter three, the duty is redundant and a source of unnecessary complexity.

In addition to denying the requirement of subjective fault, the objective fault standard in negligence involves disregarding individual strengths and weaknesses. If the legal relation between C and D is based purely on the interests or liberty rights of C and D, it should presumably depend on the relative strengths and weakness of C and D as individuals. Why should C and D be treated as typical or reasonable representatives of people in their position, as the objective approach does?[25] The content of D's duty to C should take account of the burden the duty imposes on D personally in the light of D's abilities and resources. It is said that the reasonableness standard leads to a uniform and impersonal standard of protection. This is no doubt desirable, but it is difficult to reconcile with the fact that in corrective justice the claim arises from a relation between two particular individuals, based on their competing interests in security and liberty. But an objective fault standard with uniform and impersonal protection is entirely apt for an allocation of risk under a primary liability relation.

Another feature of the law that appears inconsistent with the corrective justice approach is the absence of any restriction on liability insurance. If the justification for the claim is D's moral responsibility for a wrong, it seems doubtful whether insurance of the liability should be allowed, any more than for a criminal fine, which is uninsurable.[26] The conventional position is that insurance is not relevant to liability,[27] but this surely does not go far enough on the corrective justice

[24] D Nolan and J Plunkett, 'Keeping Negligence Simple' (2022) 138 *Law Quarterly Review* 175.

[25] According to Weinrib, under the corrective justice theory this is to do with the concept of 'personality' by which each party is treated in law as an 'abstract person', abstracting from their particular features and circumstances. 'Personality' and correlativity are the two inter-related aspects of private law: see Weinrib, *The Idea of Private Law* (n 1) ch 1.

[26] See J Morgan, 'Tort, Insurance and Incoherence' (2004) 67 *Modern Law Review* 384. It seems that liability insurance was considered problematic at one time for this reason: see K Oliphant, 'Tort Law, Risk and Technological Innovation in England' (2014) 59 *McGill Law Journal* 819, 839.

[27] *Hunt v Severs* [1994] 2 AC 350 at 363, per Lord Bridge; J Stapleton, 'Tort, Insurance and Ideology' (1995) 58 *Modern Law Review* 820.

approach. By contrast, this objection to insurance does not apply if the claim arises from a primary liability. Insurance is a natural concomitant of a legal allocation of risk.

One might ask whether the corrective justice approach could be understood in terms of primary liabilities instead of primary duties. As the corrective justice approach is normally understood, primary duties are fundamental. This is certainly how the corrective justice approach is always expressed. It is understood to be concerned with interference with C's liberty rights, rather than with allocating the risk of loss. This is thought to be necessary to account for the bilateral relations of private law. Furthermore, as between C and D, it would seem that a claim must depend on a wrong by D – why should D be responsible for C's loss if D has not wronged C?[28] An allocation of the risk of loss protects an interest with respect to harm and such interests are aggregative. It may seem that a claim based on the allocation of the risk of loss under a primary liability relation would be justifiable only as a part of a distributive justice approach involving the allocation of risk across society more widely.

The Focus on the Parties

The Standard of Care

The standard of reasonable care – the standard D must meet to avoid liability – is generally understood to depend, with respect to a certain harm to C from D's activity, principally on the three factors of the severity of the harm to C, the risk that the harm will occur, and the cost of precautions that D would have to take to obviate the risk. The traditional understanding may be, as the corrective justice approach would require, that the three factors are weighed up in arriving at a fair balance of the interests of C and D, the interest of C against harm, and the interest of D in being free to conduct himself without restraint. The three factors would depend on facts about the two parties and the interaction between them.

Sometimes in negligence it may be true that only the two parties' interests or liberty rights are relevant, where D's activity affects only one person, C. The example of assault by D against C might provide the model. But this is not always or even generally the case in negligence. One type of case that illustrates that a third party interest can be relevant is where D caused harm to C in trying to avoid harm to X, as where D swerved in his car to avoid X and in consequence hit C. X's interest in not being harmed must be relevant in determining whether D acted negligently towards C.

More generally, consider an ordinary traffic accident case. The extent and risk of harm must be assessed across the whole of the relevant population. For

[28] See eg N McBride, 'Duties of Care – Do They Really Exist?' (2004) 24 *Oxford Journal of Law Studies* 417.

traffic accidents, this must be the extent and risk of harm to any other driver or pedestrian who may be harmed, not just to C in particular. Although the law can be expressed in terms of bilateral relations, each relation is not based just on the interests of the two parties. When harm is assessed after the event, it may seem that the law takes account only of the risk and extent of harm to C, but if one considers the position in advance of the accident, at the time when the duty of care subsists, it may be unknown who the other party to a possible interaction might be. The relevant risk is the risk to any possible C, not the risk to the particular C who is harmed. The risk that C in particular would be harmed may be negligible. Imagine a case where by mistake D releases a poisonous pellet into the water supply that may harm someone in the population. The relevant risk is the risk to anyone in the population, not just the risk to C in particular. Similarly, where D's actions can cause harm to many people, in assessing whether a possible precaution that D could have taken was too burdensome, it is relevant to consider the harm that would be avoided overall, not just the harm to C in particular. This approach to the standard of care is not consistent with the corrective justice approach. The law has bilateral relations, but each relation is not based just on the interests of the two parties to it.[29]

Furthermore, as noted above, under the objective approach C and D are taken to be typical or representative of the population, but if the law were based only on the interests or liberty rights of the two particular parties C and D, it would presumably have to take account of them as particular individuals with their own strengths and weaknesses. As noted above, it is said that the rationale is to provide a uniform level of protection, but this seems to be a collective rationale, not a corrective justice rationale concerning the two particular parties. In addition, on the corrective justice approach, the social value of D's activity is irrelevant since this is a matter of benefit across society, but sometimes social value is taken into account. If D's activity is evidently socially valuable, D can create a greater risk without incurring liability. For example, in an emergency an ambulance can go faster than is justified for other drivers, without incurring liability.[30]

Thus the law of the standard of care does not seem consistent with the corrective justice approach. However, it is not clear that it is what one would expect on the distributive justice approach either. On the EAL approach, the standard of care should reflect an assessment across the population as whole of what standard would be welfare-maximising. D should take precautions to avoid possible accidents to the extent that the cost to D is just equal to the likely loss saved through the avoidance of accidents, so as to minimise aggregate loss.[31] This is not the

[29] See also Avraham and Kohler-Hausmann (n 9). See further below.

[30] *Watt v Hertfordshire CC* [1954] 1 WLR 835; *Marshall v Osmond* [1983] QB 1034.

[31] This is the Hand formula, due to Justice Learned Hand in *United States v Carroll Towing Co* 159 F.2d 169, 173 (2d Cir 1947).

approach in English law. As considered further in chapter seven, the standard of care in English law does not seem to reflect either the corrective justice or the distributive justice approach.

Policy and the 'Duty of Care'

As discussed in the last chapter, in a core case of personal injury or property damage caused by positive action by D, the issue is generally just whether D has met the standard of care, but in other cases, for example involving pure economic loss, negligent misstatements and public authority liability, there is a prior question whether there is even a possibility of liability in the circumstances. This issue is addressed in terms of the existence of a duty of care, and here, as discussed, the law appears to have developed under the strong influence of the distributive justice approach: whether there is a duty of care depends, at least in part, on the balance of policy factors. As discussed in the previous chapter, this approach has evident weaknesses and has been criticised by proponents of the corrective justice approach.[32]

On the corrective justice approach, the law should be confined to giving protection against interference with rights to property and person. On this basis, the law should revert to the core cases, and there would be no need for policy reasoning. But this seems to be an arbitrary limitation. Consider the pure economic loss rule, which is conventionally explained in terms of the balance of policy factors. If liability arises from a breach of duty by D to C, on the basis of D's responsibility for a wrong, why is it justified to exclude liability for reasonably foreseeable pure economic loss if there would have been liability for personal injury or property damage in the same circumstances? It seems that the pure economic loss rule is excluded because it concerns intangible property, and intangible property is not protected, though the consequences may be just as serious for C. Understood in this way this does seem to be an arbitrary limitation on recovery.[33]

However, there is more to the corrective justice explanation than this. It is argued that pure economic loss is not harm resulting from an interference by D, and that in fact liability for pure economic loss would amount to liability for failing to confer a benefit on C. It would be like making D liable for a failure to carry out a rescue.[34] With respect to this argument it is important to note that there is an ambiguity in the expression 'pure economic loss'. It can refer to the loss of actual financial wealth and investments, that is to say intangible property. Alternatively, it can refer to the loss of expected future profits – profits that

[32] See ch 4.

[33] Stevens (n 8) 25.

[34] P Benson, 'The Problem with Pure Economic Loss' (2009) 60 *South Carolina Law Review* 823; Beever (n 1) ch 7.

C would in the ordinary course have made but did not because of D's actions. This is not a loss of something that C already owns. The reason why these two categories have not been distinguished may be in part the failure to recognise that financial wealth and investments are a genuine form of property, as discussed further in chapter nine. But the two categories are quite different in principle. The corrective justice approach rightly takes the pure economic loss rule to refer only to the loss of expected profits. The classic examples of pure economic loss relate to expected future profits, for example where D has caused loss to C by damaging a utility belonging to a third party, or a bridge not owned by C that C uses for C's business. The argument is then that whereas C has a right to person and property, there is no right to expected future profits. A loss of future profits is not a loss caused by an interference with C's right. Holding D liable with respect to a loss of future profits might be equated with holding D liable for a failure to provide a benefit. By contrast, there is no reason why existing wealth in the form of intangible property such as money in a bank account or an investment should be treated any differently from tangible property.

The argument seems powerful but in my view is incomplete. When C claims in negligence for a loss in the form of damage to property or personal injury, the right that C relies on is a right that D act with due care. The loss suffered follows from this right with respect to D's conduct – it is the loss caused to C by D's failure to act with due care. It is the loss to C relative to the position C would have been in if this wrong had not been committed. If a wrong by D causes loss to C in the form of a loss of future profits, it is a genuine loss caused by D's wrong, whether or not it relates to a right to C's body or C's property. Why should recovery of this loss be excluded? In effect, the corrective justice account of the pure economic loss rule simply adds an ostensibly arbitrary condition that excludes recovery for a certain type of loss resulting from D's wrong. One might say that (as considered earlier) C's right is actually a right that D not cause harm by falling below the standard of care. But on this understanding, aside from the objections made to it above, the harm that is part of the duty in negligence has to be determined, and the question is why it should not encompass a loss of future profits (or some other form of pure economic loss), as a possible loss resulting from D's action.

Again, the argument is more convincing on the primary liability approach. It does make sense to say that D should bear the risk of harm to C in the form of personal injury or property damage (including intangible property), but not the risk of loss to C relative only to what C has no current right to but merely expects to receive. With respect to future profits, which C would expect to receive in the normal course of events, but might not, as a result of any of various possible events that ordinarily C would have to be alert to respond to, it is reasonable that C should bear the risk. In this form the argument is important, as discussed further in chapter seven.

Similarly, where there has been a failure by a public authority – say, where a police force has failed to protect someone in danger, or a local authority has failed to protect a child at risk of abuse – it may be difficult to deny that in the circumstances the authority has acted wrongfully towards C. Again, it is said that the corrective justice approach does not support a claim against the authority in respect of the exercise of its public duty, because the authority's duty is a duty to provide a benefit (including acting to save C from harm from a third party), not a duty against interference, and so no claim arises as a matter of corrective justice. A public authority should incur a liability only insofar as it has caused harm by interference, where an ordinary person would have been liable for causing harm in the same circumstances.[35] But again, although a duty to provide a benefit does not normally arise at common law, if liability in negligence arises from a wrong by D against C, on the ground of D's responsibility for it, and if a wrong was committed by the public authority against C, why should there not, by parity of reasoning, be liability for the wrongfully-caused loss? Why in principle should liability be confined to the traditional core case of positive action causing personal injury or physical damage by interference, here and with respect to pure economic loss? Is it simply on the basis of precedent, or is it actually a policy exclusion? It is not clear that the corrective justice approach provides a satisfactory answer.[36]

Other Wrongs

The law of negligence presents particular difficulties for the corrective justice approach because often the interests of the two parties C and D are inextricably linked to the interests of everyone in a certain population, such as road users. The corrective justice approach might be thought to do better in explaining other torts, for example assault or defamation or interference with privacy, which may seem to be concerned with a clash of interests between the two parties C and D in isolation from the interests of others and the public interest. Even here, however, it is clear that the public interest is often relevant, for example in determining what sort of everyday touching is permissible, or what sort of information should be private, or the scope of the public interest defence for criticism or the disclosure of private information.[37]

In any case, even if only the interests of the two parties are relevant to the law, it does not follow that it must be based on the corrective justice approach and not the distributive justice approach. As discussed in the previous chapter, although the distributive justice may have a problem explaining bilateral rights in negligence, it seems perfectly plausible that there can be derivative bilateral rights in cases where typically only the interests of the two parties are at stake.

[35] This position has been adopted by the Supreme Court: *Robinson v Chief Constable of West Yorkshire* [2018] UKSC 4.

[36] See NJ McBride, *Humanity of Private Law Part 1* (Hart, 2018) 4, considering *Michael v Chief Constable of South Wales Police* [2015] UKSC 2.

[37] See S Hershovitz, 'The Search for a Grand Unified Theory of Tort Law' (2017) 130 *Harvard Law Review* 942.

Some Problems with the Corrective Justice Account of Contract

The Moral Power to Undertake a Duty

The conventional understanding of contract law is the will theory, which I equate with the corrective justice approach. The standard version is that contract law arises from promising, understood as the exercise of a moral power to create a duty to the promisee, which is recognised as a legal duty. The moral duty arises purely from the party's exercise of a moral power through the expression of an intention to undertake a duty. The duty is independent of the interests of the promisor or promisee (or anyone else) in providing or receiving goods or services and so is independent of distributive justice. On the face of it, contract as promise accounts well for the bilateral rights of private law. Indeed the contract as promise theory does seem to do well on the whole in accounting for the law: the basic rule of contract law that the law should give effect to the intentions of the parties.[38]

Some commentators are sceptical that there can be such a moral power at all, that is to say a power that through a simple exercise of will – by the expression of an intention to be bound – creates a moral duty, irrespective of whether anyone else's interest, such as an interest in receiving or supplying goods or services, will thereby be advanced. If such a duty is breached, no-one's interest is harmed, other than the interest in the performance of the promise itself (if there is such an interest).[39] For some commentators, the duty is an illusion, conjured up out of nothing as if the promise were a magic spell.[40] Even if a promise can create a moral duty, the question arises whether the duty should be recognised and enforced as a legal duty, if no-one's interest would be harmed by breach. There would be no basis for this on the distributive justice approach. As discussed in the last chapter, the distributive justice approach does not rely simply on a pure exercise of will to create a duty. An agreement has effect in contract as a means of facilitating exchange.

The 'transfer theory' of contract is supposed to provide a stronger basis for contract than the simple contract as promise approach. According to the transfer theory, future actions are objects of property. When A makes a promise to B, A should be understood to make a transfer to B of a right of ownership of A's future actions, as specified in the promise. If A then fails to perform, A appropriates or destroys what is now B's property, and in giving legal effect to the contract for

[38] Ie intention in the sense of what is promised, not intention to act as opposed to promising.

[39] See the discussion in D Owens, *Shaping the Normative Landscape* (Oxford University Press, 2012) 123–27.

[40] An objection originally made by Hume, as discussed in Owens (ibid). This is 'bare wrongdoing'. See also PS Atiyah, *Essays on Contract* (Clarendon Press, 1986) 121–79. Arguments for the existence of such a moral power tend to draw on the way in which it can affect others through reliance or co-ordination, but if it is binding for this reason this is a version of the distributive justice approach. See eg N McCormick, 'Voluntary Obligations' in *Legal Right and Social Democracy* (Clarendon Press, 1982).

B's benefit the law allows B to recover B's own property, or to obtain compensation for its loss.[41] This is thought to provide a sounder justification for recognising and enforcing a promise. It is thought to overcome the objection that there is no independent interest in performance of the promise because this is supplied by the property right. It is also thought to provide a stronger basis for bilateral rights, because it is not open to the objection that promisors merely bind themselves unilaterally rather than binding themselves to the promisee, so as to give the promisee a right to performance of the promise.[42]

However, anyone who is not convinced that promisors can bind themselves, by a pure exercise of will, where no interest of anyone else is affected, is unlikely to be persuaded that the transfer theory overcomes the problem. It also depends on a theory of property that, as I discuss in chapters nine and ten, goes beyond the usual conception of property in private law, which is concerned with ownership of things in the world and not actions.[43]

Non-intention Based Aspects of Contract

Putting aside these difficulties, there are various respects in which contract law seems to depart from what one would expect on the corrective justice approach, based on the will theory. First, one might expect that all promises would be legally recognised, even promises that merely constrain the promisor's behaviour without involving the supply of goods or services. However, promises are not necessarily enforceable, in particular because of the requirement of consideration. For this reason some commentators doubt whether there is any good rationale for the doctrine of consideration.[44] By contrast, under the distributive justice theory, since the rationale for enforcing the agreement is to facilitate the exchange of goods and services there is a plausible reason for confining enforcement to contracts for exchange.

Secondly, the will theory explains only the legal effect given to what has actually been agreed.[45] It provides no basis for explaining the rules of contract law that deal with issues on which there was no actual agreement, that is to say default terms.[46] In theory, the distributive justice approach can deal with this issue. Since

[41] Benson (n 1). In property law terms it would seem to be equivalent to a grant rather than a transfer.

[42] The transfer amounts to a perfect rather than an imperfect promise: Benson (ibid) 10–11.

[43] The transfer theory would seem to give C a right over D's actions that also binds everyone else. This would justify the effect of the common law in overriding interests of third parties and the public interest. The effect of statute in reforming contact is generally to take account of such interests.

[44] C Fried, '*Contract as Promise* Thirty Years On' (2012) Vol XLV *Suffolk University Law Review* 961; SV Shiffrin, 'The Divergence of Contract and Promise' (2007) 120 *Harvard Law Review* 708. See also R Barnett, 'Contract is not Promise; Contract is Consent' (2012) Vol XLV *Suffolk University Law Review* 647.

[45] As considered further in ch 8.

[46] R Craswell, 'Contract Law, Default Rules, and the Philosophy of Promising' (1989) 88 *Michigan Law Review* 489; Barnett (n 44).

the rationale for enforcing agreements is to facilitate mutually beneficial exchange across society, one can understand the adoption of default terms that contribute to this objective.

For the same reason, the corrective justice approach has difficulty explaining the rule that contractual agreement is understood 'objectively',[47] meaning that contractors are understood to have made an agreement when their words and conduct are reasonably interpreted as indicating agreement.[48] It is not necessary that there was actual, subjective agreement. One would think that the will theory would require subjective agreement. There might separately be legal protection for reliance on the appearance of agreement, but in principle this should be distinct from the law giving effect to subjective agreement, and one might even think that it should be based on a finding that C was misled by a wrong by D. However, no such division is found in the law. On the distributive justice approach it makes more sense that the agreement is understood objectively, since the contract is essentially about the effect of agreement in facilitating exchange, through reliance on the agreement, and for reliance the appearance of agreement to a reasonable contractor is what should be required.

The Remedial Problem in Contract

As discussed previously, the remedial regime in contract reflects a primary liability approach. In particular, there is no general right to specific performance. This has long been controversial and the controversy is understood to be about why the legal duty to perform is not specifically enforced, though as argued in chapter three it would be better to understand the controversy as being about whether there is a primary duty to perform or instead a primary liability with respect to loss from non-performance.

In any case, on the corrective justice approach it would appear that D has a moral duty to perform, which is also a legal duty, though D is not treated in law as bound to perform. Shiffrin argues that, by failing to award specific performance, the law wrongly condones the promisor's failure to perform the moral duty arising from his promise.[49] She identifies this and other inconsistencies between the law of contract as it is, and what would be expected if the moral duty to perform were recognised and enforced as a legal duty. These include features mentioned in chapter three that I took to imply that there is a primary liability not a primary duty. She argues for reform of the remedial regime in contract to remove the divergence

[47] *Smith v Hughes* (1871) LR 6 QB 597.

[48] Barnett (n 44).

[49] Shiffrin (n 44). And thereby systematically undermines the moral institution of promising and at the same time has a corrosive effect on contract law because of its reliance on this institution. See also L Smith, 'Understanding Specific Performance' in N Cohen and E McKendrick (eds), *Comparative Remedies for Breach of Contract* (Hart, 2005).

between contract law and promising. Shiffrin's critique implies that if the law is justifiable as it is, it is not consistent with the corrective justice approach.

Other supporters of the corrective justice approach argue that the absence of a right to specific performance is consistent with the corrective justice approach, even though D has a legal duty to perform the promise. For example, it is argued by a number of commentators that a general right to specific performance against D would unduly impinge on D's autonomy.[50] The argument is that the value of personal autonomy provides the justification for both the power to promise and also for the right to be free from being coerced into performing the promise. Overall, weighing up the conflicting demands of the promisor D's right to autonomy, and the promisee C's right to receive what was promised, D should be liable to pay compensation to C to the value of the performance to which C was entitled, but should not be subject to coercion to compel performance of the promise.

One difficulty with this explanation is that, even if it can explain the absence of a right to specific performance, it is not clear that it can account for the other aspects of the remedial regime. If D has a duty to perform, even if the duty cannot be enforced by specific performance, why should D normally be free to retain the profits of a breach of duty?[51] Also, why should C have to act as if D has no duty, as C has to under the mitigation rule?[52] And why should a penalty clause, which has been expressly agreed as a means of protecting a contracting party's right to performance, not be enforceable?

In any case, it seems doubtful whether this argument can explain the absence of a right to specific performance. As suggested in chapter three, no doubt for certain types of contract involving personal services, specific performance could be so intrusive as to amount to an unjustified restriction of D's autonomy, despite giving effect to the agreement. Possibly also where a contract imposes a burden that is out of proportion with, or quite different in type from, what could have been expected, it could be an unjustified restriction of D's autonomy for D to be coerced into performance. But where D has a duty to do exactly what was envisaged, and where the burden is to perform an ordinary commercial service or supply, it is difficult to see why specific enforcement would amount to an unjustified restriction of D's autonomy. One should bear in mind here that the reason why C recovers compensation on the corrective justice approach is not to protect C's reliance on the promise. It is not suggested that the recovery of compensation has a different

[50] See eg M Chen-Wishart, 'Specific Performance and Change of Mind' in *Commercial Remedies: Resolving Controversies* (Cambridge University Press, 2017); D Kimel, 'Promise, Contract, Personal Autonomy, and the Freedom to Change One's Mind' in G Klass, G Letsas and P Saprai (eds), *Philosophical Foundations of Contract Law* (Oxford University Press, 2014); D Kimel, 'Remedial Rights and Substantive Rights in Contract Law' (2002) 8 *Legal Theory* 313.

[51] Putting aside the objection that disgorgement should never be available: see at n 50 in ch 3.

[52] And why should C have a claim for restitution, which allows C a measure of recovery that may exceed the value of D's performance to C, if what C is entitled to from D is the performance of the duty? See at n 58 in ch 3.

basis from specific performance. Compensation is justified on the basis that D owes C a duty to perform and this is why it is measured relative to what C would have received through performance. If there is a power to bind oneself to perform a duty, by virtue of an interest in autonomy, it is difficult to see why it should be limited such that it can generate a duty enforceable by compensation, and not a duty that can be specifically enforced, even in ordinary commercial cases.[53]

What presumably would promote autonomy would be for the contracting parties to be able to choose whether to make an agreement that is intended to give rise to duties of performance (to be enforced as such) or instead to make an agreement that is intended to give rise to a primary liability relation, allocating risk with respect to loss from non-performance, without normally creating duties to perform. It is not necessary to have a primary duty relation for the contract to provide a workable framework for a voluntary exchange (as is apparent from the fact that the law actually has a primary liability regime). But the law does not enable contracting parties to contract to establish a contractual regime that recognises duties protected by specific performance.[54]

Focus on the Particular Parties

The corrective justice approach implies that the law should give effect to the intentions of the parties, protecting their right to determine how to bind themselves. It does not take account of the interests of others (except to the extent that the parties choose to take account of them in their contract). But although contract law does seem to be based, as a rule, on giving effect to the intentions of the parties, sometimes, as mentioned in chapter four, the public interest is recognised as relevant. The doctrine of 'public policy' may be invoked to set aside certain types of contract, including contracts for prostitution or gambling, or to evade tax. This seems to be, strictly speaking, a departure from the corrective justice approach.[55]

For proponents of the distributive justice approach, as pointed out in the previous chapter, the question is why the courts cannot go further than the public policy doctrine allows in taking account of interests other than those of the contracting parties. Why can they not introduce a mandatory regime along the lines of the statutory regimes to protect certain types of contractor, for example consumers, employees and tenants? For proponents of the corrective justice approach, the problem is not merely that the public policy doctrine appears to be at odds

[53] Cf RE Scott and JS Kraus, 'The Case Against Equity in American Contract Law' (2020) 93 *Southern California Law Review* 1323.

[54] Cf the argument that parties should always have the freedom to coerce the other party to perform through a penalty clause: S Worthington, 'Common Law Values: The Role of Party Autonomy in Private Law' in A Robertson and M Tilbury (eds), *The Common Law of Obligations: Divergence and Unity* (Hart, 2015). See further in ch 8 below.

[55] See eg S Judd, 'The Unruly Horse Put Out to Pasture: The Doctrine of Public Policy in the Modern Law of Contract' (1998) 8 *Auckland University Law Review* 686.

with the corrective justice approach. What is also puzzling is that proponents of the corrective justice approach generally accept that statutory regimes to promote distributive justice are legitimately introduced by the legislature. Why then is it that the judges at common law cannot take account of distributive justice, even in principle?

A Systemic Problem for the Corrective Justice Approach

Aside from whether the corrective justice approach can satisfactorily explain traditional private law, there is an objection relating to the nature of the corrective justice approach itself. It concerns the relationship between corrective justice and distributive justice, and the roles of the courts and the legislature with respect to private law.

According to Weinrib, corrective justice and distributive justice are different 'forms of justice'.[56] However, as Weinrib acknowledges,[57] and as considered in chapter four, they do not apply in different domains or spheres of operation, corrective justice for interactions and distributive justice for institutions. They both apply to interactions, and furthermore they are both comprehensive theories of private law and are mutually exclusive. On the face of it, they are incompatible alternatives in private law.

According to the corrective justice approach, the traditional character of private law arises from the fact that it is based on moral rights against other individuals. One might infer that these rights, which the courts give effect to in their development of the common law, also in principle bind the legislature, in the sense that the legislature ought to legislate to give effect to them and not to override or curtail them. If these moral rights govern the interaction so far as the common law is concerned, one might assume that they govern the interaction so far as the legislature is concerned as well. On this assumption, the corrective justice approach amounts to a libertarian theory.[58] It rejects any role for distributive justice going beyond this, for example an egalitarian role in sharing the risks of accidents and other harms, or redistributing the wealth generated by the market.

Some critics of the corrective justice approach do object that it is libertarian in this sense,[59] but it would seem not to be the standard view of proponents of the corrective justice approach. The standard position is that, although the courts must

[56] Weinrib, *The Idea of Private Law* (n 1) ch 3. Cf Beever (n 1) 42.

[57] Weinrib, *The Idea of Private Law* 68–72. See now Weinrib, *Reciprocal Freedom* (n 1) ch 5.

[58] Associated eg with R Nozick, *Anarchy, State & Utopia* (Basic Books 1974). The libertarian approach can itself be understood as a form of the distributive justice approach but I have avoided this usage.

[59] See eg D Priel, 'The Political Origins of English Private Law' (2013) 40 *Journal of Law and Society* 481.

apply corrective justice, it is legitimate for the legislature to employ distributive justice. It can use taxation and public benefits to adjust the allocation of benefits and harms resulting from the operation of private law under the common law, and in addition it can in principle establish mandatory regimes modifying or even abolishing parts of private law. But if distributive justice applies to the interactions of private law, how can corrective justice also apply to it, since they are mutually exclusive comprehensive theories of private law? And if the legislature applies distributive justice to the interactions of private law, why do the courts not also do so? How can the corrective justice approach be the right approach for the courts to apply, on the ground that it reflects the justice of the interaction, if it is not also the justice of the interaction so far as the legislature is concerned? This is the crucial issue anticipated in earlier chapters.

Ripstein argues that there is a middle way for corrective justice in private law, according to which it is based neither on the libertarian approach, nor on a distributive justice approach.[60] According to Ripstein, following Rawls, there is a division of responsibility between societal institutions and individuals, institutions having responsibility for the fair allocation of resources and opportunities across the society, and individuals having personal responsibility for the conduct of their own lives. According to Ripstein, this must involve the recognition of basic rights of individuals as against other individuals in tort or contract or private property. This must be the case because institutions cannot justifiably allocate resources and opportunities to individuals unless individuals are accountable for what they do, both in the sense that they are responsible for advancing their own interests in the use of their resources and opportunities, and also in the sense that they are responsible for allowing others to exercise responsibility in the same way for their lives. This means that there must be basic rights against others that are compatible with and presupposed by the distributive justice approach. These basic rights give rise to the bilateral relations of private law.

This is no doubt a coherent position, but it is equivalent to a version of the distributive justice approach. It reflects a certain view of what distributive justice requires overall, and how to implement it, namely that there should be a certain division of institutional responsibility, consisting of a regime essentially in the form of traditional private law in tandem with a legislative regime for adjustment. As against a different view of what distributive justice requires or how to achieve it, the issues at stake are issues of distributive justice – whether a regime incorporating traditional private law to protect individual liberties is the best way to achieve distributive justice overall.

[60] A Ripstein, 'The Division of Responsibility and the Law of Tort' (2004) 72 *Fordham Law Review* 1811. See also SR Perry, 'Ripstein, Rawls, and Responsibility' (2004) 72 *Fordham Law Review*1845; GC Keating, 'Form and Substance in the 'Private Law' of Torts' (2021) 14 *Journal of Tort Law* 45. See also S Scheffler, 'Distributive Justice, the Basic Structure and the Place of Private Law' (2015) 35 *Oxford Journal of Legal Studies* 213. Scheffler discusses an analogous problem concerning the exclusion of distributive justice from private law under Rawls's 'division of labour', on the ground that it is outside the 'basic structure', as considered in ch 4.

Furthermore, Ripstein's approach does not explain the difference between the roles of the legislature and the courts. If it is right that private law in broadly its traditional form (or some part of it) ought to be preserved, the legislature ought not to modify it or replace it, and if instead the legislature is justified in doing this then presumably the courts ought to have developed the law in the way that the legislature has done, so far as possible.[61] To some extent, differences between the common law and statutory private law can be explained in terms of institutional limitations on what the courts can do, for example executive limitations or the inability to do policy analysis or the lack of political legitimacy.[62] But these limitations do not explain the corrective justice approach, which holds that the courts simply determine the justice of the interaction itself, as corrective justice.[63] This seems to me a serious problem for the corrective justice approach itself. It is not merely an institutional or procedural issue.

Benson has a similar approach to corrective justice, focusing on contract law.[64] He refers to his version as the 'juridical conception', which he contrasts with the libertarian approach. According to Benson, again following Rawls, contract law under the juridical conception excludes distributive justice because it is not feasible for rules based on distributive justice to apply directly to individuals, since individuals need clear and simple rules to follow. For example, it would not be practicable to incorporate Rawls's difference principle into the rules applicable to individuals. Thus, under Benson's juridical conception, the basic liberty rights of individuals do not entirely exclude considerations of distributive justice; they merely exclude them from private law as developed at common law. The legislature, operating in parallel to the common law, legislates for background justice to adjust for the adverse effects of the market system and also to ensure that everyone is in a position to participate in the market system. According to Benson, this approach allows for legislative restrictions on contract law, for example contractual disclosure rules or maximum working hours or minimum standards in employment contracts, but he insists that the legislature is bound to leave some scope for private exchange by contract in order to respect individuals' rights to contract.

Although this is no doubt a defensible vision of private law, it seems open to objection along the same lines. It holds that distributive justice must recognise something like traditional contract law in order to respect individual liberties, though it can modify traditional contract law and adjust for its effects. Again, in

[61] Some commentators point out that if it is right for the legislature to take account of distributive justice the courts should do so as well: J Stapleton, *Three Essays on Torts* (Oxford University Press, 2021) 29–32; Keating (n 60).

[62] See further ch 6.

[63] Furthermore, as mentioned earlier, if this is the right way to understand the common law, one would think that the judges would have had to make a considered decision to adopt the approach as a matter of distributive justice, on the assumption that the common law would be complemented by a legislative regime, but there seems no suggestion of this in the common law.

[64] Benson (n 1) 448–476.

response to the objection that distributive justice requires radical reform or even the abolition of private law, the issue is simply about the best regime of distributive justice. Furthermore, it is not clear why on Benson's approach the judges could not have moved away from traditional private law to promote distributive justice along the lines of the statutory reforms that have been introduced.

Weinrib makes an argument along similar lines. Private law is based on liberty rights or 'reciprocal freedom'.[65] The operation of a private law system based on reciprocal freedom may lead to the accumulation of wealth and power through contracting and property ownership, and thereby leave people impoverished and vulnerable, and this may have the effect of undermining reciprocal freedom. In order to secure reciprocal freedom, the legislature may be justified in modifying or even replacing negligence law (or other parts of private law). Just as reciprocal freedom underlies corrective justice in private law, so does it underlie distributive justice, as the legislature should promote it. Corrective justice is concerned with basic liberties and distributive justice with interests in harms and benefits, but fundamentally both protect reciprocal freedom. Again, it is difficult to see why this is not equivalent to a particular vision of distributive justice which encompasses basic liberties along with wealth distribution. It is also unclear why the courts should not take account of considerations of distributive justice as a legislature might, where appropriate to offset the adverse effects of private law (subject to institutional limitations).[66]

There is another way to understand the relationship of corrective justice to distributive justice, as mentioned previously,[67] according to which corrective justice is concerned with undoing departures from or disturbances to a prior position governed by distributive justice. Again, this seems to be in substance a distributive justice approach, with corrective justice serving merely to protect distributive justice. It does not seem to leave room for corrective justice as a distinct form of justice. The prior position may not actually be consistent with distributive justice, because of an unjust allocation across society, but it is presumed to be so, on the ground that it is not practicable for the courts actually to assess the prior position or take account of it, or because it is the sort of issue that should be determined by the legislature.[68] Corrective justice has independent significance only because of this presumption, and this seems a weak foundation for private law. If the justice of a claim in private law really lies in restoring distributive justice, it seems doubtful whether these are adequate reasons for ignoring the fact that the prior position is inconsistent with distributive justice.

[65] Weinrib, *Reciprocal Freedom* (n 1) ch 5.

[66] As mentioned earlier, Weinrib has argued that the courts are confined to applying corrective justice because this is intrinsic to the structure of private law: see ch 2.

[67] See ch 4. See J Gordley, 'Equality in Exchange' (1981) 69 *California Law Review* 1587; H Dagan, 'The Distributive Foundations of Corrective Justice' (1999) 98 *Michigan Law Review* 138. See also P Cane, 'Distributive Justice and Tort Law' [2001] *New Zealand Law Review* 401.

[68] Eg J Gordley, 'Equality in Exchange' (1981) 69 *California Law Review* 1587, 1591.

In any case, it is difficult to see how private law can be understood to be concerned only with restoring the prior position, and it does not generally aim to restore the prior position of both parties. Private law seems to be concerned with determining the rights and liabilities of the parties with respect to the harms and benefits of interactions irrespective of the prior position.

Conclusion

The corrective justice approach may do better than the distributive justice approach in accounting for traditional private law, certainly with respect to the basic feature of bilateralism, but it also has difficulty accounting for some features of private law. Although it seems clear that at common law private law does not systematically pursue distributive justice, neither is it concerned only with the liberty rights or individual interests of the two parties to the interaction, at the expense of wider interests and the public interest. Furthermore, it is not generally concerned with wrongdoing.

The biggest difficulty concerns the nature of corrective justice. It is generally accepted that distributive justice in principle applies to interactions, and that it is legitimate for the legislature to apply distributive justice to the same interactions that at common law should be governed by corrective justice, and yet the distributive justice approach and the corrective justice approach are also understood to be mutually exclusive comprehensive theories of private law. There seems to be no room left for corrective justice. It might seem that corrective justice is a 'form of justice' that must be assumed to exist because otherwise it would be impossible to explain private law in its traditional form – an ad hoc solution to the problem of explaining private law. It is not surprising that some commentators insist that the idea of corrective justice is an illusion and that any part of private law that is not justifiable in terms of distributive justice should be reformed or abolished.[69]

[69] See L Alexander and K Kessler Ferzan, 'Confused Culpability, Contrived Causation, and the Collapse of Tort Theory' in J Oberdiek (ed), *Philosophical Foundations of the Law of Torts* (Oxford University Press, 2014); LA Alexander, 'Causation and Corrective Justice, Does Tort Law Make Sense?' (1987) 6 *Law and Philosophy* 1 (1987); L Kaplow and S Shavell, *Fairness versus Welfare* (Harvard University Press, 2002). See also D Priel, 'Private Law: Commutative or Distributive' (2014) 77 *Modern Law Review* 308.

6

Distributive Justice under the Standpoint Limitation

Introduction

The previous two chapters have shown that there are objections of different kinds to both the distributive justice approach and the corrective justice approach. On the approach I set out here, the courts in developing the common law apply distributive justice to interactions subject to a constraint that I shall call the standpoint limitation, the effect of which is that the law, as they develop it, is private law in broadly its traditional form.[1]

The Standpoint Limitation

As mentioned in chapter three, a distinction can be drawn between the evidence-based (or subjective) and the fact-based (or objective) concepts of a moral duty. If one uses the evidence-based concept, D's duty depends on what D knows or ought to know, that is to say, on the facts D has access to. If one uses the fact-based concept, D's duty depends on all the actual facts, irrespective of what D knows or ought to know. For example, if D gives C a poisoned drink, according to the evidence-based concept D acts wrongfully only if D knows or ought to know that the drink is poisoned, whereas according to the fact-based concept D acts wrongfully irrespective of whether D knows or ought to know this. The two concepts are sometimes taken to be competing versions of the concept of duty, but the better view is that they are distinct concepts that are relevant in different contexts.[2] If the issue is whether D is morally responsible for the consequences of a wrongful act, one should ask whether D had a duty and committed a wrong in the evidence-based sense. By contrast, the fact-based concept is relevant to what it would be best for someone in D's position to do, in the sense of what it would be right for

[1] This chapter draws on P Jaffey, 'Two Ways of Understanding the Common Law' (2017) 8 *Jurisprudence* 435 and P Jaffey, 'Policy and Principle and the Character of Private Law' (2020) 11 *Jurisprudence* 387.

[2] D Parfit, *On What Matters*, Vol 1 (Oxford University Press, 2011) 15-1; TM Scanlon, *Moral Dimensions* (Harvard University Press) 47–52.

D to be advised or instructed to do by an omniscient person or at least someone well placed to give advice or instructions. For this purpose, the adviser or instructor should take account of all the facts, or at least all that can be ascertained, irrespective of what is known or accessible to D.

When D's remedial liability is at stake, it is D's moral responsibility that is in issue, and the evidence-based concept should apply, which would call for subjective fault for liability for wrongdoing. With respect to a primary liability, the issue is whether D should incur a remedial liability for harm arising out of an activity, and whether there is a primary liability should depend on the facts that D knew or should have known. The same is true with respect to a moral power, for example the power to make an agreement if this is to be the basis for a remedial liability. In general, if D's remedial liability is at stake, the position should be determined relative to what D knows or ought to know, ie relative to D's 'evidence base'.

More particularly, in private law the concern is with a remedial liability arising as a matter of distributive justice as it applies to an interaction between C and D. The issue is what distributive justice prescribes for C and D with respect to the interaction on the evidence-based approach. The relevant evidence base is not just what D knows or ought to know, but what both parties know or ought to know, because the law is concerned both with what D is responsible for vis-à-vis C, and also, at the same time, with what C is entitled to from D. More precisely, the legal position must depend on what each party can be taken to know that each of them ought to know – in other words, their common knowledge. This relevant knowledge encompasses, in particular, knowledge of what the parties can reasonably be expected to be capable of doing in the circumstances, since this is relevant to the justice of the interaction. Going further, with respect to the general rules of private law, which apply to anyone who may be involved in an interaction, the evidence base is the knowledge accessible to people generally with respect to such interactions, which one might describe as ordinary common knowledge with respect to such interactions.[3] Thus private law is the application of distributive justice to interactions, assessed relative to ordinary common knowledge. As I shall argue in this chapter and subsequent chapters, the distinctive character of traditional private law, including its bilateral character, is explicable on the assumption that it arises as a matter of distributive justice understood in this way.

When a court develops private law by formulating a new rule to decide a case, where no authoritative rule applies, it must formulate the rule in accordance with justice in this sense. This is because it must apply a rule that achieves a just resolution of the dispute between the parties, which means that it must apply justice as between the parties with respect to the interaction, at the time of interaction. This new rule is not necessarily the rule that a legislature would adopt if it had to lay down a rule for the same circumstances. The legislature lays down a rule for the

[3] I understand common knowledge in a common sense way, as it is presupposed (in my view) by the courts in connection with ordinary legal reasoning, as I consider below.

future, and it does not need to adopt a rule that is also the just rule to determine liability with respect to previous events. The legislature should take account of everything that can be found out about the behaviour governed by the rule and its consequences – in other words, legislation should employ the fact-based approach rather than the evidence-based approach. When a legislative rule applies, the parties are assumed to know the rule laid down and are held accountable simply for failing to comply with it. It is not relevant whether the parties knew or ought to have known the facts that provided the justification for the legislative rule.

I shall say that the law as developed by the courts is made subject to the 'standpoint limitation', because it requires that new rules be constructed from the standpoint of people to whom the law applies, on the basis of ordinary common knowledge. To say that the court must adopt the parties' standpoint in making new rules is not to say that it must apply the parties' own moral standards. In developing the law, the court applies the moral considerations that it determines are sound, but it is confined to those considerations that apply in the light of the facts that were accessible to the parties at the time of the interaction. Over time, every rule adopted by the courts is formulated in this way, so that private law as a whole embodies distributive justice in this sense, as the courts have determined it.[4]

A party may actually be aware of circumstances of injustice in society, in the light of which that party may have a moral duty to the other party to the interaction going beyond what private law would require under the standpoint limitation. Nevertheless, private law depends on what is due to C from D and what C is entitled to from D, and this must depend on what can be taken to be generally known rather than what might happen to be known to C or D personally.

The Standpoint Limitation by Comparison with Legislation

The standpoint limitation significantly curtails the ability of the courts to develop the law, compared to what the legislature can do, free of the standpoint limitation. A comparison is helpful to demonstrate the limitations of the common law. A legislature can, for example, introduce health and safety rules in the light of expert knowledge, but the standpoint limitation confines a court to devising rules that are justifiable by reference to ordinary common knowledge, which people in the parties' position can be taken to know, for example a rule not to light fires in the vicinity of dry grass. More generally, it is consistent with the standpoint limitation to have a rule requiring a reasonable standard of conduct, since this standard

[4] The justification for the general rules of private law is based on ordinary common knowledge. This is not to say that in any particular case the material facts must all be a matter of ordinary common knowledge.

implicitly depends on what people generally can be taken to know (including what it is reasonable to expect them to find out).[5]

Sometimes a convention is required to co-ordinate people's activities for the common good. A convention is required when there are different ways of achieving a certain benefit through the co-ordination of people's behaviour, and the choice between them is in some degree arbitrary. A simple example is the practice of driving on the left. Clearly it is of public benefit to have a convention about which side of the road to drive on, but which side is chosen is an arbitrary decision. A convention ordinarily develops as a matter of custom and practice, and so becomes part of ordinary common knowledge. The convention may then determine how people ought to act, and so what the law should regard as reasonable and when liability can arise. In the absence of a convention, a legislature can establish one by stipulation for the future, but, because of the element of arbitrariness, under the standpoint limitation a court cannot introduce a new convention into the law in adjudication if it is not already a matter of custom and practice. In the case of a crash between two car drivers in the absence of an established convention about which side of the road they should drive on, under the standpoint limitation a court could not resolve a dispute over liability arising from the crash by laying down a rule that drivers should drive on the left. A driver cannot justly be held responsible for the consequences of failing to conform to a convention that has not yet become established and cannot be anticipated. The court would have to apply a rule based on the reasonableness of the parties' actions in the circumstances, in the absence of a convention.

Similarly, a legislature (or a body with delegated legislative authority) could justifiably lay down a precise speed limit for a certain category of road. The speed limit would not necessarily be apt for all the circumstances or conditions in which it applies, but, despite the element of arbitrariness, it would be justifiable to impose a speed limit in the interests of guidance and ease of enforcement. However, a speed limit could not be introduced in adjudication, because, in the absence of such a legislative rule, a driver could only be expected to judge what speed is reasonable in the particular circumstances at that time, not what speed limit is appropriate for a category of road or what category of road the car is being driven on. In general, under the standpoint limitation a court has to apply a rule that depends on such a context-dependent judgement. Only a legislature can eliminate the need for such a judgement and apply a rule involving a precise quantitative limit over a range of circumstances. Although such a rule may be entirely justified, because it is in some degree arbitrary it cannot be fairly introduced in adjudication.

A similar problem arises with respect to a formality requirement, for example a requirement that certain types of contract or transfer be made in writing. There may well be good reason to introduce such a requirement, but it is not possible to do so in adjudication under the standpoint limitation. The particular form of

[5] See eg *Nettleship v Weston* [1971] 2 QB 691 and *Vaughan v Menlove* (1837) 132 ER 490 (CP).

such a requirement is to some degree arbitrary and the precise circumstances in which it would be appropriate would be impossible to determine in advance, in the absence of a legislative rule, by people making transfers or contracts, that is to say, from the parties' standpoint.

Another example is provided by a rule of corporate limited liability. Corporate limited liability is in the public interest, at least in certain circumstances, because of its effect in encouraging economic investment, but the standpoint limitation would not allow for it to be introduced in adjudication. It would entail denying the creditor C's claim against the investor D on the basis of D's limited liability, with respect to arrangements made with C before limited liability had been introduced by a legislative rule. There are of course different ways in which corporate limited liability could reasonably be implemented. The choice is to some degree arbitrary and it depends on an assessment of the benefits of limited liability across the society for different types of business. The circumstances in which it ought to be available and on what conditions could not possibly be determined from the parties' standpoint on the basis of ordinary common knowledge.

A legislative authority could introduce a new one-way traffic scheme, or a new type of traffic intersection. It could introduce planning or zoning rules allocating activities to particular areas. It could introduce a new interest rate or minimum deposit requirement or rules on disclosure or a timetable for transactions, or other procedures governing the operation of markets. It could introduce a registration scheme for property interests, or new forms of property. However, none of these changes would be open to a court laying down a new rule in adjudication.

In general, the legislature has the advantage that, free of the standpoint limitation, it can rely on expert knowledge and analysis, including empirical research – ie policy analysis – along with its capacity to co-ordinate behaviour by laying down a convention. A legislature, but not a court, can devise a scheme to co-ordinate peoples' actions in a way that is for the public benefit, but requires them to act in ways the benefit of which cannot be anticipated or justified on the basis of ordinary common knowledge. The introduction of such a co-ordinating scheme requires the people subject to it to adjust in ways that could not have been anticipated, which means that it can be introduced only with prospective effect and not in adjudication.

The standpoint limitation has something in common with the concept of polycentricity. A polycentric case is understood as a case involving many interrelated variables, sometimes compared to a 'spider's web'.[6] Following Fuller, some commentators have argued that polycentric cases are not suitable for resolution in adjudication. The issue has been discussed principally in connection with remedies in public law.[7] Consider a case where C seeks protection for a right against a public

[6] LL Fuller, 'The Forms and Limits of Adjudication' (1978–1979) 92 *Harvard Law Review* 353. See also JWF Allison, 'Fuller's Analysis of Polycentric Disputes and the Limits of Adjudication' (1994) 53 *Cambridge Law Journal* 367; JA King, 'The Pervasiveness of Polycentricity' [2008] *Public Law* 101.

[7] For example in judicial review of administrative decisions or the interpretation of legislation: see eg King (ibid).

authority, for example a right to non-discriminatory schooling or to an adequate standard of medical treatment while in prison.[8] The problem is that, although the court may be clear that the authority has failed to provide C with a benefit to which C is entitled, it cannot give an order against the public authority except in very general terms, because to specify how the benefit should be provided would involve determining how the authority should organise its resources and how the activities of different departments of the authority should be co-ordinated. With respect to matters such as resource allocation, planning and co-ordination by public authorities, in practice the court can only make an order in general terms and leave the authority to work out how to carry it out, subject to monitoring. This is to do with judicial competence to give executive directions rather than the standpoint limitation, but it involves an equivalent problem. In private law, a duty to provide a benefit could not arise where it would be impossible for the duty-holder to establish what exactly should be provided on the basis of ordinary common knowledge because of problems of resource allocation, planning and co-ordination. This is, I suggest, relevant to the rule that there is generally no duty to provide benefits in private law, as considered further in chapter seven.

The standpoint limitation can be understood as an aspect of the rule of law. According to the standard understanding of the rule of law, people are entitled to be subject only to rules that have been previously announced, and not to new rules applied retrospectively.[9] The underlying concern is that people should in principle know how the law applies to them so that they can plan accordingly. However, in the common law there are bound to be new situations arising for a court that are not governed by rules previously laid down, where the court needs to devise a new rule. Under the standpoint limitation, people are subject to new rules that are devised to give effect to distributive justice based on ordinary common knowledge, which C and D can be taken to know. Although the new rule has not previously been announced, it could at least have been anticipated by C and D by the exercise of sound moral judgement. The new rule is retrospective in a sense, but not retrospective in an objectionable way for this reason. By contrast, a new rule would be objectionably retrospective if it were devised by the court in the way that a legislature legislates, on a fact-based rather than an evidence-based approach, so that it might have been impossible for the people to whom the new rule is applied in adjudication to anticipate it, even with sound moral judgement. Such a rule would might work in an arbitrary and capricious way to people without notice. The standpoint limitation is appropriate as a matter of fairness to the parties to the dispute, and to other people in a comparable position who are also bound by the new rule with respect to events that have already occurred.

[8] See K Roach, 'Polycentricity and Queue Jumping in Public Law Remedies: A Two-Track Response' (2016) 66 *University of Toronto Law Journal* 3.

[9] This is a standard rule of law requirement, see eg L Fuller, *The Morality of Law* (Yale University Press, 1964); J Raz, 'The Rule of Law and its Virtue' in *The Authority of Law* (Oxford University Press, 1979). Cf the 'rights conception' of the rule of law in R Dworkin, 'Political Judges and the Rule of Law' in *A Matter of Principle* (Clarendon Press, 1986). See also BC Zipursky, 'The Inner Morality of Private Law' (2013) 58 *American Journal of Jurisprudence* 27.

It seems to me that the courts instinctively adopt the standpoint limitation when they consider the facts of cases. As discussed further in chapter eleven, the standpoint limitation is implicit in legal reasoning by analogy from or coherence with previous decisions. Cases are always compared in the light of ordinary common knowledge. Cases that are treated as analogous or as part of a coherent body of case law might not be understood in the same way if one took account of the additional considerations that a legislature should consider, such as knowledge that goes beyond ordinary common knowledge, or the possibility of co-ordinating behaviour through a convention. A legislature does not use analogical or coherence reasoning and a statutory regime may introduce into the law new rules and new distinctions and categories not found in the common law, which would not be justifiable from the standpoint of ordinary subjects of the law in the light of ordinary common knowledge.[10] When judges determine the common law in adjudication, I suggest that normally they instinctively adopt an 'adjudicative mindset', which implicitly involves adopting the standpoint limitation, rather than a 'legislative mindset', which is unconstrained by the standpoint limitation. However, when the law is very unsettled or open there is a danger that the legislative mindset may take over. The adjudicative mindset is part of the internal approach of judges developing the common law through adjudication.[11]

Private Law as Distributive Justice under the Standpoint Limitation

As discussed in chapter four, a standard objection to the distributive justice approach is that it cannot account satisfactorily for bilateral legal rights, because in distributive justice, it is said, rights and duties are rights against and duties to the state relating to the distribution of society's benefits and harms. It was suggested that there could be bilateral derivative rights in distributive justice. As discussed in subsequent chapters, this is the case under the standpoint limitation.[12] Private law, broadly in its traditional form, is explicable as distributive justice under the standpoint limitation. The exclusion of policy analysis and co-ordinating schemes has the effect that private law focuses on the particular interaction and the parties, and excludes, for the most part, considerations based on wider interests and the

[10] See ch 11.

[11] Cf Dworkin's focus on considerations accessible to the parties, discussed by D Regan, 'Glosses on Dworkin: Rights, Principles, and Policies' (1978) 76 *Michigan Law Review* 1213, 1261–64, and Weinrib's idea of 'immanent rationality' in EJ Weinrib, *The Idea of Private Law* (Oxford University Press, rev edn 2012) ch 2.

[12] According to Oberdiek, a contractualist account of private law can explain bilateral relations: see J Oberdiek, 'Structure and Justification in Contractualist Tort Theory' in J Oberdiek (ed), *Philosophical Foundations of the Law of Torts* (Oxford University Press, 2014). See also E Voyiakis, *Private Law and the Value of Choice* (Hart, 2017). I suggest that a contractualist approach would have to incorporate the standpoint limitation to account for bilateral relations.

public interest. In other words, it explains why the law is a matter of principle and not policy, or private rights and not distributive justice (as normally understood) or community welfare or public policy.[13] The corrective justice approach purports to explain this feature of the law, but as considered in chapter five it does not explain it satisfactorily, since the law does not take account of only the liberties or interests of the two parties to the interaction, as the corrective justice approach would require. Under the standpoint limitation, as discussed in later chapters, the law can take account of the interests of others in a comparable position and of the public interest or public policy, to a limited extent, as it is apparent from ordinary common knowledge.[14]

The corrective justice approach is sometimes criticised for focusing exclusively on the common law and failing to account for private law as it has been reformed by the legislature,[15] but in this respect the suggested approach follows the corrective justice approach. A theory applicable only to the common law is justified because the traditional character of private law is linked to the common law through the standpoint limitation. Unlike the corrective justice approach, however, the suggested approach does not rely on the idea that private law is based on a distinct realm of justice, autonomous from distributive justice. Nor is the suggested approach a version of the libertarian approach, which holds that private law is based on individual moral rights that not only govern interactions so far as the common law is concerned, but ought also to constrain the legislature from reforming private law. The standpoint limitation explains why it is justified for the courts to develop the common law in the constrained way that gives rise to traditional private law, even though it is also justified for the legislature to adapt and reform or even abolish it.

The suggested approach leaves no room and has no need for a concept of corrective justice in the substantive sense, meaning the justice of interactions in the common law. The justice of interactions is explicable in terms of distributive justice subject to the standpoint limitation. There remains the question how the right to a remedy relates to the primary right, that is to say remedial corrective justice. This is a matter of remedial consistency, as discussed further in the following chapters.[16]

As discussed in chapter four, the distributive justice approach, unqualified by the standpoint limitation, for example EAL, cannot explain the traditional

[13] Dworkin's distinction between principle and policy has in common with the standpoint limitation that it does not rely on corrective justice or rights independent of distributive justice: see RM Dworkin, *Taking Rights Seriously* (Duckworth, 1977) 22–28, 90–100, 294–330.

[14] The standpoint limitation provides a response to the challenge that 'fairness' arguments cannot justify departing from the ideal welfare approach: L Kaplow and S Shavell, *Fairness versus Welfare* (Harvard University Press, 2002) 77.

[15] J Stapleton, *Three Essays on Torts* (Oxford University Press, 2021) 29–32; GC Keating, 'Form and Substance in the 'Private Law' of Torts' (2021) 14 *Journal of Tort Law* 45. See also P Cane, 'Taking Disagreement Seriously: Courts, Legislatures and the Reform of Tort Law' in M Bryan (ed), *Private Law in Theory and Practice* (Routledge-Cavendish, 2007).

[16] Though the standpoint limitation does not rule out claims based on responsibility for wrongdoing.

character of private law, including bilateral relations and the focus on the interaction and the parties' interests. Proponents of EAL complain that the judges use an artificial form of legal reasoning, either formalism or analogical reasoning, which has wrongly constrained them from exercising moral judgement to its fullest extent to take account of distributive justice.[17] They also complain that the judges wrongly focus on 'social norms' rather than policy and public purposes in accordance with policy analysis as a matter of distributive justice.[18] But under the standpoint limitation the judges are rightly concerned with the 'everyday morality' of interactions,[19] not the political morality of collective action based on policy analysis, which is the preserve of the legislature.

Proponents of EAL also object that the judges make the mistake of using an 'ex post' rather than an 'ex ante' analysis.[20] They have in mind that the judges look at the aftermath of the interaction and consider what justice requires at this point in the form of an appropriate remedy, whereas they ought to consider the position in advance of the interaction to establish in the first place how the parties ought to have acted or what risk they were subject to at this time. It would seem that the ex post analysis wrongly focuses on a particular narrow set of facts instead of applying policy analysis in accordance with an ex ante analysis. But under the standpoint limitation the judges do apply an ex ante analysis, though by virtue of the standpoint limitation it rightly focuses largely on the interaction and the parties.

Under the standpoint limitation, on the one hand private law is not formalist – it does not deny that the judges exercise moral judgement – nor, on the other hand, does it imply that the courts should exercise political judgement in the same way as a legislature, as a matter of distributive justice.[21] The standpoint limitation offers a middle way. Justice subject to the standpoint limitation may be sub-optimal, in the sense that a legislature legislating prospectively, free of the standpoint limitation, could make better law for the future. Nevertheless private law represents genuine distributive justice in the absence of legislation.

Institutional Constraints

Institutional constraints have been suggested to explain why the courts do not draw on the full range of considerations of distributive justice in developing the common law. It is said that the judges may lack the necessary evidence, or the right

[17] Eg H Collins, *Regulating Contracts* (Oxford University Press, rev edn 2004) ch 3.

[18] Eg Kaplow and Shavell (n 14) 62–81. See also D Priel, 'Land Use Priorities and the Law of Nuisance' (2015) 39 *Melbourne University Law Review* 346, 383.

[19] This does not mean that conventional social morality should be accepted, merely that the moral position is considered on the basis of ordinary common knowledge.

[20] Kaplow and Shavell (n 14) 48–51.

[21] Cf D Kennedy, 'The Distinction between Adjudication and Legislation' in *A Critique of Adjudication (fin de siècle)* (Harvard University Press, 1997).

sort of training and expertise, or the necessary executive power or administrative resources to apply distributive justice as they should.[22] But these supposed constraints do not explain the traditional character of the common law. Nor can the traditional character of the common law be explained on the basis that it saves the courts from making political decisions without a democratic mandate. There seems no reason to think that, in developing private law in the common law, the judges have systematically refrained, for institutional or political reasons, from considering issues that they would otherwise regard as relevant to the justice of the case. If this were the case, the implication would be that there should not be a common law at all.

One might object that, so long as a common law does exist, and the legislature does not act, it is more important for judges to make law in the way that will best advance distributive justice, even at the expense of injustice in the particular case and in other disputes that are pending or may arise with respect to past events. However, if it is right for the judges to legislate in the same way as a legislature can, free of the standpoint limitation, they should do this in a separate, second stage of decision-making, after they have made the decision in adjudication in the matter between the parties. Such a second stage would not do any injustice to the parties or other people relying on the decision as to the current law. By the same token, however, it would mean that the parties would not have any interest, as litigants, in arguing for or against a proposed new rule, and the court would have to seek the assistance of other parties to represent wider interests, including the public interest. It would also be necessary to consider whether judges are competent or can be trained to act as legislators, and it would be necessary to establish how broad the power to legislate should be.[23]

Most importantly, however, having such a second stage would also mean giving the judges a separate form of authority – an authority with respect to political morality – going beyond the authority they traditionally have had in the common law.[24] It would seem far better for such authority to be exercised by a body with democratic legitimacy, combining this with support from policymakers expert in policy analysis.[25] The limited authority that the judges have to develop the law is based on their competence to deal fairly with the issues in adjudication, on the basis of their understanding of justice in the light of ordinary common knowledge.

[22] See eg Collins (n 17).

[23] See T Keren-Paz, *Torts, Egalitarianism and Distributive Justice* (Ashgate, 2007). See also Fuller (n 9). It would also presumably be necessary to have a more formal process for the proclamation of new rules. But this would not be 'hybrid legal reasoning', combining traditional legal reasoning with policy analysis in the same exercise, as advocated by Collins (n 17). Cf J Gava and J Greene, 'Do We Need a Hybrid Law of Contract? Why Hugh Collins is Wrong and Why It Matters' (2004) 63 *Cambridge Law Journal* 605.

[24] See ch 11.

[25] See A Beever, *Rediscovering the Law of Negligence* (Hart, 2009) 8.

Statutory Private Law

When private law is modified by statute, it is useful to distinguish in principle between, first, a modification that corrects what the legislature deems to be an error by the courts, or clarifies the law, and puts the law in a state that the courts could have achieved subject to the standpoint limitation (where the legislature in effect adopts the adjudicative mindset); and, secondly, a reform that is distinctively legislative and goes beyond the standpoint limitation. Reform of the latter sort may depart from the traditional characteristic features of private law. It may entirely abandon the private law model, involving bilateral relations, as when negligence law is replaced by an accident compensation fund, or it may modify the traditional law to create a form of private law recognisable as a relation of private law though beyond the powers of the common law to achieve – for example employment or consumer contract legislation, as discussed in chapter eight. Law in a form described as regulatory or as 'policy regulation' or 'social and economic regulation' is law of this sort. It may be devised or overseen by administrative agencies with specialised policy makers.[26] Codification of the law, by contrast, would on my understanding normally be confined to laying down with statutory effect rules that the courts might have achieved under the standpoint limitation, though they are not open to development in the same way as the common law.

How the legislature should reform private law, or more generally how it should provide for interactions, is a political question of distributive justice, free of the standpoint limitation. An egalitarian legislature might be drawn towards replacing the law of negligence with an accident compensation fund or social insurance, and increasing regulation of contract law and the centralised allocation of goods and services, whereas a libertarian legislature might promote self-insurance and liability only for genuine wrongdoing and unregulated contract. Private law in its traditional form may look rather more like the libertarian approach than the egalitarian approach, but this is not the result of political judgement by the judges. It has emerged without political judgement by virtue of the standpoint limitation.[27]

Reform of the common law also raises practical and empirical issues, for example the reliability of policy analysis and the cost and effectiveness of different methods of regulation. From the legislative point of view, this includes the cost and efficacy of the common law as a means of securing distributive justice. There is considerable scepticism over the tort system as a means of advancing distributive justice,[28] not only because of the cost, but also because it is arbitrary and selective

[26] See Collins (n 17) 7–8.

[27] Another concern about statutory regulation may be that, if the common law is replaced by legislation, governments might undermine distributive justice through misguided policies, for example because of excessive influence from particular sectors promoting their own interests ('regulatory capture').

[28] As considered in ch 4.

as a matter of distributive justice considered from the legislative standpoint. There may be more confidence in the system of contract and markets, at least subject to statutory modification. There are also practical limitations on what it is feasible to require of individuals with respect to interactions. Rules applicable to individuals must meet standards of simplicity and practicality, as noted in chapter four. For example, imposing regulation in contract that differentiates between different types of contracting parties may not always be feasible in practice. However, it is not these considerations but the standpoint limitation that gives rise to the traditional character of private law.

7

Negligence under the Standpoint Limitation

The Character of Negligence

Under the standpoint limitation, private law depends on what is required by distributive justice – justice with respect to benefits and harms across society – on the basis of ordinary common knowledge, that is to say, given what the parties to an interaction can reasonably be expected to know and be capable of doing, at the time of the interaction. On this basis, what duty do the parties have, or what risk ought they to bear, with respect to a possible accident? I suggest that what is required is a fair allocation of the risk of loss from the accident as between the people involved in it. Under a fair allocation of risk, D typically bears the risk of loss to C if an accident results from D's having fallen below a reasonable standard of care.[1]

This approach generates bilateral rights as between the parties to an accident. The fair allocation of risk between the parties is a primary liability relation. As discussed previously, it is generally assumed that the primary relation in negligence is a primary duty relation, with a right of C correlated with a duty on the part of D. It may be said that it would be unjust for D to be liable to C unless D has committed a wrong against C, but there is no injustice in the fair allocation of risk. This approach reflects the structure for private law proposed in chapter three. C's primary right is a right that D bear the risk of harm caused to C when D falls below the reasonable standard of care, and the claim for compensation follows as a matter of remedial consistency, not by virtue of a principle of responsibility for wrongdoing. It makes sense of the fact that there is no subjective fault requirement, and that harm is an element of the cause of action. There are a number of other features of the law of negligence that are easier to understand on this approach, as considered in this chapter.

This approach does not mean that it is not also possible for D to have a duty to C. Such a bilateral duty with respect to an interaction presupposes a prior

[1] Cf R Dworkin, *Law's Empire* (Hart, 1998) ch 8; GP Fletcher, 'Fairness and Utility in Tort Theory' (1972) 85 *Harvard Law Review* 537; N Jansen, 'The Idea of Legal Responsibility' (2013) *Oxford Journal of Legal Studies* 1; A Ripstein, *Equality, Responsibility and the Law* (Cambridge University Press, 1999) ch 3.

allocation of risk with respect to the interaction. The allocation of risk is the legal basis on which the interaction occurs. D may then also have a duty to do what D reasonably can to avoid or prevent the harm for which D bears the risk, and D may commit a wrong by failing to do so, but the wrong is not the basis for the claim for compensation. Breach of duty would be relevant to the award of an injunction or disgorgement of profits or punishment.[2]

The suggested approach has no room for the public policy objectives that a legislature might pursue. The interest of someone who has suffered loss, simply by virtue of its being a loss and a hardship, cannot generate a bilateral moral right against the other party to an accident in order to take advantage of the fact that D is a 'deep pocket' with financial resources or is in a position to pass on the loss by loss spreading.[3] This would not reflect a fair allocation of the risk of loss. Similarly, giving C the right to secure a sanction against D as a deterrent for others in order to reduce accident losses does not reflect a fair allocation of the risk of loss. (It is not concerned with C's loss at all.) Furthermore, there is no room for policy reasoning to determine the balance of policy factors, that is to say weighing up the effects that a possible rule will have on harms and benefits across the society, by way of policy analysis. This goes beyond what is possible by reference to ordinary common knowledge. In particular, there is no room for the policy factors of alleviation of hardship from accidents (favouring payment of compensation), and reduction of accident losses (favouring liability as a sanction): these are the policy factors of 'compensation' and 'deterrence'.[4]

Standard of Care

The standard of care is what is reasonable, taking into account the risk of harm, encompassing its likelihood and seriousness, and the cost of precautions to reduce the risk of harm. Consistently with the standpoint limitation, the standard of care should take account of risks assessed relative to ordinary common knowledge, and disregard risks that are apparent only on the basis of specialist or esoteric knowledge, as at the time of the interaction. Similarly, the law is bound to treat C and D as typical or representative and assume reasonable competence and reasonable foreseeability.

On the suggested approach, the standard of care should take account of risk to anyone who, as a matter of ordinary common knowledge, may be affected by D's activity; for example, with respect to traffic accidents, this would be the population

[2] In Y Adar and R Perry, 'Negligence Without Harm' (2022) *Georgetown Law Journal*, the allocation of risk approach is rejected because of the absence of a duty.

[3] Furthermore, compensation on this basis is not a sanction but nor is it a remedy in the sense of a measure that protects C's right against D and resolves an interpersonal injustice.

[4] Following the corrective justice approach: EJ Weinrib, *The Idea of Private Law* (Oxford University Press, rev ed 2012) 39–42.

of road users. The risk to C personally from D's actions may be negligible; it is the risk to anyone in this population of possible claimants that counts.[5] Similarly, whether it is reasonable that D should bear a certain cost in order to reduce the risk of harm depends on the likely reduction of harm across this population. This approach also allows for the standard of care to accommodate the social value or public benefit of D's activity, insofar as this benefit is apparent on the basis of ordinary common knowledge, as it is in the case of the speeding ambulance. In such a case, D can subject others to an increased risk without falling below the reasonable standard. This seems to reflect the way that the standard of care is understood in English law.[6]

On the distributive justice approach, free of the standpoint limitation, the standard of care should depend on the interests of everyone across the whole society. This appears to be the approach under the Hand formula applying EAL, according to which the reasonable standard is the standard that will minimise aggregate net loss, assessed across the whole society. This involves policy analysis and is excluded under the standpoint limitation. On the suggested approach, a fair allocation of risk is normally assessed across the relevant population and furthermore the standard does not have to be based on the minimisation of aggregate net loss. It may be reasonable that D should be able to impose a greater risk on C if this is necessary to enable D to perform a socially beneficial activity (as in the ambulance example), but it does not follow that C should have to bear a greater risk in order that D should be able to avoid a cost to himself, even if this would minimise aggregate net loss. Arguably, this would not be consistent with a fair allocation of risk.[7]

Because it involves an allocation of risk in advance of an accident on the basis of ordinary common knowledge, on the suggested approach the assumption should be that the parties are of equal wealth and have equal capacity to bear loss, and more broadly that distributive justice is otherwise satisfied across the society, or at least that separate provision will be made for it. Thus a claim should arise even if it is a claim by a rich person against a poor person.[8] If disparities in wealth were taken into account, one might take the view that the level of compensation should vary with the disparity. If, free of the standpoint limitation, the law operated an accident compensation fund or a public benefits system in the interests of distributive justice, it might be appropriate to require different levels of contribution to the fund according to wealth. Similarly, it might be justified for a legislature to take account of the public benefit generated by the parties' activities, but this is not normally possible from the parties' standpoint. The assumption must be that

[5] Cf R Stevens, *Torts and Rights* (Oxford University Press, 2007) 108.

[6] See Stevens (n 5) 107–11.

[7] Stevens (n 5) 94; A Ripstein, *Equality, Responsibility and the Law* (Cambridge University Press, 1999) 63–70; GC Keating, 'Principles of Risk Imposition and the Priority of Avoiding Harm' (2018) 36 *Revus* 7.

[8] Cf JL Coleman, 'The Mixed Conception of Corrective Justice' (1991) 77 *Iowa Law Review* 428.

the parties' respective activities are of equal value to them and to the society, except where they are directed at an obvious public benefit, like driving an ambulance. These assumptions have to be made under the standpoint limitation because, in the absence of legislative regulation, people are bound to interact on this basis if they are to interact at all.

Negligence and Strict Liability

As discussed in chapter three, strict liability means liability for loss suffered by C in certain circumstances irrespective of whether it was caused by D's conduct falling below a standard of care. An example is where D is liable for loss caused by water escaping from a reservoir on D's land, even though there was nothing that D was required and failed to do that caused or would have prevented the loss.[9] The traditional objection to strict liability is that it is unfair to D because it involves making D liable without fault, or where D has not committed a wrong. This is why strict liability is conventionally regarded as having a completely different basis from negligence, and this is also the objection under the corrective justice approach (though, as discussed in chapter three, if D's liability is based on moral responsibility for wrongdoing, the objection applies equally with respect to negligence since it is subjective fault not objective fault that should be required.) On the EAL approach, whether strict liability or negligence is preferable is a matter for policy analysis, in order to determine which rule is more likely to minimise aggregate net loss across the society. This is incompatible with the standpoint limitation.

On the suggested approach, neither an ordinary claim in negligence requiring objective fault, nor a strict liability claim, is based on a wrong; both are based on a fair allocation of risk. The difference between the two is that they involve different allocations of risk, appropriate for different situations. It is commonly said that the reasonable standard of care is apt for ordinary everyday activities, the risks of which lie where they fall, provided that the activity is carried on to a reasonable standard, whereas strict liability is apt for an abnormal activity that people should be free to carry on only at their own risk, meaning that they are liable for any harm caused.[10] This understanding is compatible with the suggested approach: it is at least plausible to say that these are different allocations of risk that are fair in the different types of case, and that the difference between the two types of case is apparent on the basis of ordinary common knowledge.[11] With respect to strict liability, the suggested approach also allows for liability to arise from an action and from an activity that D is legally entitled to carry out. The recognition of strict liability and the treatment of strict liability and negligence as variants of the same

[9] *Rylands v Fletcher* [1983] CLJ 65.
[10] Stevens (n 5) 111–13.
[11] See eg A Ripstein, *Equality, Responsibility and the Law* (Cambridge University Press, 1999) ch 3; N Jansen, 'The Idea of Legal Responsibility' (2014) 34 *Oxford Journal of Legal Responsibility* 221.

type of liability is difficult to reconcile with the conventional understanding of the law or the corrective justice approach but makes sense on a fair allocation of risk approach under the standpoint limitation.

Strict liability is contrary to the standpoint limitation if it is justified in terms of hardship alleviation as such, or loss spreading. This would be the case if the rationale is to use D as a means of securing compensation for C because D is in a position to pass on losses to consumers or because D is a 'deep pocket' who can absorb losses. Similarly, it would be contrary to the standpoint limitation for D to be made subject to strict liability on the ground that D can recover through insurance, with the introduction of a requirement to insure at the same time. These arrangements are contrary to the standpoint limitation, not only because they involve policy analysis concerning the effects of the rule in achieving loss spreading, but also because they involve a co-ordinating scheme designed to make D, and others in D's position, adjust their position as necessary in order to be able to bear the liability by passing on or absorbing the loss. It might be justified for a legislature to introduce such arrangements with prospective effect, but not for a court to do so in adjudication.

Vicarious Liability

Vicarious liability is understood to be the most important form of strict liability. The standard case is where D is liable to C because D's employee, X, fell below the reasonable standard of care in the course of X's employment by D and as a result caused loss to C. The rationale and scope of vicarious liability has long been controversial and this controversy has been intense in recent years.[12] The puzzle is why the employer D should be liable. The traditional understanding of negligence, reflected in the corrective justice approach, is that D must be a wrongdoer who is liable for a personal wrong. If the wrongdoer is actually X, why should the employer D be liable?[13] The employer D may sometimes be personally responsible for a failure of control over the employee X or for a poor appointment, but neither of these factors is relevant to the doctrine of vicarious liability. This is an additional problem for the corrective justice approach.

Proponents of the corrective justice approach argue that the mistake is to think that the doctrine relies on attributing X's wrong to D, which is a fiction. Instead, it is argued that it is X's action that is attributed to D, and D commits the wrong personally because the action is D's. It is said that this is like the case where X is an agent who contracts on behalf of D, and the contract binds D though it was X's communication to the other contractor through which the contract was made.

[12] See P Giliker, 'Can the Supreme Court halt the ongoing expansion of vicarious liability? *Barclays* and *Morrison* in the UK Supreme Court' (2021) 37 *Professional Negligence* 55.

[13] PS Atiyah, *Vicarious Liability in the Law of Torts* (Butterworths, 1967) 181.

This is the 'agency theory' of vicarious liability.[14] But this is also a fiction so far as vicarious liability in negligence is concerned. In the case of contractual authority, the contract binds D because the agent had D's authority. It is not necessary to say that making the contract was literally the action of D. But if D's personal responsibility for a wrong is in issue, it is necessary for the action to be actually D's action (or for D to be liable for having instigated the particular action by X).

The conventional position now seems to be that versions of the distributive justice approach, free of the standpoint limitation, provide the rationale for vicarious liability.[15] One view is that vicarious liability promotes hardship alleviation by loss spreading, imposing liability because the employer is more likely to have the financial resources to pay. Another version of the distributive justice approach is the EAL approach, according to which the imposition of liability on D will create an incentive for D to exercise control over D's workforce to reduce the likelihood of losses caused by negligence. As considered above, neither loss reduction by deterrence nor hardship alleviation as policy factors are consistent with the standpoint limitation and neither supports a fair allocation of risk between the parties.

To understand how vicarious liability should apply on the suggested approach, it is necessary to revert to the ordinary case of two individuals C and D, where there should be a fair allocation of risk between them. The rationale for liability in the ordinary case is that D, who chooses to carry on an activity for D's own benefit, should be subject to a fair allocation of the risk of loss from the activity, which normally means that D should bear the cost of loss resulting from a failure to meet a reasonable standard of care in performing the activity. Where C is harmed by an employee X, acting on behalf of D and for D's benefit, as part of an activity that D chose to undertake, D should similarly bear the risk of loss caused to C by X resulting from X's failure to meet the standard of care. The allocation of risk is between C and D as the business owner, with respect to any activity of D's business that falls below the standard of care. The implication is that vicarious liability should apply to losses arising from risks that are 'reasonably incidental to' or 'characteristic of' the business.[16]

This suggested approach under the standpoint limitation might be understood as a version of the 'benefit and burden' theory of vicarious liability,[17] but only in the sense in which this is behind the idea of fair allocation of risk in negligence generally. It could also be understood as a version of the enterprise risk approach, though confined to the 'fairness' rationale for enterprise risk rather than the deterrence rationale.[18] The fair allocation of risk is on the basis of ordinary common

[14] See eg Stevens (n 5) ch 11.

[15] See generally P Giliker, *Vicarious Liability in Tort* (Cambridge University Press, 2010) ch 8; A Gray, *Vicarious Liability* (Hart, 2021).

[16] Atiyah (n 14) 171. See also GC Keating 'Enterprise Liability' in M Petrin and C Witting (eds), *Research Handbook on Corporate Liability* (Edward Elgar, 2023) 22.

[17] Keating (ibid).

[18] D Brodie, 'Enterprise Liability: Justifying Vicarious Liability' (2007) 27 *Oxford Journal of Legal Studies* 493; Jane Stapleton, *Product Liability* (Butterworths, 1994) 193.

knowledge, not policy analysis across society generally. It is not based on promoting distributive justice across society by reducing losses through deterrence or harm alleviation by loss spreading.

Understood in this way, D's liability is not really strict or vicarious in the ordinary sense: it is a liability of the business owner arising from the fact that the business has been conducted in a way that fell below a reasonable standard of care. It has in common with the agency theory of the corrective justice approach that it involves attributing the actions of X to the business owner D, but this is not in order to treat D as having committed a wrong, and it does not rely on the idea that either X or D is a wrongdoer. The implication of the suggested approach is that X need not be a wrongdoer and need not be personally liable in order for D to be liable. This appears to reflect industry practice, though the conventional understanding and the corrective justice approach base D's liability on a wrong by X.[19]

Insurance

Is it relevant to liability whether D had liability insurance, or should have had liability insurance? This has always been controversial because it goes to the heart of the controversy over the character of the law. The traditional position is that it is irrelevant.[20] This is consistent with the corrective justice approach, since whether D has or should have liability insurance is irrelevant to whether D has committed a wrong in negligence. But, as pointed out earlier, the implication of the corrective justice approach would appear to be that insurance should be prohibited rather than merely disregarded, just as it is for a criminal liability. Whether or not it is taken into account in determining liability, the effect of insurance is to eliminate the effect of liability on the wrongdoer D, and on the corrective justice approach D is personally responsible and it would seem important that D should personally bear the loss. But the law does not prohibit liability insurance.[21] Similarly, it would seem that liability insurance conflicts with the EAL approach, under which liability is supposed to operate as a sanction on D and a deterrent for others.

The practical effect of liability insurance is pervasive (along with direct insurance for the loss). Often the litigants are the insurers of the victim and tortfeasor. From a certain perspective, one can understand negligence law as playing an ancillary role in the insurance industry, the role of which is to alleviate hardship by spreading loss across society.[22] This seems very much at odds with the corrective

[19] See eg E Voyiakis, 'Means, Rights, and Opportunities: on Arthur Ripstein's Private Wrongs' (2018) 9 *Jurisprudence* 607.

[20] *Hunt v Severs* [1994] 2 AC 350 at 363, per Lord Bridge; J Stapleton, 'Tort, Insurance and Ideology' (1995) 58 *Modern Law Review* 820.

[21] Ibid. It seems that liability insurance was considered problematic at one time for this reason: see K Oliphant, 'Tort Law, Risk and Technological Innovation in England' (2014) 59 *McGill Law Journal* 819, 839.

[22] R Merkin, 'Tort, Insurance and Ideology: Further Thoughts' (2012) 75 *Modern Law Review* 301.

justice approach, as commentators have argued. It might seem to support instead the harm alleviation or loss-spreading version of the distributive justice approach, which would favour adapting the law of negligence to make defendants liable if they are or should be insured. There does seem to be support for this in occasional judgements that suggest that liability in negligence should depend on whether D is or ought to be insured.[23]

The availability of insurance is consistent with the suggested fair allocation of risk approach. This approach does not rely on personal responsibility for wrongdoing or on deterrence as the basis for liability. There is no reason why someone who bears the risk of loss under a fair allocation of risk should not anticipate a liability by taking out insurance. Indeed, this is generally how someone ought reasonably to respond to a primary liability. The suggested approach is consistent with the way in which insurance operates in tandem with the law of negligence.[24] Nevertheless, whether D is or ought to be insured is not relevant to liability. Liability cannot depend on whether D is actually insured for the loss, since this is something about D that may not be known to C in advance. The law cannot take advantage of the fact that D happens to be insured in order to make D liable. Nor is it relevant whether D ought to be insured, except in the sense that one might say that D ought to take out insurance if D bears the risk of the loss. It would not be right for liability to depend on whether D ought to be insured if this means whether D can insure the loss in question more cheaply than C. This involves policy analysis going beyond ordinary common knowledge. As commentators have pointed out, it is not easy to say whether it is more appropriate for C or D to insure or even whether insurance is available at all or at a viable rate to either party.[25]

A legislature can legislate for mandatory liability insurance for negligence to promote loss spreading in the interests of hardship alleviation. It could do this for loss caused by certain types of activity, at the same time as imposing strict liability for that type of loss on people involved in the activity. However, the courts cannot achieve this consistently with the standpoint limitation. The courts cannot make D liable to C in order that people in D's position will take out insurance so as to ensure, for the future, that people in C's position will be able to recover through the insurance held by people in D's position. This would be a co-ordinating scheme requiring adjustment.

The Duty of Care and Pure Economic Loss

As discussed previously, a duty of care is normally assumed for the core case of positive actions causing personal injury or property damage. Whether there is a

[23] J Morgan, 'Tort, Insurance and Incoherence' (2004) 67 *Modern Law Review* 384.

[24] Merkin (n 23); R Merkin and J Steele, *Insurance and the Law of Obligations* (Oxford University Press, 2013) ch 1.

[25] Merkin (n 23). There may be a convention governing who should insure, which becomes part of ordinary common knowledge.

duty of care may be controversial in other cases. As discussed in chapter four, on one view whether there is a duty of care depends on the balance of policy factors, which reflects the distributive justice approach. This is how the rule excluding recovery for pure economic loss is usually understood, for example recovery of loss of profits where C's business has been disrupted by a power cut or by damage to a bridge that has prevented supplies reaching C's business. The policy factor is said to be the 'floodgates argument', which is taken to outweigh the countervailing policy factor favouring compensation. This policy-factors approach is excluded under the standpoint limitation, along with policy analysis. Under the standpoint limitation, the issue has to be addressed in terms of a fair allocation of loss as between the parties in the light of ordinary common knowledge.

As considered previously, pure economic loss normally refers to the loss of expected future profits, that is to say profits that C would have made if events had proceeded as they would generally have been expected to do in the absence of D's actions. C has no right to these profits as against other people generally. They are not C's existing property. This is a point emphasised in the corrective justice literature and taken to explain why it is justified to exclude liability, as considered in chapter five.[26] It is said that, because the future profits do not belong to C, holding D liable would amount to making D liable for the failure to provide a benefit to C, and on the corrective justice approach D has only a negative duty not to cause harm to C. But as pointed out in chapter five, if the claim is based on a wrong by D against C, there is no reason why pure economic loss should be excluded if it is the reasonably foreseeable consequence of the wrong. The pure economic loss is still a genuine loss caused by D's wrong, measured relative to the position that C would have been in if the wrong had not been committed.

The rule does make sense on a fair allocation of risk approach. Liability under a fair allocation of risk does not depend on a wrong. The issue is not whether the loss or a part of the loss caused by D's wrong should be recoverable, but who should bear the risk of this type of loss. It makes sense to say that with respect to possible future benefits that are not owned by C, C rather than D should bear the risk of the loss. The expected future profits may be what C has good reason to expect, but they are not yet C's and they are also profits that C is responsible for securing by continuing work and by anticipating events that may jeopardise them or by insuring against the prospect of not getting them.

It would be possible in theory to have a right of ownership over future profits. In effect, C owns certain future profits when C owns intellectual property, for example the profits of working a patented invention. It would be possible in theory to give C ownership of future profits more generally. For example, where C has an established business, if the law prevented a new competitor from setting up in competition, C would in effect have a property right over future profits of the

[26] P Benson, 'The Problem with Pure Economic Loss' (2009) 60 *South Carolina Law Review* 823; A Beever, *Rediscovering the Law of Negligence* (Hart Publishing, 2007) ch 7.

business. Of course, the common law does not do this. The pure economic loss rule is in effect a rule concerning or presupposing what things are owned. This is a matter of property law, to be touched on later, in chapters nine and ten. This issue, of what things can be owned, is in principle a matter of distributive justice. This is another reason why the pure economic loss rule is inconsistent with the corrective justice approach.

As pointed out previously, some confusion arises from the fact that the expression 'pure economic loss' is used to refer to loss of intangible property, such as an investment or right of payment, as well as to expected future profits. The rule makes sense only with respect to expected profits not owned by C.[27] The problem in distinguishing the two types of case may be that the common law has unfortunately sometimes failed to recognise that a debt or right to payment or other intangible, including intellectual property, can be a form of property.[28]

There has been controversy over the exception to the pure economic loss rule where C has received carelessly mistaken advice or information from D, and C suffered pure economic loss in the form of expenditure incurred in reliance on the advice or information. The leading case is *Hedley Byrne v Heller*, where C did work under a contract with a third party in reliance on a credit reference for the third party from D. C can recover such a loss, which is a form of pure economic loss, if C can make out a claim for negligent misstatement. The claim is understood to depend on establishing that there was an 'assumption of responsibility' by D, though there is controversy over exactly what this requires. Whether there has been an assumption of responsibility is sometimes taken to depend on a balancing of policy factors.[29] The various policy factors that may be relevant in this sort of case were listed by way of illustration in chapter four. This approach is also excluded by the standpoint limitation.

Another approach to negligent misstatement is that D is liable where C reasonably relies on the information or advice, and D knows or ought to know that this is the case and so acts wrongfully in giving the negligent information or advice.[30] This is a version of the corrective justice approach, at least to the extent that it treats liability as based on a wrong. But the fact that C reasonably relies on D's information or advice does not imply that D should be liable, since C could reasonably rely on it at C's own risk. Even if D knows that C is relying on the information or advice, there is no implication that D should be liable, since D may be entitled to

[27] Together with pure economic loss in the form of voluntary expenditure, as considered below. In *Ministry of Housing and Local Government v Sharp* [1970] 2 QB 223, C lost the right to a payment of money from a third party as a result of D's negligence, and C was rightly allowed to recover compensation. This is said to be an exception to the pure economic loss rule, but if the rule is understood as suggested the case does not fall under the rule. See also the discussion of *OBG v Allan* [2007] UKHL 21 in P Jaffey, 'Private Property and Intangibles' [2022] *Conveyancer and Property Lawyer* 47.

[28] See further ch 9. See also Jaffey (ibid).

[29] K Barker, '*Hedley Byrne v Heller*: Issues at the Beginning of the Twenty-First Century' in K Barker, R Grantham and S Swain (eds), *The Law of Misstatements: 50 Years on from* Hedley Byrne v Heller (Hart, 2015) 3.

[30] Barker (ibid).

assume that C is relying at C's own risk.[31] The difficulty here is again the focus on whether what D has done is wrongful.

The issue is really whether the ordinary business risk that C normally runs – the risk that expenses that C chooses to incur will be wasted – should be transferred to D. C's loss is a loss voluntarily incurred, in the sense that C chose to rely on the information or advice from D. This is why it is apt to equate it with future profits as a form of pure economic loss for which C ordinarily bears the risk. In principle, the transfer of risk to D should depend on an agreement between C and D that D is to bear the risk, so that C can act at D's risk. Without this understanding, there is no reason why D should bear the risk rather than C, or why C should be entitled to act at D's risk. This is the natural way to understand the requirement of assumption of responsibility in this context. In *Hedley Byrne v Heller* itself, there was an agreement between the parties, but it was not contractually enforceable for lack of consideration. In principle, it would be better if the claim were treated as contractual.[32]

Causation and 'Scope of Duty'

The fair allocation of risk approach can explain certain puzzling aspects of the law broadly relating to loss and causation. As the pure economic loss rule shows, D may be liable for a certain loss to C resulting from conduct of D's that gave rise to C's claim, but not other loss to C that resulted from the same conduct and was equally likely and foreseeable, and this seems incongruous if the claim is wrong-based. Similarly, the orthodox understanding in terms of wrongdoing by D has difficulty explaining the case where D's action causes reasonably foreseeable loss to both C1 and C2, but only C1 has a claim. It seems natural to think that, if wrongfulness is a property of an action, D's action must be wrongful vis-à-vis C2 as well as C1. As pointed out in chapter five, on an allocation of risk approach it is possible to say that, as between C1 and D, the risk of loss resulting from D's action is allocated to D, but as between C2 and D the risk is with C2. This approach is possible under the standpoint limitation.

On this approach, furthermore, there is a symmetry, as logically there ought to be, between the risks of loss for which D is liable, and the risks that are relevant to determining D's standard of care. The risks that D should take account of in D's activities, as risks that may give rise to liability, are the same risks for which in due course D will be liable if they materialise. In determining D's standard of care, the risk of loss to C1 should be taken into account but not the risk to C2, and the

[31] See also D Campbell, 'The Dog that Did Bark in the Night-time: What Mischief does Hedley Byrne v Heller Correct?' in Barker, Grantham and Swain (ed) (n 30), following JA Weir, 'Liability for Syntax' (1963) *Cambridge Law Journal* 216, 218–19. See also P Jaffey, 'A New Version of the Reliance Theory' [1998] *Northern Ireland Legal Quarterly* 107.

[32] Campbell (ibid); Jaffey (ibid). Cases like *Murphy v Brentwood DC* [1991] UKHL 2, which are not discussed, also involve pure economic loss in the form of voluntary expenditure.

risk of property damage and personal injury but not pure economic loss. This is said to be the implication of the 'risk principle',[33] but in fact, as mentioned in chapter five, if D can be liable for the reasonably foreseeable consequences of D's action as a wrong, this symmetry may be lost, or at least can be retained only with unnecessary complexity.

Consider a case where D's negligence was in giving mistaken advice or information. Here it is said that loss is not recoverable where it is outside the 'scope of the duty' under the 'SAAMCO principle'.[34] Say D negligently overvalues property for C. C relies on the valuation in lending to X on the property as security. When X defaults, the property provides inadequate security. If the property had been properly valued, C would not have accepted it as security and would not have made the loan. Under the SAAMCO principle, C can recover for loss resulting directly from D's overvaluation of the property, by virtue of which the security was inadequate, but C cannot recover for any further loss resulting from the fact that the property market has fallen. However, if D committed a wrong against C in making the mistaken valuation, it is difficult to see why C should not be able to recover for this loss as well, since it is certainly a loss that resulted reasonably foreseeably from the wrong. Another example might be where D mistakenly advises that C's knee is fit and, in reliance on the advice, C goes on a mountaineering expedition.[35] C is injured on the expedition, but the injury is unrelated to the fact that C's knee is weak. C cannot recover for the loss though, again, it is certainly a consequence of D's mistaken advice in the sense that if the advice regarding the knee had been correct and C had stayed at home the injury would not have been suffered, and furthermore the fact that an injury might occur while mountaineering was reasonably foreseeable. One might infer from this example that, although reasonably foreseeable, the loss should be excluded because it is only coincidentally related to the advice, but this does not apply to the valuation example.

The SAAMCO principle is understandable only if the liability arises from an allocation of risk under a primary liability relation, rather than a breach of duty. The issue is, when D advises C, what risk of loss D is – implicitly or explicitly – agreeing to bear. The liability is not for loss caused by D's wrong, but for loss for which D bore the risk under a primary liability relation. That the SAAMCO principle is about the fair allocation of risk between the parties has been explicitly stated.[36] Again, the difficulty arises from the recognition of a redundant duty and

[33] See D Nolan and J Plunkett, 'Keeping Negligence Simple' (2022) 138 *Law Quarterly Review* 175.

[34] Derived from *South Australia Asset Management Corp v York Montague Ltd* [1997] AC 191 ('the SAAMCO case').

[35] A hypothetical example suggested by Lord Hoffmann in the SAAMCO case (ibid) at [19]–[20].

[36] Eg per Lord Burrows in *Khan v Meadows* [2021] UKSC 21 at [71]. The 'counterfactual test', which is used to indicate whether the harm is within the 'scope of the duty', would seem to work only on this assumption. According to the test, if the harm would have occurred even if the advice given had been correct (ie if the same advice had been given, but it was correct), it is not within the scope of the duty. This is because the implication is that the risk of this harm was not relevant to why the advice or information was given or sought. It does not imply that the harm in question was not caused by the provision of advice or information or was not reasonably foreseeable.

the assumption that the claim is for loss caused by a wrong. On the suggested approach, liability should depend (in the absence of an expressly agreed allocation of risk) on whether reasonable parties would have understood that D was to take account of the particular risk in question in giving the advice, or whether this was a risk that was to stay with C, given the professional roles and expertise of the two parties and the purpose of the provision of information or advice.[37] Furthermore, the reason why the SAAMCO principle applies only with respect to professionals providing information and advice is that only in this sort of case can the issue arise of an expressly or impliedly agreed allocation of risk.[38]

The suggested fair allocation of risk approach under the standpoint limitation also casts light on the 'wrongful birth' cases.[39] If C becomes pregnant and gives birth as a result of D's negligence (for example, mistaken medical advice about fertility or contraception), the courts have been unwilling to allow compensation for the cost of upbringing, one reason being that it involves disregarding or offsetting the benefit to the mother of the birth and the life of the child. However, they have found it possible to award compensation for particular loss to the mother such as pain and discomfort and loss of earnings during pregnancy. But the difficulty does not arise if D bears the risk of liability for some part of the cost of bringing up the child under a primary liability relation. There is a rationale for making D responsible for such a risk on a distributive justice approach. Similarly, take the case where C is a child born disabled as a result of D's negligence (in the sense that without the negligence C would not have been born). The claim is said to be for 'wrongful life' and it would seem that there should be no claim because it involves treating C's existence as a disabled person as itself a loss to C. However, it is not inconsistent for C to be able to claim compensation for the costs of care created by the disability under a fair allocation of risk, even if C has overall benefitted from D's actions (by being born). Furthermore, it would make sense to allow compensation only for those costs of upbringing that arose from a risk for which D was responsible for giving warning, and not for the costs of upbringing arising from other risks, even if these were also reasonably foreseeable.[40]

Going further, on the suggested approach it is not illogical to give up altogether, in some circumstances, the requirement that C's loss be caused by D's actions. If D's liability to compensate for harm is based on a wrong, it follows that the harm must have been caused by the wrong. But this is not necessarily the case with respect to a primary liability. The causation requirement is not a logical

[37] As held in *Khan v Meadows* [2021] UKSC 21 and *Manchester Building Society v Grant Thornton* [2021] UKSC 20.

[38] But it is not confined to cases where D relies by incurring expenditure and extends to, eg, medical advice as in *Khan v Meadows* [2021] UKSC 21.

[39] *Khan v Meadows* [2021] UKSC 21; *McFarlane v Tayside* [2000] 2 AC 59; *Rees v Darlington* [2003] UKHL 52.

[40] See *Khan v Meadows* [2021] UKSC 21.

or conceptual requirement; the issue is whether it is appropriate in the context. Consider so-called 'market share' liability.[41] If a consumer suffers loss from a defective product, but cannot establish which supplier put the defective product on the market, according to the principle of market share liability each supplier to the market can be liable for a share of the loss corresponding to his share of sales on the market. Market share liability is generally understood to be incompatible with the corrective justice approach because liability is not based on a wrong by D that caused the loss to C.[42] On the suggested approach, however, one can argue that a party who enters the market as a supplier should be liable to make a proportionate contribution to compensation for such harm. The supplier should know that there is a risk of harm associated with the product and that it may be very difficult to determine which supplier is responsible for a particular harm because of the interchangeability of different brands. This involves treating the suppliers as a group who should share the risk of harm to consumers, on the ground that, in effect, they cause losses collectively though they have separately identifiable profits. This is apparent under the standpoint limitation, on the basis of ordinary common knowledge. The appeal of market share liability must lie in an argument along these lines, as a possible extension of ordinary liability in negligence, understood in terms distributive justice under the standpoint limitation.

A similar approach can be applied to the mesothelioma litigation cases.[43] Here, C has suffered serious illness and early death resulting from an exposure to asbestos many years earlier in the course of employment, but since C has had various employers for whom C worked with asbestos, and it is impossible to establish when C was exposed to asbestos or which exposure led to the fatal condition, it is impossible for C to show that any particular employer is liable on the balance of probabilities. However, the courts have found that the various employers can all be liable and have to make a contribution to C's compensation. It is very difficult to see how this can be defended on the conventional approach according to which D must have committed a wrong that caused the harm, proved on the balance of probabilities. But on the suggested approach it is not unreasonable to say that there is an allocation of risk amongst the various employers, as a matter of distributive justice subject to the standpoint limitation.[44]

Conventionally, the appropriate measure of compensation in negligence is taken to be the loss caused by C's wrong, since this is what will undo the effects of the wrong so far as this is possible. But on the primary liability approach, as

[41] As adopted in *Sindell v Abbott Laboratories* 607 P 2d 924 (Calif, 1980).

[42] See eg Arthur Ripstein and Benjamin C Zipursky, 'Corrective Justice in an Age of Mass Torts' in GD Postema (ed), *Philosophy and the Law of Torts* (Cambridge University Press, 2001).

[43] *Fairchild v Glenhaven Funeral Services Ltd* [2002] UKHL 22 and following cases.

[44] Cf Steel's argument for sharing liability arising because each manufacturer has contributed to causing the evidential difficulty: S Steel, 'Justifying Exceptions to Proof of Causation in Tort Law' (2015) 78 *Modern Law Review* 729, and Voyiakis's argument that it is fair to C to allow a lower standard of proof of the wrong, but the arguments are more persuasive if liability does not depend on a wrong by D: E Voyiakis, 'Causation and Opportunity in Tort' (2017) 38 *Oxford Journal of Legal Studies* 26.

discussed above, it is not necessarily the case that D should be liable for all the loss or even all the reasonably foreseeable loss caused by D's action. It may be that D should bear the risk of part of the loss as various examples above show. One might also say that C should have 'fair' recovery rather than necessarily having 'full' recovery,[45] though full recovery (for foreseeable losses) may seem more appropriate for a wrong. Another example might be that, where C is seriously disabled, C should recover the costs of care, rather than the amount assessed speculatively as the value of the lifestyle and activities that C has lost,[46] though the latter might seem more apt as compensation for a wrong. The cost of care approach is defensible as a matter of distributive justice subject to the standpoint limitation.

Provision of Benefits

The law traditionally makes a distinction between causing harm and failing to provide a benefit. There is no claim for failing to provide a benefit, even, it would seem, in an extreme case such as failing to rescue a baby drowning in a shallow pool. As mentioned earlier, supporters of the corrective justice approach say that the reason is that the law is concerned only with rights against interference with person and property.[47] Liability can arise only from active interference (misfeasance) and not failure to assist (non-feasance). By contrast, it is said, the distributive justice approach cannot explain this traditional position, because it is concerned with aggregate net benefit, and this does not distinguish between causing a harm and failing to provide a benefit.[48] However, it is not true of the distributive justice approach in general that it cannot distinguish between benefits and harms.

With respect to loss caused by interference, it is clear that it is the person who causes the loss who is at risk of liability. But with respect to the provision of benefits it is often not clear who should be responsible for providing the benefit or at risk of liability for failing to do so. If anyone who might possibly be able to provide the benefit is at risk of liability, some conscientious people would be constantly providing or taking steps to provide benefits and others would free-ride by standing back or taking steps to avoid being in a position where a liability might arise. There would be an unfair distribution of the burden, and a wasteful replication of work, and a great deal of uncertainty, and the curtailment of freedom would go far beyond the limited burden of actually conferring the benefit in the particular instance. Non-liability for the failure to provide a benefit is certainly explicable on a distributive justice approach.[49]

[45] JCP Goldberg and BC Zipursky, *Recognizing Wrongs* (Harvard University Press, 2020) 163–68.

[46] As suggested, as 'fair compensation', by Lord Denning in *Lim Poh Choo v Camden and Islington Area Health Authority* [1979] QB 196 at 216.

[47] See ch 4. See Stevens (n 5) 9–10; Beever (n 26) 52.

[48] See Stevens (n 5) 9.

[49] Cf the reference to polycentricity in ch 6.

The problem arises for individuals acting on the basis of ordinary common knowledge. It is a problem of co-ordination to determine who should provide the benefit, if anyone should. There is no solution under the standpoint limitation. There may sometimes be salient facts to identify the appropriate person to provide a benefit. There may be a customary practice that determines who takes responsibility, which may be recognised as a common law rule – for example the duty of an innkeeper to travellers. Where someone has come forward and taken responsibility for providing the benefit, it makes sense that this person should be liable for failing to do so, and this is the role in this context of 'assumption of responsibility'.[50] However, in general, the solution is for an authority to make arrangements for a benefit to be provided where appropriate. To save people from drowning, the solution is to have a lifeguard. In general it is the role of public authorities to provide benefits on behalf of the community where this is what distributive justice requires.

Liability of Public Authorities

Where the police have failed to intervene to protect a member of the public from harm at the hands of a third party, should the member of the public be able to claim compensation from the police?[51] The police have a duty to provide certain services to the public. This is a public duty, but in some cases it seems very tempting to say that the public duty also generates a duty owed to an individual, for example where pursuant to their public duty the police D should assist a particular individual C who is in danger, and there is no conflict between assisting C and other aspects of D's public duty.[52] On the corrective justice approach, duties to provide a benefit do not arise at all and proponents of the corrective justice approach argue that there should be no liability in common law negligence. Nevertheless, a problem arises because it is generally assumed that, when a liability to pay compensation does arise at common law, it arises from the breach of a duty. Thus it seems natural to assume that, if the police have committed a breach of duty towards a member of the public, a claim for compensation is an appropriate response.[53]

At the same time, there seem good reasons to deny liability for compensation. It may seem objectionable for public funds designated for use by the police to be diverted from this use to the payment of compensation. One might also object that

[50] See generally Tofaris and Steel (2016) 75 *Cambridge Law Journal* 128.

[51] See eg *Hill v Chief Constable of West Yorkshire* [1989] AC 53; *Michael v Chief Constable of South Wales Police* [2015] UKSC 2. See F Du Bois, 'Human Rights and the Tort Liability of Public Authorities' (2011) 127 LQR 589; Tofaris and Steel (n 51).

[52] See NJ McBride, *Humanity of Private Law, Part 1* (Hart, 2018) 4.

[53] Tofaris and Steel (n 51) 137–38.

liability is likely to encourage the police to act defensively, in order to avoid liability, rather than pursuing their public duty as they understand it. Counting in favour of a liability for compensation, in addition to the policy of promoting compensation for loss, is the policy of promoting accountability. This policy reasoning approach has been influential, though, as mentioned earlier, English law has now retreated to the position that a public authority should not generally be liable for a failure to provide a benefit, on the basis of the traditional rule of the common law that there is no liability for omissions.[54]

The suggested approach, of a fair allocation of risk based on ordinary common knowledge, is a distributive justice approach, subject to the standpoint limitation. This common law approach cannot be used to determine the liability of a public authority with respect to the exercise of its public duty.[55] This is a matter of distributive justice, free of the standpoint limitation, as determined by the public authority's constitution or legal basis. Furthermore, in the light of the earlier discussion of primary duties and liabilities, there is no reason to assume that a breach of duty by the public authority should give rise to a claim for compensation. Whether there is a liability for compensation is a separate question from whether there is a breach of duty. It also a matter of distributive justice, free of the standpoint limitation, determined by the public authority's constitution or legal basis. Considered as a matter of distributive justice, it would seem quite plausible for the police not to be liable for any loss caused by a breach of duty, on the ground that the public purse should bear the cost only through the provision of public services such as the NHS, social services and welfare benefits, on which C will be able to draw in any case.[56] It would seem more likely, by contrast, that a local authority building control department might be responsible for loss caused to a house owner who has relied on a mistaken determination of the adequacy of the foundations of the new house by the building control officer.[57]

In addition, one might ask whether C should have locus standi to take proceedings, not for compensation, but to hold the authority accountable by establishing that it did breach a duty to C, or at least a public duty particularly affecting C, in order to ensure that appropriate steps are taken, for example disciplinary measures or measures to prevent a recurrence.[58] On the suggested approach, there is a lacuna in the law, since as things stand it would seem that the only way for an individual to hold the authority accountable is by way of a claim for compensation.[59]

[54] *Robinson v Chief Constable of West Yorkshire* [2018] UKSC 4; *CN & CN v Poole BC* [2019] UKSC 25.

[55] However, it does apply with respect to liability of the authority with respect to harm caused by the actions of its staff.

[56] See AJE Jaffey, *The Duty of Care* (Dartmouth, 1992) 240.

[57] *Murphy v Brentwood DC* [1991] UKHL 2.

[58] See RA Duff, 'Repairing Harms and Answering for Wrongs' in J Oberdiek (ed), *Philosophical Foundations of the Law of Torts* (Oxford University Press, 2014); Tofaris and Steel (n 51) 146–47.

[59] In some circumstances there may be an action based on human rights or misfeasance in public office.

Statutory Reform

Evaluated in terms of distributive justice from the standpoint of the legislature, free of the standpoint limitation, negligence is difficult to make sense of. It is said that no coherent vision of its function has been offered.[60] The availability of compensation appears arbitrary and inefficient. Compensation provided through negligence reaches only a small proportion of accident victims, through an expensive process and independent of hardship or need. Negligence also appears to have a marginal effect on reducing accident losses and the burden placed on a defendant is unrelated to culpability or to deterrent effect. Arguably negligence should be replaced by a combination of the prohibition of dangerous conduct enforced by punishment and social insurance for accident losses, irrespective of fault.[61] This would be, in effect, an extension of the criminal justice and social security or welfare benefits systems to apply more comprehensively to accidents.

However, these are not relevant considerations for the courts or the common law, and it does not follow that negligence at common law is incoherent or unjust. Negligence understood in terms of distributive justice subject to the standpoint limitation is a coherent body of law with a sound basis in justice as it applies in the absence of legislation. This approach provides a better account of the traditional common law than the corrective justice approach. Furthermore, it shows that the arguments for reform can be consistent with the fact that decisions reached in the common law are just in their own terms.

[60] S Hedley, 'The Unacknowledged Revolution in Liability for Negligence' in S Worthington, A Robinson and G Virgo, *Revolution and Evolution in Private Law* (Hart, 2018).

[61] Hedley (ibid); see eg L Alexander and K Kessler Ferzan, 'Confused Culpability, Contrived Causation, and the Collapse of Tort Theory' in J Oberdiek (ed), *Philosophical Foundations of the Law of Torts* (Oxford University Press, 2014); L Alexander, 'Causation and Corrective Justice, Does Tort Law Make Sense?' (1987) 6 *Law and Philosophy* 1; R Avraham and I Kohler-Hausmann, 'Accident Law for Egalitarians' (2006) 12 *Legal Theory* 181, 186.

8

Contract Law under the Standpoint Limitation

Introduction

On the distributive justice approach, the justification for enforcing contractual agreements is that they facilitate the mutually beneficial exchange of goods and services for payment. Agreements for the exchange of goods and services for payment are likely to be mutually beneficial because generally the parties can determine what goods or services will be beneficial to them and at what price. As discussed in chapter four, some features of traditional private law seem to be at odds with the distributive justice approach. Contract law focuses almost exclusively on the interests of the parties and ignores factors relating to other people's interests and the public interest that would appear relevant on the distributive justice approach. It may also seem that the distributive justice approach cannot account for bilateral relations and the remedial regime in contract. As discussed in this chapter, applying the standpoint limitation can overcome these difficulties.

The Character of Contract Law

Although often private exchange by agreement is mutually beneficial and does not adversely affect third parties or the public interest, at times it may unfairly exclude some people from certain goods or services, or allow certain goods and services to be acquired only on excessively onerous terms, and it may also lead to an excessive concentration of wealth. In the interests of distributive justice, free of the standpoint limitation, a legislature might adopt a system of public provision of some goods and services to avoid these adverse consequences. At common law, however, on the basis of distributive justice subject to the standpoint limitation, the question is what people know and what they can do, in the light of ordinary common knowledge, with respect to the acquisition and supply of goods and services. The option of public provision is not available and the courts cannot introduce it in adjudication (even if they had the executive and administrative means to do so). The only possible regime under the standpoint limitation would seem to be a regime for private exchange based on agreement.

The justification for the enforcement of the agreement is not the will theory, by which the parties are bound simply by virtue of their moral power to make promises, independently of their purpose of making an exchange, but the contribution that the mutually beneficial exchange by agreement makes to distributive justice. Contracting may have adverse effects, as mentioned above, and the legislature may choose to introduce mandatory terms and compensate for adverse effect in the interests of distributive justice, but under standpoint limitation contracting parties are not affected by the considerations that justify such legislative provision. At common law, on the basis of ordinary common knowledge, contract law is normally concerned only with the justice of the particular contract between the two parties, based on the principle of agreement. This is why contract has its traditional form, in which only the interests of the contracting parties are relevant, as they are reflected in their intentions, as expressed through the agreement. Under the standpoint limitation, it is not unjust for the parties to contract on this basis. The contract does not have to take account of the existing societal distribution, nor the adverse consequences for the societal distribution which the legislature might have to make adjustment for. (I return to this point in the final section.)

The common law does take account to a limited extent of interests other than those of the two parties under the public policy doctrine. As considered previously, the doctrine is controversial because its limits and rationale are unclear. The ordinary distributive justice approach would favour an expansive doctrine applying policy in a wide sense, tending towards legislative policy, which encompasses the policy behind the mandatory regimes, whereas the corrective justice approach would favour a very narrow doctrine, if any. As suggested previously, the doctrine would appear to be limited in the sense that the scope of the doctrine is determined by the fact that it is triggered only by what is apparent from the performance of the contract without any need for careful calculation or investigation of its effects.[1] In other words, the doctrine draws on distributive justice based on ordinary common knowledge. The standpoint limitation explains why the public policy doctrine at common law applies distributive justice to this extent and no further.[2]

As mentioned in chapter four, some commentators have objected that in its traditional form contract law has gone astray in failing to take adequate account of distributive justice, and have argued that the courts should develop (and should in the past have developed) the common law in the way that the legislature has reformed it. The thinking is that the courts have failed to do this because they are in the grip of the will theory, under the corrective justice approach, and in

[1] See ch 4.

[2] On this approach, the restraint of trade doctrine should be understood to be based on the public interest, not with respect to competition in general, like competition law or antitrust law, which depends on policy analysis of the market, but the public interest in the rights of individuals to pursue their livelihood. See eg S Smith, 'Reconstructing Restraint of Trade' (1995) 15 *Oxford Journal of Legal Studies* 566; RB Grantham and D Jensen, 'The Proper Role of Policy in Private Law Adjudication' (2018) 68 *University of Toronto Law Journal* 187, 213–20.

consequence they mistakenly think that distributive justice has no place in contract law.[3] This has given rise to a debate in the literature about whether distributive justice is best promoted through contract law or through arrangements outside contract law that adjust for unfairness arising out of contracting, for example through social welfare benefits funded by taxation.[4]

There is something curious about this debate because it seems to assume that legal relations in contract arise on the corrective justice approach and therefore exclusively on the basis of the parties' intentions by virtue of the will theory, and the question then is how far the position should be modified to take account of considerations of distributive justice. But if contractual relations are indeed based exclusively on the parties' intentions under the will theory, it is not clear that it is justified to impose terms that the parties did not agree to in the interests of distributive justice. On the suggested approach, contract law is based on distributive justice and confined, subject to the exception of the public policy doctrine, to giving effect to the parties' intentions by virtue of the standpoint limitation. How far contract law should be modified to take account of distributive justice beyond this is a debate only for the legislature.

Bilateral Relations

On the corrective justice approach, bilateral legal rights are understood as the direct reflection of bilateral moral rights arising from promising. On the distributive justice approach, bilateral legal rights appear to be a device to give effect to a public duty to perform the contract, based on the public interest in promoting the exchange of goods and services for money. It was suggested in chapter four that it might be possible to have derivative bilateral moral rights based on distributive justice, where the principle of agreement contributes to a regime that promotes distributive justice overall. I suggest that there are indeed derivative bilateral moral rights based on distributive justice under the standpoint limitation. The effect of the standpoint limitation is that considerations other than the interests of the parties as expressed through the agreement may normally be disregarded and so the law is concerned purely with the justice of the particular contract between the parties, based on the principle of agreement, not the public interest or other individual interests across society.

[3] AT Kronman, 'Contract Law and Distributive Justice' (1980) 89 *Yale Law Journal* 472; A Bagchi, 'Distributive Justice and Contract' in G Klass, G Letsas and P Saprai (eds), *Philosophical Foundations of Contract Law* (Oxford University Press, 2014). H Collins, *Regulating Contracts* (Oxford University Press, 1999) chs 3 and 4, treats contract law as an instrument of distributive justice the efficacy of which is limited because of its excessive generality and abstraction and lack of differentiation which mean that it is weak at providing guidance. See also P Kincaid, *Privity: Private Justice or Public Regulation* (Ashgate, 2001).

[4] L Kaplow and S Shavell, *Fairness versus Welfare* (Harvard University Press, 2002) 33–34.

Substantive Fairness

A distinction is drawn in contract law between procedural and substantive unfairness. There is 'procedural unfairness' where there is a 'vitiating factor' such as mistake, duress or undue influence, or lack of authority with respect to a contract made by an agent.[5] Procedural unfairness relates to the formation of the contract – it implies that there was no true agreement. By contrast, substantive unfairness is unfairness in the exchange itself, as defined by the contractual terms of exchange.

The common law provides a remedy for procedural unfairness, but the conventional position is that there is no remedy at all for substantive unfairness. The absence of any remedy for substantive unfairness is readily explicable in terms of corrective justice based on the will theory. The contract is binding because the parties have the moral power to bind themselves, which they do by expressing their intention to do so, and if there is procedural unfairness the contract is not a true expression of their intentions. By contrast, the idea of substantive unfairness hardly makes sense. Since the justification for enforcing the agreement is that it gives effect to the parties' intentions, if the agreement was genuine it should be enforced whatever the terms of exchange may be.[6] There is always the risk that the contract may not prove as beneficial as was hoped or expected, but that is a risk involved in contracting and a bad contract is not on this understanding in any sense an unfair contract. A remedy for substantive unfairness would appear to be subversive of party autonomy and contrary to the principle of freedom of contract.

However, intuitively it does seem that a contract can be unfair even though there was no flaw in its formation. Many commentators argue that there ought to be protection against substantive unfairness, and indeed that substantive unfairness is often tacitly influential in decisions on procedural unfairness.[7] But how should substantive unfairness be understood? It seems to be to do with an imbalance or lack of equivalence in the agreed terms of exchange. There is an imbalance in the exchange where a contracting party pays an excessive price for what that party receives or the price is inadequate for what that party provides. There is no basis for this in the corrective justice approach understood in terms of the will theory. It also appears inexplicable under the ordinary distributive justice approach because, although the contract takes the form of bilateral legal relations, the moral basis is understood to be a public duty to perform the contract, to protect the public interest contracting, and contract is not fundamentally a matter of interpersonal justice or fairness as between the contracting parties.[8]

[5] See eg M Chen-Wishart 'The Nature of Vitiating Factors in Contract Law' in G Klass et al (eds), *Philosophical Foundations of Contract Law* (Oxford University Press, 2014) 295–97.

[6] The 'sanctity of contract'; see eg Chen-Wishart (ibid) 297–98.

[7] See eg S Waddams, *Sanctity of Contracts in a Secular Age* (Cambridge University Press, 2019); TD Rakoff, 'The Five Justices of Contract Law' (2016) *Wisconsin Law Review* 733; PS Atiyah, 'Contract and Fair Exchange' in *Essays on Contract* (Oxford University Press, 1990); Chen-Wishart (n 5).

[8] See eg SA Smith, 'In Defence of Substantive Fairness' (1996) 112 *Law Quarterly Review* 138.

One suggestion has been that a contract is substantively unfair when it is liable to push the contractor into destitution,[9] or when it disrupts the contractor's ability to make plans because, owing to its unfairness, the contractor's expectations are not met.[10] However, it would seem that a contract that is not unfair can have these effects. It may be simply ill-judged or rash. In any case, these suggestions would seem to reflect unfairness as a matter of distributive justice in the ordinary sense, that is to say in terms of the contractor's position relative to other people generally. They do not capture the sense in which there can be an imbalance between the contracting parties.

Gordley offers an account of substantive unfairness in terms of 'equality in exchange'. According to Gordley, private law, including contract law, is a matter of corrective justice,[11] which he understands as the justice of preserving or restoring distributive justice (as considered in chapter five). A contractual exchange should not disturb the prior distribution, and where there is equality in exchange the prior distribution is preserved. On Gordley's approach, equality in exchange does not mean that the value C places on what C gets is equal to the value that D places on what D gets, which is unlikely to be the case. There is equality in exchange when the contractual exchange is at the market price. At the market price, the exchange leaves each party with the same purchasing power in the market place, since what one contracting party receives is worth the same, in terms of purchasing power, as what that contracting party has lost to the other contracting party.

There are difficulties with this approach, as some commentators have pointed out.[12] One problem is that it seems wrong to assess the distribution before or after the exchange simply in terms of levels of purchasing power. If marketable property is exchanged for money, it may be true that purchasing power is unaffected (at least at the time of the exchange). But both parties may obtain a benefit beyond the market price because one needs cash and the other the particular property, for their own purposes. An exchange at market prices may also reduce purchasing power because – as in the case of a haircut, for example – it does not provide a contractor with anything marketable, but this would surely not be unjust to this party on the ground of inequality in exchange.

More importantly, as pointed out in chapter four, there is the problem that the prior position may not in fact be defensible as a matter of distributive justice. According to Gordley, although the justification of a remedy is to restore the prior position in order to uphold distributive justice, the courts are precluded from considering whether the prior position actually accords with distributive justice, because a court is not an appropriate body to make such a judgement. But if it is

[9] Considered and rejected by Smith (ibid).

[10] Smith (ibid); P Saprai, 'Against Equality of Exchange' (2010) 21 *King's Law Journal* 71.

[11] See J Gordley, 'Equality in Exchange' (1981) 69 *California Law Review* 1587. Gordley refers to 'voluntary commutative justice', which he distinguishes from corrective justice but as I understand it is a version of corrective justice as I have discussed it in this book. Cf Rakoff (n 7).

[12] Smith (n 8); Saprai (n 10).

relevant to the justice of the claim, it is difficult to see why the court should disregard it for a procedural or institutional reason. The implication is really that the court should not be adjudicating at all.[13]

The approach suggested here does have something in common with Gordley's approach, but it is not open to the same objections. Voluntary exchanges are valuable because they generate benefit for the parties, but the moral basis for the enforcement is to uphold distributive justice subject to the standpoint limitation, not to uphold distributive justice in the sense of restoring the prior position. As noted above, under the standpoint limitation the societal distribution of wealth and the relative wealth of the parties is irrelevant. Distributive justice in the ordinary sense has difficulty accounting for bilateral moral rights, whereas distributive justice subject to the standpoint limitation can account for bilateral moral rights. It is relative to these rights that it makes sense to think of substantive fairness as an imbalance or lack of equivalence in contract.

Each party benefits from the contract because that party values the benefit received under the contract sufficiently to justify the expense and labour put in, or the payment made, under the contract. The possibility of substantive unfairness arises because the contract does not contribute to distributive justice under the standpoint limitation where the exchange is not mutually beneficial in this way. This might be the case where the exchange is not beneficial at all to one party, or possibly where the two parties do not receive comparable benefits because the 'contractual surplus' is allocated in a one-sided way. This is the sense in which there can be a lack of equivalence or imbalance or inequality in exchange. This understanding is not available under the will theory, nor as a matter of distributive justice free of the standpoint limitation.

Protection against Substantive Unfairness

This approach shows in what sense there can be an imbalance or a lack of equivalence in a contract, but it does not follow that where this is the case there is necessarily substantive unfairness, or that there ought to be a remedy. For various reasons, it is very difficult to say in any particular case that there ought to be a remedy based on substantive unfairness.

A contract may turn out not to be beneficial because events do not happen as expected, but of course this does not mean that it was imbalanced. Furthermore, whether and to what extent each party benefits from the contract depends on that party's circumstances, objectives, and tastes, which are largely subjective. In particular, contractors may vary in their willingness to take on risk, which depends on their personal circumstances. This is why it is sensible to rely on the agreement of

[13] See ch 5 above.

the parties to ensure that the exchange is likely to be mutually beneficial. It also means that it may be very difficult to say objectively whether the contract is imbalanced. It may seem that a contract is unfair to C because C is unable to secure a benefit on terms that ought to be available to C as a matter of distributive justice free of the standpoint limitation, but D is not responsible for C's predicament and this does not mean that the contract is imbalanced.

Even if one can conclude that the agreement is imbalanced, each party has a right to act on the basis of the agreement and a right to protection for reliance on the agreement. If the contract is imbalanced to C's detriment, the imbalance may be due to circumstances relating to C or to the market that D does not know and cannot be expected to know.[14] Generally D is entitled to assume that it is C's responsibility to determine that the contract is a good contract for C. Once the contract has been made and D has acted in reliance on it, it may be unfair to D to upset the contract even if it is imbalanced.

However, there may be some exceptional circumstances in which it is justified to set aside an imbalanced contract on the basis of substantive unfairness. If C makes a misjudgement in assessing the terms of the exchange which has the effect that the contract is obviously imbalanced – ie no reasonable party would have made such a contract – and the other party D must realise this, then one might say that D should not be able to be able to rely on the contract on these terms or enforce it. There is no vitiating factor in the ordinary sense, because C made a misjudgement about the benefit of the exchange on the agreed terms, and this judgement is normally C's responsibility. The basis for setting aside the contract in such a case is substantive unfairness.

A possible example is where there is a well-functioning market with an ascertainable market price, and the contract price is far from the market price. Another possible example might be where D has the benefit of an exclusion of liability clause in circumstances where it is obvious that D is clearly better placed than C to take steps to prevent or insure against the type of loss for which D's liability is excluded, so that reasonable parties would certainly not have included such a clause.[15] But even in these cases it may not be obvious that the terms are imbalanced, since the provision in question may be compensated for in the other terms of the contract, and the particular circumstances of the parties may be complex and unknown to the other party.[16]

The doctrine of unconscionable bargains can be understood to recognise a remedy for substantive unfairness that is consistent with this approach. On one formulation, such a claim should arise where (as the doctrine was originally

[14] Policy analysis of the relevant market may show one party is receiving a disproportionate benefit or that despite appearances he is not, but this cannot affect the parties if it is not apparent on the basis of ordinary common knowledge. According to Collins there may sometimes be an 'illusion of unfairness': see Collins (n 3) 258.

[15] See Gordley (n 11) 744–55; Collins (n 3).

[16] Collins (n 3) 258–66.

formulated) C is 'poor and ignorant', and D exploits C's weakness in a way that is morally culpable and makes the contract oppressive.[17] This would reflect the approach above if it were interpreted to require the following: (1) C is someone who might be expected not to be capable of assessing whether the contract is beneficial, and possibly also someone who by virtue of difficult circumstances may be under pressure to secure a benefit that is really unaffordable; (2) the contract is significantly imbalanced to C's detriment; and (3) D is aware of these circumstances. If D goes ahead in these circumstances D may be acting culpably in taking advantage of C. The implication is that, in such circumstances D has a responsibility to assess whether the contract is beneficial to C. This may put D in a difficult position because, as considered above, it may sometimes be difficult to say whether a contract is imbalanced.

This approach might also be helpful in connection with standard form contracts with consumers, which consumers may have no practical choice but to accept. Standard form contracts may be an efficient way of managing contracting, but the danger is that the terms may be imbalanced to the detriment of the consumer. Possibly the law should take the position that, if a supplier chooses to use a standard form contract that a consumer is in practice bound to accept, so that the consumer is not genuinely able to exercise judgement about the contract terms or whether in the light of the terms the contract is beneficial, the supplier should be responsible in the same way to ensure that the terms are not imbalanced.[18] In any case, for present purposes, the point is that an approach along these lines is not available on the will theory or corrective justice approach or on the ordinary distributive justice approach.

The Remedial Regime

As discussed previously, contract law has a primary liability rather than a primary duty regime. This is reflected in the general absence of a right to specific performance, and in related aspects of the law such as the mitigation rule. It is controversial why this is, and whether the law should be reformed to recognise a primary duty regime instead. (As mentioned earlier, the debate is usually understood to be about how to enforce a primary duty.) The absence of a primary duty is difficult to explain under the corrective justice approach, because on this approach the contract is based on promises that give rise to moral duties to perform, which are recognised as legal duties to perform. The distributive justice approach seems better placed to provide an explanation.

[17] *Alec Lobb (Garages) v Total Oil* [1983] 1 WLR 87 at 94–95, per Millett J.

[18] And that there is no 'unfair surprise' that might have led to reconsideration: see the last section of this chapter, text accompanying n 44.

As considered in chapter four, according to EAL the theory of efficient breach explains the remedial regime. The primary liability approach is justified because, if the contracting parties are free not to perform, subject to the payment of compensation, so that they are free to take up an alternative more profitable opportunity or avoid an excessively burdensome contract, aggregate net benefit through contractual exchange across society will be maximised. This approach is excluded under the standpoint limitation. This is because it involves policy analysis and also, more importantly, because under the standpoint limitation the law is concerned not with what would promote contracting across society, but rather with what is justified with respect to the particular contract, that is to say with the interests of the two contracting parties under the contract.

The distributive justice approach under the standpoint limitation is distributive justice applied to the particular contract in isolation. Distributive justice should be understood in terms of the harms and benefits of the particular exchange. This supports the reliance theory version of the distributive justice approach. If the contract breaks down, the contract should protect C's reliance interest – the interest in being paid for work and expenses and other losses incurred under the contract, measured according to the contractual valuation, that is to say, as performance is valued under the terms of exchange (and also taking into account any benefit received). This is why contract adopts the primary liability approach. The primary relation is an allocation of risk with respect to the reliance interest. A legal duty to perform the contract, enforced by way of specific performance, would go beyond what can be justified as a matter of distributive justice, except where it is necessary to protect C against uncompensable loss relative to C's reliance interest. The distributive justice approach can in this way explain the remedial regime in contract through the reliance theory.

As discussed in chapter four, there are different versions of the reliance theory. The reliance theory is often equated with the death of contract theory and dismissed because of the implausibility of this version of the reliance theory, but there is no reason to understand the reliance theory in this way. As discussed previously, this would disregard the contractual valuation and the reliance interest in being paid for work done. The reliance theory can be understood instead to hold that the parties' promises to perform give rise to moral duties, but these moral duties are not recognised as legal duties, and instead there is a primary liability relation that protects only the reliance interest with respect to performance. The reliance interest is protected in accordance with the valuation placed on it by the contractual exchange. It could also be that the parties make an agreement that, by its own terms, limits its effect to the protection of their reliance interests, that is to say they agree to accept responsibility for the other party's reliance interest in performing the agreement. This makes sense, at least for sophisticated commercial contractors who understand their legal position and intend to commit themselves just to the extent that they will be legally bound. On this understanding there is no divergence between what the parties have committed themselves to under the agreement and what the law requires of them.[19] Either of these versions of the reliance theory is consistent with distributive justice subject to the standpoint limitation and provides a plausible account of the established remedial regime as a primary liability regime.

There is another aspect of the law that is better captured by the primary liability approach. On a primary duty analysis, there are two primary right–duty relations – which are logically independent of each other – relating to each party's performance. In theory, each could be valid and enforceable irrespective of the position with respect to the other. As the law is understood, if D's duty to C is breached and lapses, C's duty to D lapses as well. However, it would be possible for C to remain subject to a duty and to have to perform it before suing D.[20] On the primary liability, reliance theory approach, by contrast, the two relations are necessarily interdependent because each is protected only with respect to reliance on the progress of their mutual exchange. If one party withdraws, the other party cannot continue to act on the basis that the contract is in force.

The rule against penalties is sometimes understood to give protection against substantive unfairness, based on a principle of unconscionability,[21] but I suggest this is not how the rule should be understood. According to the traditional form of the penalty rule, it is permissible to have a liquidated damages clause, which in the event of a breach gives to C the right to a payment intended as a genuine estimate of expected loss, that is to say, as compensation, but not a penalty clause, which allows for a sum intended as a deterrent against non-performance. The penalty gives C a windfall, and so one might say that it involves an imbalance in the contract. However, on the traditional understanding the objection to the penalty clause seems to be not that it gives C a windfall, but that it is intended to impose a sanction on D rather than giving C a remedy.[22]

Under the new rule in English law, a penalty clause is permissible if it is designed to protect a legitimate interest in the actual performance of the contract.[23] This implies that the objection to the penalty clause rule is not to penalties as such, but to their use as a matter of course in the ordinary case, where a penalty is not appropriate. As discussed in chapter three, this is explicable on the basis that ordinarily there is no duty to perform the contract and no right to performance. There is a right to performance and a duty to perform only exceptionally, and the 'legitimate

[19] Cf SV Shiffrin, 'The Divergence of Contract and Promise' (2007) 120 *Harvard Law Review* 708.

[20] This seems to have been the position at one time: see eg TA Baloch, *Unjust Enrichment and Contract* (Hart Publishing, 2009) ch 5.

[21] As discussed in M Chen-Wishart, 'Controlling the Power to Agree Damages' in PBH Birks (ed), *Wrongs and Remedies in the Twenty First Century* (Oxford University Press, 1996).

[22] The origin seems to lie in the unconscionability of a 'penal bond'; see *Dunlop Pneumatic Tyre Co v New Garage* [1915] AC 79. Furthermore, the imbalance is not really in the exchange itself. If the contract were performed as envisaged there would be no imbalance.

[23] *Cavendish Square Holding v El Makdessi* [2015] UKSC 67.

interest in performance' is the right to performance in such a case. The current rule reflects the primary liability and the reliance theory understanding of the remedial regime.

On the corrective justice approach, applying the will theory, there is no reason to disallow a penalty clause. The role of contract is fundamentally to give effect to whatever terms the parties have agreed to govern their performance, and they should be able to agree on a penalty clause.[24] By contrast, on the suggested approach, the rationale for enforcing the contract is to facilitate an exchange, and a contracting party should not be subject to a sanction to compel performance where this goes beyond what is necessary to protect the other party's interest in the exchange itself, ie the reliance interest. Even on this approach, however, one might argue that the parties should be given a wide margin to determine for themselves whether the breach of a contractual term may cause loss for which damages would be an inadequate remedy.

Objective Agreement and Implied Terms

Under the will theory, on the corrective justice approach, one would expect a promisor, D, to be bound only by what D subjectively intended to promise. One might expect D to be at risk of liability, beyond this, where C relied on a reasonable belief about what D had promised, at least if D was responsible, and one would expect to see a distinction in the law between these two types of case, but no such distinction is found. The law simply adopts an objective approach to agreement.[25] As suggested in chapter five, the distributive justice approach seems to have more potential to explain the objective approach. The justification for enforcing the agreement is not simply that the contractors had the moral power to bind themselves by an exercise of will, but the effect of the agreement in facilitating a mutually beneficial exchange by protecting reliance on the agreement. On this basis, it makes sense to use an objective test. It is fair to the two contractors for each of them to be responsible for reliance by the other on a reasonable interpretation of how they have presented themselves in making an agreement. In effect, it is an aspect of substantive fairness, in the sense discussed, between the contracting parties.

Another problem for the corrective justice approach, drawing on the will theory, is how to deal with a gap in the contract, where circumstances arise for

[24] This is implicit in S Worthington, 'Common Law Values: The Role of Party Autonomy in Private Law' in A Robertson and M Tilbury (eds), *The Common Law of Obligations: Divergence and Unity* (Hart, 2015).

[25] *Smith v Hughes* (1871) LR 6 QB 597.

which no provision has been made – in other words, how to determine a default term or default rule. Default terms present a problem for the will theory because they are not based on the parties' intentions (unlike genuine implied terms or terms implied 'in fact'). One approach is to say that 'background norms' should be incorporated into the contract, though under the will theory this would seem to make sense only on the assumption that this is what was implicitly agreed, which presumably cannot always be assumed.[26] The will theory also seems to be behind the restrictive rule that terms should be required only where necessary to give business efficacy to the contract rather than on the basis of what would have been agreed by reasonable parties.[27]

It is said, more realistically, that since default terms are not agreed it should be openly recognised that they should be selected according to what would best promote mutually beneficial exchange by contracting – as it might be put, according to considerations of policy.[28] This reflects the distributive justice approach. An example of a policy-oriented default rule is a 'penalty default' rule.[29] A penalty default rule is intended to encourage one contracting party to propose an agreed term to avoid the risk that the penalty default rule will apply. It is argued that the penalty default rule may be efficient because the express term actually agreed will be more apt for the contract than what might have been applied as a standard default rule. A possible example suggested is the rule that compensation is available only for reasonably foreseeable loss, but if a contracting party notifies the other party of a particular risk of loss not otherwise reasonably foreseeable, then compensation will extend to this loss if it occurs.[30] If notice of such a risk is given, the contract terms are more apt because the other party will take care to avoid loss arising from this identified risk.

Penalty default rules may work in the interests of contractors generally, and it is open to a legislature to legislate to this effect, but they cannot be introduced by a court under the standpoint limitation.[31] Under the standpoint limitation, the court can rely only on the interests of the two parties to the particular contract, or other considerations apparent on the basis of ordinary common knowledge.

[26] See C Fried, 'Contract as Promise: Lessons Learned' (2019) 20 *Theoretical Inquiries in Law* 367, 357.

[27] *Marks & Spencer v BNP Paribas* [2015] UKSC 72.

[28] E Peden, 'Policy Concerns Behind Implication of Terms in Law' (2001) 117 *Law Quarterly Review* 459. According to Fried, default terms are a matter of political morality, i.e., distributive justice, though the justification for the actual duties is purely the promise of the parties, apparently departing from his original view: C Fried, 'Contract as Promise, 30 Years On' (2012) XLV *Suffolk University Law Review* 961. If the justification for the actual duties is quite independent of distributive justice, it is unclear why the default terms should be based on distributive justice.

[29] I Ayres and R Gertner, 'Filling Gaps in Incomplete Contracts: An Economic Theory of Default Rules' (1989) 99 *Yale Law Journal* 87.

[30] I leave aside whether this rule should be understood as a default rule.

[31] Cf EA Posner, 'There Are No Penalty Default Rules in Contract Law' (2006) 33 *Florida State University Law Review*. According to Posner the courts in the US have not actually introduced any penalty default rules, though not for this reason.

Under the standpoint limitation, it would seem appropriate to use hypothetical contracting, in the sense of what reasonable and fair-minded people would have agreed on, in order to achieve a fair exchange.[32] This reflects the rationale of facilitating a mutually beneficial exchange, in the parties' interests, according to the substantive fairness rationale. Hypothetical contracting in effect preserves the implicit contractual allocation of risk, whereas the introduction of a policy-based rule, such as a penalty default rule, involves adjustment in the interests of distributive justice free of the standpoint limitation, taking account of the public interest, and amounts to the reallocation of contractual risk. Similarly a court cannot adopt an arbitrary rule of interpretation in the interests of certainty, not aimed at determining what was actually agreed.[33] Relying on certainty as being valuable in itself is, like a formality rule, contrary to the standpoint limitation.[34]

It is said that in recent years the English courts have made increasing use of implied terms, introducing for example an implied term of trust and confidence in employment contracts, and in some circumstances a duty of good faith (requiring honesty and fairness). If the justification for introducing such an implied term is that it will improve the practice of contracting generally and increase the benefits obtained through it, then it is beyond the power of the courts under the standpoint limitation. It would be consistent with the standpoint limitation if the reason for introducing the implied term is that it merely recognises an existing customary practice amongst contractors, or if it is based on what reasonable contractors would have agreed.[35]

Imputed Contracts

In some circumstances C can claim payment from D for providing D with a benefit where there was no agreement. For example, under the doctrine of necessitous intervention, or more particularly in the case of maritime salvage, C can claim payment for the salvage of D's ship without an agreement, if no agreement was possible in the circumstances.[36] This clearly cannot be a contractual claim. It seems

[32] Cf Rakoff (n 7).

[33] Consistently with this it is said that the English courts nowadays favour informal methods of interpretation rather than rigid and artificial rules based on a concern with certainty: R Catterwell, 'Autonomy and Institutionalism in the Law of Contract' (2022) 42 *Oxford Journal of Legal Studies* 1067.

[34] Morgan argues that remedies should be understood as default rules: J Morgan, 'Contract Remedies as Default Rules' in R Halson and D Campbell (eds), *Research Handbook on Remedies in Private Law* (Edward Elgar, 2019). But any departure from what is required as a matter of remedial consistency, presumably based on policy considerations, would amount to a reallocation of risk.

[35] See Catterwell (n 33). For example, a duty of good faith was implied as a matter of fact in *Yam Seng v International Trade Corporation* [2013] EWHC 111, but some would say this was really a matter of legislating in the public interest. See also H Collins, 'Implied Terms: The Foundation in Good faith and Fair Dealing' (2014) 67 *Current Legal Problems* 297.

[36] See eg *The Goring* [1988] AC 831, which held that the doctrine does not apply in inland waters.

difficult to explain in any way on the corrective justice approach. It is not about agreement, and nor is it justifiable in terms of the protection of individual liberty rights, since it does not arise from any interference.

Such a claim is, however, concerned with facilitating a mutually beneficial exchange. It is reasonable to say that because there is very clearly a mutually beneficial exchange, the parties would have contracted if they had been in a position to do so. Where the parties are in a position to make an agreement, liability for payment should depend on an agreement in order to respect each party's right to determine what to pay for and at what price. But where it is not possible for the parties to negotiate, typically because it is an emergency, and it is also clear that an exchange is mutually beneficial, it makes sense to enforce an exchange by allowing C to do the work and claim for payment from D without a contract. This is understandable under the suggested approach of distributive justice under the standpoint limitation. It is a natural extension of contract in the sense that it has the same fundamental rationale of securing a mutually beneficial exchange. For this reason one might call it an imputed contract.[37]

EAL offers a different explanation for liability,[38] in terms of a policy of encouraging maritime salvage. This is not consistent with the standpoint limitation, because it involves policy analysis and it is not about the justice of the interaction between the parties in the light of their interests.

Statutory Regulation of Contract

Under the standpoint limitation, the common law can advance distributive justice only in a limited way. The legislature can do much that is beyond the judges. It can replace common law private contracting by arranging for publicly owned providers or subsidised private providers to provide benefits at no or limited cost. It can compensate for any adverse effects of private exchange by contract, such as the exclusion of some people from certain benefits, or disparities in wealth or excessive wealth accumulation, by way of redistributive taxation for social benefits.

The legislature can also modify common law contract in ways that are beyond the judges at common law under the standpoint limitation. It can promote successful contracting by taking steps to mitigate market failure and improve the general functioning of the market, for example by laying down rules on price displays or on the disclosure of information, or by laying down a timetable for a complex transaction.[39] It can introduce rules on competition law to promote market competition in the interests of consumers. Statutory regulation might also

[37] See further P Jaffey, *The Nature and Scope of Restitution* (Hart, 2000) ch 3.

[38] See WM Landes and RA Posner, 'Salvors, Finders, Good Samaritans and Other Rescuers: an Economic Study of Law and Altruism' (1978) 7 *The Journal of Legal Studies* 83.

[39] See generally Collins (n 3) 279–86.

promote contractual performance, for example by introducing a general duty to perform (with sanctions or specific performance to enforce it). Under the standpoint limitation, the rationale of contract law is merely to facilitate a mutually beneficial exchange in the particular case. It may be that policy analysis can show that overall it would be welfare-enhancing to promote actual performance in more cases than will occur at common law under the standpoint limitation. Similarly, it may be desirable to introduce a duty of good faith in contracting even if the judges are unable to do this.[40] The optimal level of contracting and performance may not be what emerges from common law development under the standpoint limitation.

As mentioned above, the legislature can also impose mandatory rules, for example banning exclusion of liability clauses or early termination clauses, or imposing a minimum wage or maximum rent, for the benefit of certain categories of contractor, such as consumers, employees or tenants.[41] Such mandatory regimes may advance distributive justice in the sense of increasing the benefits obtained overall through contracting, but the courts cannot impose such mandatory terms under the standpoint limitation. It is not simply that they may be contrary to what has actually been agreed. If it were possible to establish that what was agreed is unjustified as a matter of distributive justice relative to ordinary common knowledge, and that the mandatory term is justified, there might sometimes be good reason to override the agreement, but it is not possible to do this. One problem is that determining whether such mandatory terms are justified involves policy analysis of the effects of possible rules on the types of contract to which they would apply, which is not possible on the basis of ordinary common knowledge.[42] In addition, the mandatory term is not necessarily intended to achieve a contract that the parties themselves acting reasonably would have agreed on, or that is substantively fair as between the two parties. It is concerned with distributive justice with respect to a sector of the population. Thus the parties would have to adjust to it, as they can when such a term is introduced by statute with prospective effect. For example, the effect of introducing or increasing a statutory minimum wage may be that businesses have to reorganise their activities in order to remain profitable at the new minimum wage, say by increasing prices to consumers, reducing the number of employees, or investing in technology. If it is introduced at common law in adjudication, however, such a term is liable to be unjust because contractors have no opportunity to adjust to it. These types of statutory contract regime are

[40] See n 35.

[41] See eg JN Adams and R Brownsword, 'The Ideologies of Contract' (1987) 7 *Legal Studies* 205. Adams and Brownsword draw a distinction between 'consumer welfarism' and 'market individualism' as general approaches to contract law. Consumer welfarism holds that contract should promote fair terms, protect weaker parties against unfair terms or bad deals, and reduce risk or disproportionate loss. I would equate this with the ordinary distributive justice approach. The law is said to have evolved towards consumer welfarism but this is principally through statutory reform. The market individualism approach is associated with the classical theory and so might be equated with the will theory, but since it ties contract to its role in the market it might be better equated with the suggested approach of distributive justice under the standpoint limitation.

[42] Collins discusses 'regulatory backfiring': Collins (n 3) 274.

aimed at improving distributive justice across society, but they would not necessarily be justified in the interests of substantive fairness in a particular case as between the parties under the standpoint limitation, in the absence of the statute. It is not necessarily the case that applying a rent cap or a minimum wage retrospectively to a particular contract makes that contract substantively fairer.

A statute may provide explicitly for protection against substantive fairness, for example, by providing that 'unfair terms' are unenforceable.[43] If the courts are competent to apply such a provision under the statute, could they not have done the same thing at common law, without the authority of a statutory provision, with respect to a particular contract in the interests of substantive fairness? As mentioned above, some commentators think that the courts could have gone much further to develop the common law to give protection against substantive unfairness, but this is difficult to reconcile with the standpoint limitation. The standpoint limitation requires the law to be based on considerations relating to the particular contract in the light of its own particular circumstances, and as pointed out above in the case of a particular contract it may be very difficult to say whether a particular contract is unfair in the sense of being imbalanced. It may be possible to identify types of clause that are typically unfair or liable to operate unfairly: examples might be a discretionary termination or alteration clause, a power of one party to determine compliance by the other, and an exclusion of liability for negligence or non-compliance.[44] This is not a matter of establishing imbalance or substantive unfairness in a particular case. The effect is to reduce the likelihood of unfairness, though at the (no doubt small) risk of causing unfairness in a different way by preventing a possible contract from taking place in which the parties genuinely and reasonably want to use such a clause.

Common law contract under the influence of the standpoint limitation is largely confined to giving effect to a principle of agreement. This is why it is characterised by uniformity with little differentiation between contract types. In general, at common law, the rules do not differ according to the type of contract or contractor, for example whether it is a contract for goods or services, or employment, shipping or licensing. Some differentiation may arise from the terms implied by custom and practice for certain types of contract. Statute has created more differentiation between different types of contract and contractor. The statutory regimes are no doubt superior regimes as a matter of distributive justice, free of the standpoint limitation. They differentiate between different types of contract on the basis of policy analysis and judgements of distributive justice across the society or sectors of society that is not possible under the standpoint limitation.[45]

[43] See the Consumer Rights Act 2015.

[44] In the Consumer Rights Act 2015, it is taken to be reasonable to exclude unfair terms such as these unless they have actually been negotiated and agreed.

[45] See Collins (n 3) 46–55. Dagan and Heller argue that the law should provide a menu of different regimes for different contract 'types' between which contractors can choose, though this would not be an option for the common law under the standpoint limitation: H Dagan and M Heller, *The Choice Theory of Contracts* (Cambridge University Press, 2017).

Some commentators argue that contract in its traditional form, which simply applies a principle of agreement without differentiation between types of contractor or contract and takes no account of any interests other than those of the contracting parties, except very narrowly under the public policy doctrine, reflects a failure of legal development at common law. It results from a failure to escape from formalism and from the will theory, which means that judges have not considered how contract law can be developed to achieve distributive justice, drawing on policy analysis to show how the function of contract in facilitating mutually beneficial exchange can be promoted.[46] But on the approach I have suggested it is not possible for judges to do this, not because of formalism or the will theory, but because of the standpoint limitation.[47]

[46] Collins (n 3). Kronman (n 3); Bagchi (n 3). See also J Gava and J Greene, 'Do We Need a Hybrid Law of Contract? Why Hugh Collins Is Wrong and Why It Matters' (2004) *Cambridge Law Journal* 605.

[47] Even where the issue arises for the legislature, some would argue that taxation is more effective than adapting contract law for effecting distributive justice (with respect to overall distribution): L Kaplow and S Shavell, 'Why the Legal System Is Less Efficient than the Income Tax in Redistributing Income' (1994) 23 *Journal of Legal Studies* 667.

9

Property Rights and Remedial Consistency

Introduction

In this chapter and the next, drawing on the earlier discussion, I discuss the implications of the requirement of remedial consistency and the standpoint limitation for the law of private property.

C's property right is conventionally understood as a right against interference with respect to a thing legally recognised as an 'object of property' ('the property' for short) correlated with a duty against interference on the part of others. Interference includes entering, taking or using the object of property. On this conventional understanding, a property right is a right in tort with respect to an object of property. This is how the 'right of exclusion' theory of private property is generally understood.[1] It also corresponds to the understanding of a property right as a basic liberty right against interference under the corrective justice approach. It is reflected in the common law of trespass and conversion, by which property rights are protected by way of claims arising from wrongful interference.

It is helpful to distinguish between a right of ownership and a lesser property right. A right of ownership is a property right with respect to the whole object of property, subject to derogations, and a lesser property right, such as an easement, a charge or a restrictive covenant over land, is a right with respect to a particular aspect or part of the object of property, typically by way of a derogation from the right of ownership. On the right of exclusion approach, rights of ownership and lesser property rights are correlated with duties against interference with respect to the whole or the relevant part of the object of property.

There is generally (though not always) a right in tort with respect to interference with property. As discussed previously, there is a distinction between a right against interference by others and a right that others bear the risk of loss from interference. However, the property right itself cannot be equated with a right

[1] See eg JW Harris, *Property and Justice* (Oxford University Press, 1996); J Waldron, *The Right to Private Property* (Clarendon Press, 1988); JE Penner, *The Idea of Property in Law* (1997); TW Merrill, *Property and the Right to Exclude* (1998) 77 *Nebraska Law Review* 730 (1998); HE Smith, 'Property as the Law of Things' (2012) 125 *Harvard Law Review* 1691.

against interference in either sense. The property right itself is a right to the benefit of the object of property or some part of it. A right of ownership is a right to all the benefit and a lesser property right a right to a particular part of the benefit. A right to the benefit of the property is necessarily presupposed by a right against interference.

The idea of the benefit of an object of property seems perfectly well defined in principle – it is the benefit of the uses and applications to which the object of property can be put, by which it can provide a benefit – and to say that C has a legal right to the benefit of the property is to say that the law provides for C to have and to be able to secure this benefit, or the opportunity to have it, or its value, as against anyone else. On the conventional legal understanding, however, private property involves a right to the benefit of property only in the sense that the owner C is free to make use of the property, and others are not, because C has the right to prevent others from using it or interfering in C's use. In other words, C's right to the benefit is merely a liberty to use the property that is exclusive because it is protected by a right against interference.[2] It is the right against interference, and not the protected liberty, that gives rise to a claim against others. It is thought that there cannot be a right to the benefit of a thing, except in this insubstantial sense. But the right to the benefit of the property is not simply the protected liberty to use the property. This becomes apparent when we consider what claims C has or should have in the light of the requirement of remedial consistency. The remedial position is inexplicable without the recognition of a distinct and basic right to the benefit of the property.[3]

Remedial Consistency and Claims to Protect Property

Compensation and the Measure of Loss

The recognition of a right to the benefit of the property is necessary as a matter of remedial consistency to understand the primary right from which a claim to compensation arises. A claim for compensation for loss of or damage to property arising from interference presupposes a logically prior right to the benefit of the property. Say C has a share of the ownership of an object of property or a lesser property right in the property, and D damages the property, through an act of negligence or trespass. One cannot say what C's loss is without first establishing what C's property right is, as a right to some part of the benefit of the property. C's right with respect to the property cannot be merely a right against interference or against loss from interference. Even if C is the absolute owner, if C suffers loss to

[2] See eg S Douglas and B McFarlane, 'Defining Property Rights' in J Penner and HE Smith, *Philosophical Foundations of Property Law* (Oxford University Press, 2013).

[3] There is an approach along broadly the same lines in P Jaffey, *Private Law and Property Claims* (Hart, 2007).

the property through D's negligence, it is clear that C's right that D bear the risk of loss resulting from a failure to meet the standard of care, or C's right that D meet the standard of care, is not the same as C's property right. There is a separate question of what counts as a loss to C, which depends on C's having a separate right to the benefit of the property. Similarly, a right against interference by trespass or a right to compensation for loss from trespass is not the same as the right to the property itself, which is the right to the benefit of the property. When C acquires property, C can now suffer a loss that C could not have suffered previously, but one cannot sensibly say that C has simply acquired a right against loss. C must first have acquired a right to the benefit of the property.

C can have a claim for compensation for loss of the benefit of a thing only if C has a property right to it. Consider confidential personal information. In the law of privacy, C can recover compensation for personal harm resulting from the disclosure of such information. This does not involve recognising the information as an object of property. C does not recover loss representing a deprivation of the benefit of the information itself as an object of property. By contrast, consider the disclosure of a trade secret or confidential commercial information. Here C may be entitled to recover compensation for the loss of the benefit of the information itself of which C is deprived, that is to say the value of using it, or the licensing revenue that would have been received. If so, this is because C has a right to the benefit of the information as an object of property. The measure of compensation is different in the two types of case, according to whether the information is an object of property owned by C.

Restitution

Say C is the owner of land or goods that are transferred invalidly to D, that is to say possession or control passes to D without the valid exercise of a power of transfer by or on behalf of C as the owner. This is a typical example of a situation calling for the protection of a property right. C should in principle have a claim to recover the property – a claim for restitution (as I shall call it). However, in the light of the requirement of remedial consistency, the claim for restitution is not explicable as a claim arising from a right against interference (whether understood as a right correlated with a duty against interference on the part of D, or a right that D bear the risk of loss caused by interference).

The claim for restitution does typically have the effect of compensating C for a loss incurred through the invalid transfer, but it is not based on D's having caused the loss to C. Often D will have had no part at all in the transfer. The transfer may have been made by C or C's agent, not by D. The primary right from which the claim arises, as a matter of remedial consistency, cannot be C's primary right against interference by D or C's right that D bear the risk of loss caused by interference. The reason for making D liable is that D has received and retains the property transferred. The implication is that, as a matter of remedial consistency, the primary right from which the claim arises, following an invalid transfer, is C's right to the benefit of the property. This right of C's survives the invalid transfer and binds D.

It might seem that C's claim for restitution is a right correlated with a duty on the part of D to return the property, and one might say that this duty of return is the form that the duty against interference takes after an invalid transfer. But D may not actually be physically capable of returning the property; it might be a tangible thing that is very heavy and unwieldy. D may also not know of the transfer or may not know where the property is. D's duty with respect to a transfer received must be to take reasonable care to locate and not to destroy or dispose of property that D knows or ought to know is someone else's, until such time as it is retrieved. This, one can say, is a version of the duty against interference persisting in accordance with remedial consistency, but this duty is not the correlate of the right to restitution. C has a right all along to the property. This is the right to the benefit of the property, and it is not correlated with a duty against interference or a duty of return. The right to the benefit of the property is one side of a primary liability relation, correlated with a liability on D's part to have the property returned to C if it is received. C's claim for restitution is a power to secure the return of the property. It is a power to put in train legal proceedings that, with the assistance of the state, will secure the return of the property.[4]

As a matter of remedial consistency, since the claim for restitution arises from the primary right to the benefit of the property, it should arise simply from the receipt by D of the property, and it should lapse if or insofar as the property has been destroyed or passed on by D. By contrast, with respect to a claim for compensation for loss caused by D, the claim should arise in consequence of what D has done – for example causing damage, or misappropriation of the property, or, when the property has come into D's possession, disposal or consumption – not from the fact of D's receipt of the property, and it should be irrelevant whether the property remains with D.

Furthermore, as a matter of remedial consistency, C's right to the benefit of the property, which persists in the event of an invalid transfer, should bind the whole world, since if the transfer is invalid it is necessarily invalid as against all the world, and C retains the right to the benefit of it as against all the world, not just the immediate recipient D. Thus a claim for restitution arising from an invalid transfer should be proprietary, that is to say that it should be unaffected by the claims of D's creditors if D goes bankrupt, and should be capable of binding further recipients. By contrast, a claim for compensation based on C's right against interference by D must be a personal claim against D alone as the person responsible for the interference.[5]

[4] Cf for the primary liability with respect to loss as considered in ch 3.

[5] A claim for compensation for loss caused by an appropriation of property could take the form of a claim to have the property returned to C, as an apt way to compensate C, but this would be a personal claim against D with respect to the property, which, in the event of D's bankruptcy, should in principle lapse into an ordinary pecuniary claim.

The claim for compensation for loss from interference and the claim for restitution of property following an invalid transfer are distinct and arise from different primary rights. The differences between the claims follow, as a matter of remedial consistency, from the nature of the primary rights. It is a weakness of the common law that it does not distinguish between them. It explicitly recognises only a claim for compensation caused by wrongful interference, such as trespass or conversion, which does service for both types of claim, but at the cost of injustice in some cases.[6] For example, a claim in conversion is a strict liability claim, which is appropriate where D still has the property and the claim is in substance a claim for restitution to recover it, but if D no longer has the property a claim for its value is justifiable only as a claim for compensation for loss, which should normally require that the loss was caused by D's conduct.[7] The law may also be unjust in failing to provide a proprietary claim in D's bankruptcy if D still has the property. As considered below, the law has managed to distinguish between the two types of claim in equity with respect to the protection of trust property, where the law has recognised a proprietary claim for restitution of the property.

Licence Fee Damages

There is another remedy that, like restitution of an invalid transfer, cannot be understood as a form of compensation for loss caused by interference. If D has used C's property without permission, C is entitled to a pecuniary remedy in the measure of the amount that might reasonably have been agreed between the parties as a fee for a licence to do what D actually did without permission, which I will refer to as licence fee damages. It has been controversial how the licence fee damages remedy should be understood.[8] It is sometimes understood as a form of compensation for loss caused by interference. However, C is entitled to licence fee damages for unauthorised use even if C has not suffered any loss at all from the use, whether by damage to the property, or by being prevented from using or licensing the use of the property. Licence fee damages do not serve to correct a loss from an interference in the sense of undoing or negating its effects on C through compensation. C's licence fee damages cannot be understood to arise from a primary right

[6] See eg T Weir, *Introduction to Tort Law* (Oxford University Press, 2nd edn 2006) 166–67; A Tettenborn, 'Coercion, Tort and Remedies' in N Palmer and E McKendrick (eds), *Interests in Goods* (Routledge, 2nd edn 1998) 825.

[7] This leaves aside the issue of tracing considered below, where D still has the value of the property received.

[8] Also referred to as 'restitutionary damages' and by various other expressions. The approach here follows P Jaffey, 'Licence Fee Damages' (2011) *Restitution Law Review* 95. See also S Waddams and R Sharpe, 'Damages for Lost Opportunity to Bargain' (1982) 2 *Oxford Journal of Legal Studies* 290; F Giglio, 'Restitution for Wrongs: a Structural Analysis' (2007) 20 *Canadian Journal of Law and Jurisprudence* 5, 16; EJ Weinrib, 'Restitutionary Damages as Corrective Justice' (2000) 1 *Theoretical Inquiries in Law* 1.

that D bear the risk of loss resulting from interference or from a duty on the part of D not to commit an interference. This would be impossible to reconcile with the requirement of remedial consistency.

Furthermore, if licence fee damages were an appropriate remedy to protect a right against loss caused by interference, there is no reason why they should not be available for interference generally,[9] for example for interference with personal rights by way of assault or breach of privacy. In fact, licence fee damages have traditionally been confined to claims arising from the unauthorised use of property, in particular land, goods and intellectual property.[10]

Licence fee damages are explicable as a remedy to protect C's primary right to the benefit of the property. They secure to C the benefit of the property made by D through D's use of it, even when C would not have received this benefit because C would not have used the property or licensed its use in this way, and so has suffered no loss. When D uses C's property, the benefit that D derives from it is due in part to D's application of work and resources to the property, and in part to the use value of the property, which is a part of the benefit to which C is entitled as owner. Licence fee damages, in the measure that would have been agreed between reasonable parties as a licence fee, are a measure of that part of the benefit obtained by D through the unauthorised use of the property that belongs to C as owner.[11] On this understanding, although an unauthorised use may be an interference, the claim for licence fee damages arises, like the claim arising from an invalid transfer, in order to protect C's right to the benefit of the property, not C's right against interference or for compensation for loss from interference.

This is particularly important with respect to intellectual property. Say D sells a product that infringes C's intellectual property rights. C may suffer no loss from the infringement because C did not have any equivalent product for sale and has not lost any sales, nor has it lost any licensing revenue. Nevertheless C is entitled to a royalty on D's sales. This is said to be ordinary damages, but it is clear from the way that the measure is determined that in fact the remedy is licence fee damages.[12] This is in fact the standard measure of damages for intellectual property, and it is explicable only on the basis that the intellectual property owner has a right to the benefit of the intangible thing as an object of property.[13]

Similarly, if confidential information is treated as property, as in the case of a trade secret or commercial know-how, there should be a claim for licence fee

[9] As argued in J Edelman, 'The Measure of Restitution and the Future of Restitutionary Damages' (2010) 18 *Restitution Law Review* 1.

[10] It is found in contract in the form of 'negotiating damages': As to whether this can be explained in the same way, see P Jaffey, 'Disgorgement and "Licence Fee Damages" in Contract' (2004) 20 *Journal of Contract Law* 57.

[11] Licence fee damages cannot plausibly be explained as a measure of disgorgement of wrongful profits, since they deprive D of only a fraction of the benefit received. See Weinrib (n 8); Jaffey (n 8).

[12] See eg *General Tire & Rubber Co v Firestone Tyre & Rubber Co Ltd* [1975] 1 WLR 819. See M Spence, *Intellectual Property* (Oxford University Press, 2007) 32–33.

[13] See further P Jaffey, 'Private Property and Intangibles' [2022] *Conveyancer and Property Lawyer* 47.

damages in respect of the unauthorised use of the information.[14] By contrast, with respect to liability for breach of privacy by disclosure of private information, C should be limited to compensation for personal harm, because the claim does not depend on treating the private information as property belonging to C that was used by D.[15]

Specific Enforcement

Normally with respect to property there is a right against interference, correlated with a duty against interference, not merely a right to compensation for loss resulting from interference. C can prevent interference even where it would not have caused any loss, for example where it would not have interfered with C's use, nor caused any damage, nor prevented C from licensing use of the property. An injunction is not confined to the case where 'damages are inadequate'. This may be justifiable because of the difficulty of demonstrating loss through interference, but more importantly it is normally justified simply to protect the right of the owner to secure the benefit of the property (including any benefit to be obtained through licensing its use).

It would be possible to have an arrangement under which there is no right against interference and anyone is free to enter or make use of the property, and C's right to the benefit of the property merely generates a right against anyone who uses the property to a reasonable sum as payment for the use, equivalent to licence fee damages. One might say that in such a case C's property right falls short of a full right of ownership since it does not give C a right of exclusive use. Such an arrangement might make good sense for intellectual property. It would enable C to get a financial return on the intellectual property, whilst allowing others to use it as well.[16] As discussed below, intangible property in the form of an investment or receivable or right of payment may not need protection against interference at all.

Objects of Property and Property Rights

The requirement of remedial consistency implies, given what is found or what one would expect to find in a remedial regime for property, that the basic form of a property right is a right to the benefit or some part of the benefit of an object of property, not a right against interference or loss from interference.[17] This makes

[14] See eg *Seager v Copydex* [1967] 1 WLR 923.

[15] By contrast, a celebrity right or 'publicity right', which can be licensed for use and transferred, does amount to a form of ownership of reputation. See generally G Black, *Publicity Rights and Image: Exploitation and Legal Control* (Hart, 2011).

[16] For intellectual property, this would be similar to compulsory licensing: as to which see Spence (n 12) 18–19.

[17] Proponents of the right of exclusion theory may say that property law is fundamentally concerned with an interest in using things: see eg Smith (n 1); Penner (n 1) ch 5.

sense of the fact that a property right is a right to a thing as an object of property. A right to the benefit of an object of property necessarily attaches to a particular thing. It is an exclusive right, in the sense that it cannot be held by different people at the same time (except by sharing in some way). A right of exclusive use or possession must refer to a right to the benefit of the property, not a right against interference.[18] By contrast, it is logically possible for two people both to have, quite independently of each other, a right against interference with respect to the same thing, empowering each of them to exclude everyone else from it.[19]

A right against interference need not relate to a thing as an object of property – it could be a right against interference with a person. Equating a property right with a right against interference implies that property is not necessarily concerned with things at all.[20] Possibly to avoid this implication, it is sometimes said that an object of property must be a tangible thing from which people can be physically excluded.[21] On the right to the benefit approach, a thing is capable of being an object of property if it is something that can be used for benefit. The availability of restitution or licence fee damages, or a measure of compensation that encompasses benefit to be obtained, implies that there is a right to the benefit of property. These types of claim are indicative of property and an object of property can certainly be an intangible thing.

It is often said that intellectual property is not truly a form of property, and more particularly that the intangible thing such as the invention or work of art that is the subject of intellectual property protection is not an object of property.[22] This may be simply because the intangible thing cannot be possessed and the intellectual property right is not a right against physical interference with it. It may seem instead that intellectual property is concerned not with property but with controlling the behaviour of people in order to create an economic monopoly for the right-holder's benefit. But on the suggested approach there is no reason to deny that intellectual property is a form of property. The right-holder has a right to a defined part of the benefit of the intangible thing, as an object of property, and the economic monopoly is the means for realising the value of this benefit.

[18] Cf J Penner, *Property Rights – A Re-Examination* (Oxford University Press, 2020) 139.

[19] As Stern says, property rights involve 'mutual exclusivity' in this sense, which is not the case for the right against interference: JY Stern, 'The Essential Structure of Property Law' (2017) 115 *Michigan Law Review* 1167, 1188.

[20] The Hohfeldian concept of a property right is a right correlated with a duty imposed on all the world, or strictly speaking a distinct right against each other person, with no requirement for a 'thing' in the definition: WH Hohfeld, 'Fundamental Legal Conceptions as Applied in Judicial Reasoning' (1913) 23 *Yale Law Journal* and (1917) 26 *Yale Law Journal* 710. Cf Honoré, who insisted that property is concerned with things: AM Honoré, 'Rights of Exclusion and Immunities Against Divesting' (1959–60) 34 *Tulane Law Review* 454. See also C Webb, 'Three Concepts of Right, Two of Property' (2018) 38 *Oxford Journal of Legal Studies* 246.

[21] See eg Douglas and McFarlane (n 2). See also TW Merrill and HE Smith, 'The Architecture of Property' in H Dagan and BC Zipursky (eds), *Research Handbook on Private Law Theories* (Edward Elgar, 2020) 6. Some say that, whilst tangible things provide the core case of property, intangible things can be peripheral or secondary examples of property: see eg Waldron (n 1) 33–37.

[22] See also Penner (n 1) 118; Spence (n 12) 13–15.

The benefit of an object of property can in principle be divided up into aspects of benefit protected by different property rights. There can be a right of ownership, which is a right to all the benefit, and a lesser property right, which is a right to a particular aspect of the benefit. Examples of lesser property rights in land law are, as mentioned above, easements, charges, restrictive covenants. In the case of intellectual property, the statute creating the intellectual property right specifies the particular benefit encompassed in the intellectual property right (by stipulating what constitutes infringement).[23] The recognition of the right to the benefit of property as the basic form of the property right naturally leads to the idea that the benefit can be divided up amongst different property rights to aspects of the benefit of the object of property in innumerable different ways.[24] This is one way of understanding the 'bundle of rights' theory of property.[25]

One objection made of the bundle of rights theory is that it rejects the assumption that property rights are rights to things as objects of property.[26] Behind the objection may be the thought that a right to an aspect of the benefit of property is simply a right to a certain use, and that this is equivalent to a right relating to an action or activity such as a contractual performance or a standard of conduct in negligence, which are not necessarily related to things. But on the approach suggested, a property right is indeed a right to the benefit of a thing, or an aspect of the benefit of a thing, as an object of property, and if this is expressed as a right to a use it means the use of an object of property. As pointed out above, it is actually the idea that a property right is a right against interference that opens the way to the rejection of the traditional assumption that a property right is a right to a thing as an object of property.

A more important concern is that the traditional approach in the common law, at least for land and goods, has been to recognise only a dominant right of ownership with a limited number of lesser property rights. According to the 'numerus clausus' principle, the courts cannot add new lesser property rights in the common law.[27] This calls for an explanation, particularly if a property right is a right to the benefit or some aspect of the benefit of the object of property, since

[23] It is sometimes thought that because the intellectual property right does not encompass all the benefit of the intangible, without limit in time, it cannot be a property right: see Spence (n 12) 13–14; MA Lemley, 'Faith-Based IP' (2015) 62 *UCLA Law Review* 1328.

[24] Famously Honoré enumerated the different aspects of benefit encompassed in the standard right of ownership: AM Honoré, 'Ownership' in *Making Law Bind* (Oxford University Press, 1987).

[25] For versions of the bundle of rights theory, see TC Grey, 'The Disintegration of Property' in *Nomos XII: Property* (New York University Press, 1980); SR Munzer, *A Theory of Property* (Cambridge University Press, 1990) 23; SN Glackin, 'Back to Bundles: Deflating Property Rights, Again' (2014) 20 *Legal Theory* 1; H Breakey, 'Two Concepts of Property: Ownership of Things and Property in Activities' (2011) *The Philosophical Forum* 239, 239.

[26] Examples of criticism of the bundle of rights approach include J Penner, 'The "Bundle of Rights" Picture of Property (1996) 43 *UCLA Law Rev* 711, 714–15, 721–22; TW Merrill and HE Smith, 'What Happened to Property in Law and Economics?' (2001) 111 *Yale Law Journal* 357.

[27] See generally B Rudden, 'Economic Theory v. Property Law: The "Numerus Clausus" Problem' in J Eekelaar and J Bell (eds), *Oxford Essays in Jurisprudence: Third Series* (Oxford University Press, 1987).

it would seem that the benefit of an object of property can in theory be divided up into different aspects of benefit protected by distinct property rights in any number of possible ways. The bundle of rights theory suggests that this restriction may be misconceived. It might be thought to have arisen instead from the right against interference approach, on the assumption that, if a property right is a right against interference, it should normally or ideally be a right to the whole object of property.[28] The basis for the numerus clausus restriction is considered in the next chapter.

The Right of Control Approach

Some commentators argue that a property right should be understood fundamentally not as a right against interference but as a 'right of control' over the object of property, or, as it has also been put, a power to determine the use of the property, or a right of private 'sovereignty' or 'agenda-setting authority' over the property.[29] The right of control or power approach is preferable to the right against interference approach. The right of control of property is, like the right to benefit, a right necessarily related to a particular thing. These two approaches may seem equivalent, since a right of control confers a right to determine how the benefit is applied. But in my view the right to benefit approach is the more fundamental, and the right to control approach is not always apt.

A right to all the benefit of an object of property – a right of ownership – by implication carries with it a right of control over its use, as an aspect of the entire benefit of the property, but a lesser property right may not carry a right of control over any part of the property. The property right carries a legal power to secure the benefit but the benefit may be obtainable only by taking action against the owner, who has control. This may be true of a restrictive covenant, for example. This does not mean the right is a personal right against the owner. It is a right to part of the benefit of the property, enforceable against the owner for the time being, whoever that may be. A beneficiary under a trust has a property right with respect to some aspect of the benefit of the trust property, without any right of control over the

[28] The dominant right of ownership approach tends to be associated with but is distinct from the idea of a property right as a right against interference. In other words, the 'information costs' theory of property rights (concerning strong ownership rights) can be distinguished from the 'gatekeeper' theory (concerning the right against interference), though it seems difficult to pin down the difference without recognising the right to the benefit of property. See eg JY Stern, 'What Is the Right to Exclude and Why Does It Matter?' in J Penner and M Otsuka (eds), *Property Theory: Legal and Political Perspectives* (Cambridge University Press, 2018); HE Smith 'Exclusion versus Governance: Two Strategies for Delineating Property Rights' (2002) 31 *Journal of Legal Studies* 453.

[29] See eg L Katz, 'Property's Sovereignty' (2017) 18 *Theoretical Inquiries in Law* 299; ER Claeys, 'Property 101: Is Property a Thing or a Bundle?' 32 *Seattle University Law Review* 617 (2009); A Dorfman, 'Private Ownership' (2010) 16 *Legal Theory* 1; KM Wyman 'The New Essentialism in Property' (2017) 9 *Journal of Legal Analysis* 183.

trust property. The beneficiary can take action against the trustee to secure the benefit to which the beneficiary is entitled (or have the trustee replaced), but the beneficiary has no right of control of the trust property. It is a characteristic feature of a trust, as considered further below, that the right to the benefit of the property is dissociated from the right to control it. The trustee has the right to control the trust property but is not the full owner in the ordinary sense because trustees do not have the right to apply the trust property for their own benefit. Similarly, in a case of public ownership or public stewardship, the public authority has the right of control of the property but is not genuinely the owner (or at least the private owner) of that property because it does not have right to the benefit of the property.

Where a claim arises to protect a property right, the remedial right arises as a matter of remedial consistency out of a primary right to the benefit of the property. As discussed above, this is the case with respect to the claim for licence fee damages and the claim for restitution. Furthermore, as considered further below, where C has a proprietary claim for restitution against D, C can invoke the tracing rules to establish a proprietary claim against replacement property and this must also be based on a right to the benefit of the property.

Finally, it is surely the benefit of the property that is fundamentally valuable rather than the right of control. The right of control must be derivative of the more fundamental right to the benefit of the property. When property is considered in the context of a theory of distributive justice, it is the allocation of the benefit of things that property is understood to be fundamentally concerned with, as considered further in the next chapter.

Personal Rights as Objects of Property

Claims to recover money are commonplace but not straightforward. Typically nowadays money takes the form of a contractual right such as the right to the balance on a bank account. Take the standard case of a payment from C's bank account to D, made at C's direction where C has made a mistake, or at the direction of C's agent or trustee with the apparent but not actual authority of C. C has a claim against D to recover the payment, nowadays described as a claim for restitution.[30] In dealing with this claim, the law has faced problems arising from the conventional understanding of private property. It is thought that the claim cannot be based on C's ownership of the money as property, since it is thought that C's right to the money in a bank account is purely a contractual matter between C and the bank, and so no property rights are involved. This is one reason why it is thought that the claim must have an entirely different basis in a principle of unjust

[30] *Lipkin Gorman v Karpnale* [1991] 2 AC 548 is taken to be the standard authority, though it is also clearly concerned with property.

enrichment.[31] But, if C's right to the money is indeed purely contractual, there can be no basis for a claim against D at all, unless there has been a breach of contract to which D is an accessory, or D is liable for procuring a breach of the contract. As a matter of remedial consistency, the claim for restitution against D must arise, by virtue of the mistaken or unauthorised payment, from a prior right of C's against D relating to the money, and this cannot be C's contractual right against the bank.

It is true that, as between C and the bank, the position is purely contractual, but this is not the entirety of the legal position concerning C's money. Consider first a contractual right of payment such as a bank draft or bond or other financial instrument. Such a right of payment is sometimes thought of as a form of property – for example, trust property often consists of such rights as investments, which are interchangeable as investments with land or goods. The right to payment is not itself a property right – it is not a right against the debtor to the benefit of an object of property. The creditor has a personal right against the debtor, which can be enforced against the debtor's general property, in competition with other such claims. The distinction between a personal right and a property right is fundamental.[32]

However, such a contractual right to payment can itself be an object of property.[33] The creditor, though having a purely personal right against the debtor, can also own this personal right as an object of property: the creditor has a right to the benefit of the right to payment as an object of property. As property owner, the creditor has a power to transfer this object of property and so to realise its value, and also a claim for restitution to recover the object of property from a recipient of an invalid transfer. Similarly, a bank account can be an object of property. The right to payment in the form of a bank account is divisible, and a payment from the account, which is a transfer of a right of payment to the recipient, is a transfer of property. An unauthorised transfer from the account is an invalid transfer of property, which should give rise to a claim for restitution to recover the transfer. The property right over the contractual right as an object of property is not itself a right against interference. There is no need for a right against interference at all.[34]

[31] See eg C Webb, *Reason and Restitution* (Oxford University Press, 2016) 93–94; D Fox, *Property Rights in Money* (Oxford University Press, 2008) [1.77]; TRS Cutts, 'Modern Money Had and Received' (2018) 38 *Oxford Journal of Legal Studies* 1.

[32] See eg RM Goode, 'Ownership and Obligation in Commercial Transactions' (1987) 103 *Law Quarterly Review* 433, 433. There are analyses that doubt the basic distinction in part because of the difficulty of explaining property with respect to personal rights: see eg Penner (n 1) 130–32; S Worthington, 'The Disappearing Divide Between Property and Obligation: The Impact of Aligning Legal Analysis and Commercial Expectation' (2007) 42 *Texas International Law Journal* 917.

[33] Historically English law did not recognise contractual rights as property rights that could be transferred by assignment. Assignment as a matter of course was allowed in s 136 of the Law of Property Act 1925, though the effect of assignment has been achievable for much longer in equity.

[34] As noted by Penner (n 1) 128. The creditor as property owner may have a claim against someone who has wrongfully procured an invalid transfer, for example by deception or duress, as a property owner would have with respect to other forms of property, but this is not a matter of interference with the ownership of the right to payment as an object of property. The creditor can have a right against interference in the performance of the contract by the debtor, but this is a matter of protecting the

The Trust

The trust is an important part of private property law, but it cannot be satisfactorily explained under the conventional analysis of private property in terms of a right against interference or a right of control. In a trust, the trustee T holds the trust property for the benefit of a beneficiary B or beneficiaries on the terms of the trust. An express trust is established by a settlor, who creates the trust by transferring the trust property to T on the stipulated terms. T has control of the property and is the owner, or appears to be, as far as third parties are concerned. T is registered as owner, where the trust property is the sort of property for which registration of ownership is required, and T has the legal power to sell the property to a third party. However, T has a duty to B to use and apply the trust property (or its proceeds of sale, which become trust property) for the benefit of B, in accordance with the terms of the trust. The nature of the trust has been controversial, in particular with respect to B's right to the trust property. On the conventional understanding, it would seem that T must be the owner of the trust property because T exercises the owner's right against interference and right of control. B has neither a right against interference nor a right of control. It would seem that B must have merely a personal right against T correlated with T's duty to use and apply the property for B's benefit.

However, this understanding is impossible to reconcile with the remedial position. If B has only a personal right against T, and the trust property is owned by T, then if T fails to transfer trust property to B in breach of trust, B is merely a personal creditor of T's in competition in the event of T's bankruptcy with T's other creditors. In fact, the trust property is not available for the payment of T's liabilities to personal creditors. It is available exclusively for the satisfaction of B's claim to the trust property under the trust, and B is not in competition with T's creditors with respect to the trust property. Furthermore, if T makes an unauthorised disposal of trust property, B has a proprietary claim against the recipient to recover the property. As a matter of remedial consistency, the legal position is inconsistent with B's having merely a personal right against T. A personal right against T cannot give rise to a proprietary claim binding creditors and third party recipients. B must have a property right in the trust property.[35]

It is indeed the orthodox understanding of trusts law that B has a property right in the trust property, even though this is difficult to reconcile with the conventional understanding of private property. The legal position is readily explained on the suggested approach. B has a right to a certain part of the benefit of the property as defined in the terms of the trust. The beneficiaries between them have the right or

creditor's contractual right against the debtor; it is not a right with respect to the creditor's ownership of the right to payment as an object of property: see also Jaffey (n 13).

[35] Supporters of the right of exclusion theory argue instead for the 'persistent right' theory: see B McFarlane and R Stevens, 'The Nature of Equitable Property' (2010) 4 *Journal of Equity* 1.

rights to all the benefit of the trust property, apart from the right of control over it, which is an aspect of benefit given to T, and includes the power to enforce the right against interference by third parties. The separation of the right to benefit (other than control) and the right of control is what characterises the trust. Where there is more than one beneficiary, and there is an allocation of benefit amongst different beneficiaries, it is possible to have arrangements for the allocation of benefit that would not be possible if the property were in the control of the property right-holders themselves and not a trustee. There can be consecutive or conditional or discretionary interests in the property, for example. This is the practical advantage of the trust as a device for property-holding.[36]

The trust illustrates the point that a property right is fundamentally a right to the benefit of the property. However, there is more to an express trust than property rights. In an express trust, there is an appointed trustee who has agreed to assume the position of trustee, and becomes responsible for investing and taking care of the property and distributing it in accordance with the terms of the trust. The trustee surely could not incur this responsibility merely by virtue of having a right of control of the property, as a matter of property ownership: the duty arises only because the trustee has agreed to assume the position of trustee. This is clear from the fact that the recipient of an unauthorised transfer of trust property does not incur such a duty through the receipt of the property, though the beneficiary's property right does persist and bind the recipient. The beneficiary's personal right to the performance of the trust against an express trustee is in the nature of a contractual right, in the sense that it arises from the trustee's agreement or consent (regardless of whether there is also a contract under the common law rules). In consequence, B can have a personal claim against the trustee for compensation for loss of trust property. As a matter of remedial consistency, such a claim must arise from a personal right against the trustee. As considered further below, a personal right to compensation can arise against a recipient who has disposed of or used up trust property if the recipient knew or ought to have known that the transfer was unauthorised.

Thus the requirement of remedial consistency implies that the express trust has two dimensions, in the sense of separate bodies of law that operate in tandem – one governing property rights in the trust property and the other personal rights against the trustee. The property right generates the proprietary claim for restitution of trust property, and the personal right generates the claim for compensation against the trustee for the loss of trust property. The property right arises from the act of the settlor, the original owner of the trust property, in transferring the property to the trustee and creating the interests of the beneficiaries, and the personal right arises from the trustee's agreement to act as trustee on the terms of the trust.

[36] This account follows P Jaffey, 'Explaining the Trust' (2015) 131 *Law Quarterly Review* 377.

On the traditional understanding, the trust is a product of the ancient division between common law and equity. The trustee has legal title and the beneficiary has an equitable interest or equitable title, and the relevant law developed in equity appears to be a sort of hybrid of property and contract, based on the idea of 'conscience', as a peculiarly equitable form of moral principle that is said to be behind the rules of equity. On the suggested analysis – which follows directly from the requirement of remedial consistency and from the distinction in principle between property and contract – the division between law and equity, and the associated concepts of conscience and unconscionability, should be understood as particular ways of understanding contract or property rights as they were developed in equity. It would be better, on this understanding, if the archaic language were jettisoned.[37]

Proprietary Claims and Tracing

A proprietary claim is available to a trust beneficiary to recover an unauthorised transfer because a beneficiary has a right to the benefit of the trust property and this right survives an unauthorised transfer of trust property. The recipient of an unauthorised transfer has not undertaken to act as an express trustee; as noted above, the recipient does not incur the duty of distribution or investment of an express trustee. The proprietary claim is simply the property dimension of the trust, without the contractual dimension. The recipient has the right of control of the property and the beneficiary retains the right to the benefit of it in the form of the proprietary claim. This arrangement is traditionally described as a constructive trust. If the property is disposed of or used up by the recipient, the beneficiary's proprietary claim will be reduced or eliminated as the property is lost.

Under the law of tracing, if the recipient D exchanges the trust property for different property, the proprietary claim of the beneficiary, C, attaches to the exchange property; and if the trust property is a fungible and D mixes it with equivalent property, the claim attaches to a part of the mixture. C can assert the proprietary claim over the traceable proceeds of the original trust property. Although the tracing rules have a long history, their rationale is not obvious. Why does the claim to the original trust property jump from one object of property to another, as it is said to do under the tracing rules? If a property right is a right to a specific object of property, should it not simply lapse or disappear if the original object of property is no longer identifiable in D's hands, because it has been disposed of or absorbed into a mixture?[38]

[37] Though to the contrary it may be enjoying something of a revival: see eg SC Agnew, 'The Meaning and Significance of Conscience in Private Law' (2018) 77 *Cambridge Law Journal* 479; I Samet-Porat, *Equity: Conscience Goes to Market* (Oxford University Press, 2018).

[38] There is a considerable literature on this contentious topic: see eg A Nair, *Claims to Traceable Proceeds* (Oxford University Press, 2018); M Raczynska, *The Law of Tracing in Commercial Transactions*

The right to benefit approach I have suggested above indicates how tracing should be understood in principle. With respect to a mixture – where the trust property is a fungible – if C has a right to the benefit of the property and if the original property is interchangeable with other property in the mixture, it is fair for the benefit to which C is now entitled to be a part of the benefit of the mixture. The exchange property rule can be understood in a similar way if any object of property, for the purposes of determining an appropriate remedy, is treated as simply a repository of wealth equivalent to another object of property of comparable value, which is surely the assumption behind tracing.[39]

The crucial practical question in tracing is what property the tracing claim should attach to. In principle, it would seem that it should be that part of the benefit of D's general property that is derived from the invalid transfer, or in other words the value of the transfer less any loss to D consequent on the transfer. This would mean that C's proprietary tracing claim is a distinctive type of lesser property right: a right over D's general property to an abstract part of it defined under a causation test. This can explain tracing and is possible in principle. By contrast, it seems impossible to make sense of tracing if a property right is a right against interference or a right of control.

Restitution of Money Payments

In principle, the claim for restitution of a money payment should be a proprietary claim based on a right to the benefit of the property, but the claim for restitution at common law, nowadays said to be an unjust enrichment claim, is personal. This is contrary to the requirement of remedial consistency. A beneficiary under a trust has a proprietary claim to recover trust property invalidly transferred by the trustee, but an absolute owner whose money has been invalidly transferred normally has only a personal claim.

The problem at common law is that the common law never developed the conceptual tools required to give effect to a proprietary claim. At common law, title to money paid into an account necessarily passes to the recipient as the account holder of money in the account. With respect to tangible money as cash, title passes to the recipient, even if the transfer was invalid, in order to protect the role of money as currency. Money cannot perform the role of currency unless the person who has possession and control has the legal authority to transfer it. Since title to money is lost in a transfer at common law, no proprietary claim is possible.

(Oxford University Press, 2018); J English and J Hafeez-Baig *The Law of Tracing* (Federation Press, 2021).

[39] This reflects the approach taken in P Jaffey, 'Proprietary Claims to Recover Mistaken and Unauthorised Payments' in P Devonshire and R Havelock (eds), *The Impact of Equity and Restitution in Commerce* (Hart, 2018).

A proprietary claim requires the recognition of a right to the benefit of the money separate from the right to control it as ostensible owner, which goes with common law title. A right to the benefit of property developed in equity as a beneficiary's right under a trust and allows for a proprietary claim in equity. Some commentators are convinced that proprietary claims should not be available except with respect to trust property. But there is no reason why the concept of a right to the benefit of property, along with the separation of the right to benefit from the right of control, cannot be employed to provide a proprietary claim for all invalid transfers. This is necessary to give effect to the requirement of remedial consistency with respect to invalid transfers of property. Indeed, as pointed out above, the concept of the right to the benefit of the property is necessary to give a satisfactory explanation of any claim to recover an invalid money payment.

At common law, where the claim has always been personal, it is sometimes said that the court can allow a proprietary claim by way of a 'remedial constructive trust'.[40] The expression is used to signify that the trust is created by the court through its award of a remedy, instead of arising directly from the invalid transfer, as where there is an unauthorised transfer of trust property by a trustee. The usage is confusing: it would be appropriate to describe the constructive trust as remedial in the latter case also, because the beneficiary's claim is a remedial right not a primary right. The award of a remedial constructive trust is widely regarded as illegitimate because it is understood to involve a judicial power to create and to expropriate property rights. It gives C a proprietary right, at the expense of creditors who lose the right to share in this part of D's general property, which would otherwise have gone to satisfy the debt to them. This is an example of a remedial discretion, in the sense of a discretion to depart from the subsisting legal position, which is not normally acceptable, as discussed in chapter three. It involves remedial inconsistency, because the remedial right recognised and ordered is inconsistent with the subsisting legal rights.[41]

This objection to the remedial constructive trust is sound if one accepts the conventional understanding that C's property right did not survive the transfer, so that from that time C had only a personal right, until a new property right was created by the court. But the remedial constructive trust is defensible if it is understood to recognise and enforce the property right that C ought to have had or, one might say, implicitly did have, as a matter of remedial consistency, from the time of the invalid transfer. On this assumption, there is no objection to the remedial constructive trust on the ground of remedial inconsistency.

[40] See eg *Re Omegas Group* 16 F.3d 1443 (US 6th Cir, 1994). See E Sherwin, 'Topic II: The Availability and Justification of Property-based Remedies in Restitution' (2012) 92 *Boston University Law Review* 885; A Kull, 'Restitution in Bankruptcy: Reclamation and Constructive Trust' (1998) 72 *American Bankruptcy Law Journal* 265.

[41] For the same reason some commentators have regarded tracing rules as rules governing the distribution of D's money, equivalent to rules governing distribution in bankruptcy. See eg H Dagan, *The Law and Ethics of Restitution* (Cambridge University Press, 2004) 303–04; C Rotherham, 'The Metaphysics of Tracing: Substituted Title and Property Rhetoric' (1996) 34 *Osgoode Hall Law Journal* 321.

To the contrary, remedial consistency requires that the remedial constructive trust should be awarded to give effect to the proprietary claim.

Where C has a proprietary claim for restitution to recover an invalid transfer, C should also in principle have a personal claim for compensation for loss where any part of the property to which C is entitled has been lost, in circumstances in which it is justified to hold D responsible for the loss. As discussed above in connection with conversion, the requirement of remedial consistency shows that a remedial regime should distinguish between these two types of claim. The distinction is not recognised at common law: claims in conversion are understood as purely wrong-based claims for compensation, and claims to recover money payments at common law are understood purely as restitutionary claims arising from the receipt of the transfer. In equity, however, in connection with unauthorised transfers of trust property, the law does distinguish between two claims, roughly along the lines suggested: these are the equitable proprietary claim and the claim for knowing receipt.[42] The equitable proprietary claim is a claim to recover the traceable proceeds of the transfer, and by means of the knowing receipt claim the beneficiary can in effect recover the value of trust property lost, if the recipient knew or ought to have known that the transfer was invalid.

Summary

The requirement of remedial consistency has important implications for property law. It implies that there is a right to the benefit of the property. The right to the benefit of property is one side of a primary liability relation, in the sense that it binds others by way of a primary liability not a primary duty. It is the basic form of property right. It gives rise to the basic claims to protect property, the claim for restitution of an invalid transfer and the claim for licence fee damages for unauthorised use. It is intrinsically related to things as objects of property. It may be accompanied by a right against interference or a right to compensation for loss from interference, but this right cannot be equated with the property right itself. The recognition of the right to the benefit of the property assists in explaining the requirement for an object of property, and the possibility of lesser property rights as well as the right of ownership. It also helps to explain tracing, proprietary claims, the trust, and intangible things as objects of property, including intellectual property and rights of payment as objects of property.

[42] See further Jaffey (n 3) and (n 36).

10

Private Property and the Standpoint Limitation

Introduction

Property rights are rights, good against everyone, to the benefit of things as objects of property. A property right is directly protected through a claim for restitution to recover property, or a claim for licence fee damages for payment for the unauthorised use of property, or specific enforcement to exclude other people from the benefit of the property. It may also be indirectly protected by a right against interference or loss caused by interference, which presupposes the right to benefit.

The basic issues in property law include what things should be recognised as capable of being objects of property in which a property right can subsist; what types of property right should be capable of subsisting; and how someone can acquire a property right. One can distinguish two broad approaches, corresponding to the corrective justice and distributive justice approaches, and they face problems comparable to those discussed in earlier chapters in connection with contract and negligence. Just as for negligence and contract, my suggestion is that an approach based on distributive justice subject to the standpoint limitation can help to explain how private property law has developed at common law.

The Distributive Justice Approach

On the distributive justice approach, all things from which people can derive a benefit belong fundamentally to everyone in society and should be subject to a property regime governing rights in things as objects of property based on distributive justice.[1] According to EAL, the regime should allocate the benefits of things in such a way as to maximise the aggregate benefit derived from them. This is understood under EAL to involve maximising benefit through the use of things by way of incentives for investment in the creation or improvement or productive

[1] See eg D Attas, 'Private Property' and P Vallentyne, 'Taxation, Redistribution and Property' in A Marmor (ed), *The Routledge Companion to the Philosophy of Law* (Routledge, 2015); L Murphy and T Nagel, *The Myth of Ownership* (Oxford University Press, 2002).

use of things. Other distributive justice regimes might in addition take account of considerations such as need, equality or fairness, reward, and personal autonomy or personal development in designing the property regime. A property regime might provide for common use and access to property, or state control of property, as well as private property.[2]

Property rights under a regime based on the distributive justice approach might appear to lack the characteristic features of property rights in the law (just as for contract and negligence as discussed previously). It would seem that fundamentally each person has a right against and a duty to the state with respect to the property regime, and accordingly a right to some part of society's property, rather than a fundamental right to particular property prevailing over the interests of others and the public interest.[3] On this understanding, it may seem that if C loses property to D through an invalid transfer, C's claim should in principle be a claim against the state to restore C's property entitlement, rather than a claim against D with respect to the property transferred. D may be accountable to the state for any surplus over D's due share of the society's property, which should be allocated to someone else. It would be possible also to have criminal sanctions against wrongful interference. It may be convenient to allow C a claim against D to recover the property transfer and restore the prior allocation, but it would seem that this is really a device for upholding C's entitlement vis-à-vis the state. Thus it would seem that if a bilateral claim is allowed, C should have to show that restoring the prior position would actually be in accordance with distributive justice, so that if the prior allocation of property to C was excessive, or fell short with respect to D, relative to what distributive justice would prescribe, full recovery of the invalid transfer would not be justified. There would be no right to specific property binding others independently of the justice of the prior distribution.

It would seem that the distributive justice approach cannot explain the most basic features of private property law as it developed at common law,[4] that is to say an individual right to specific property giving rise to bilateral rights and remedies, independent of the societal distribution of property, on the basis of which an owner has a claim in interpersonal justice to recover specific property. One might conclude that the only way to explain private law claims to recover property must be that they serve to protect the public interest in the ordinary use of property by discouraging unauthorised seizures rather than by reference to any genuine bilateral individual property rights.[5]

[2] The regime also has to resolve practical questions such as whether a possible object of property has well-defined boundaries: see eg K Gray, 'Property in Thin Air' [1991] *Cambridge Law Journal* 252.

[3] See L Murphy, 'The Artificial Morality of Private Law' (2020) 70 *University of Toronto Law Journal* 453, 483; see also Murphy and Nagel (n 1). See also JL Coleman, 'Corrective Justice and Property Rights' (1994) 11 *Social Philosophy and Policy* 124.

[4] See generally Murphy (n 3). This reflects the objections to the distributive justice approach made in the corrective justice literature, as discussed in ch 4.

[5] See eg J Waldron, 'Property Law' in D Patterson (ed), *A Companion to Philosophy of Law and Legal Theory* (Blackwell, 2nd edn 2010) 22–23.

But can it really be the case that under a regime based on distributive justice there can be no genuine right to specific property supporting bilateral rights? Can there not be such a right in the form of a derivative right in distributive justice, in the sense discussed earlier? If private property is recognised in a distributive justice regime, it is because the regime recognises the principle that an individual should receive the benefit of an investment made in particular property. One might call this the private property principle. Such a principle cannot be given effect in isolation. The regime has to determine to what extent and in what way it should be given effect. It has to take account of considerations of distributive justice that weigh against the operation of the principle, as well as considerations in favour, and it has to specify accordingly what can be an object of property and what property rights there are and how they are acquired. The private property principle is a principle of distributive justice in the sense that it contributes to the allocation of benefits and harms as a component of a distributive justice regime. This principle would seem capable of giving rise to bilateral rights with respect to specific property, as derivative rights in distributive justice.

However, it is difficult to see how this can explain the common law. There is a problem that such a regime would have to be constructed in a single exercise as an integrated regime with interdependent parts, and this could not have happened over a series of decisions at common law. On the distributive justice approach, it would seem that a private property regime must be constructed 'top-down' by the legislature, and not 'bottom-up' by the courts, incrementally rule by rule.[6]

Furthermore, even though a claim under the private property principle is based on C's right to the benefit of an investment in the property, and so in principle can bind others, this would presumably be the case only as part of an appropriate regime. In particular, although the claim does not in principle require C to establish that it restores a prior position consistent with distributive justice, the claim would nevertheless seem to be in tension with other considerations of distributive justice if the distribution of property across society is not justifiable as a matter of distributive justice. Thus it seems doubtful whether this approach can actually account for the bilateral rights of private law.

A further problem concerns the particular form of the property regime. The possible benefits of things as objects of property can be divided up in many different ways. A regime can recognise different types of property right, as rights to different aspects of the benefit of an object of property. As discussed in the previous chapter, this is recognised in the 'bundle of rights' theory. There are many different forms that a property regime could take, for example, as mentioned above, as to which things can be objects of property, what sort of property rights are recognised, and how property rights are acquired, and also how use is regulated. The possibilities include common ownership and public ownership. The

[6] See eg RA Epstein, *Design for Liberty: Private Property, Public Administration and the Rule of Law* (Harvard University Press, 2011) 99.

issue under the distributive justice approach is which arrangement will best promote distributive justice. The common law developed a regime with a dominant ownership right, along with, in land, a limited number of lesser property rights (the numerus clausus principle), and little or no public interest regulation of use or public rights of access, as considered in the previous chapter. It did not adopt a complex, 'fragmented' regime, involving, for example, a division of the benefit of objects of property amongst various parties with different lesser property rights, public rights of access and regulation of use, and residual weak rights of ownership, or even a division of benefit that involves nothing amounting to a right of ownership, as some supporters of the bundle of rights theory argue might be preferable, at least in some circumstances.

There is a strong economic efficiency argument for the dominant ownership model.[7] A dominant ownership right creates a strong link between an owner's investment in an object of property and the return from it, and so promotes the most productive use of the object of property. It also promotes the marketability of objects of property for sale or rent because for a buyer or renter there is a single owner to deal with and fewer lesser property rights to be concerned with, and this means that the property is likely to reach the hands of the most productive owner. This seems a powerful argument; indeed it is surely irresistible with respect to constantly circulating forms of property such as goods and in particular money. Under a fragmented regime, by contrast, objects of property are less marketable and the link between an individual right-holder and the return from his investment in the property is weaker. However, 'progressive property' theorists argue that the dominant ownership model is inflexible and may operate unfairly, and that a fragmented regime may be preferable for certain types of property in certain contexts. With respect to land, it might be appropriate to allow public access or to facilitate more complex use of land involving multiple interests that may provide other types of benefit that are not available under a dominant ownership regime, even at the cost of hindering investment and marketability.[8]

Even if the efficiency argument is correct, it cannot plausibly explain the common law since the judges have never been in a position to determine the overall form of the private property regime, and they do not seem to have actually considered and adopted the economic efficiency argument, or considered and

[7] See TW Merrill and HE Smith, 'Optimal Standardisation in the Law of Property: The Numerus Clausus Principle' (2000) 110 *Yale Law Review* 1; H Hansmann and R Kraakman, 'Property, Contract and Verification: the Numerus Clausus Problem and the Divisibility of Rights' (2002) 31 *Journal of Legal Studies* 373.

[8] See eg GS Alexander et al, 'A Statement of Progressive Property' (2009) 94 *Cornell Law Review* 743; GS Alexander, 'The Human Flourishing Theory' in H Dagan and BC Zipursky, *Research Handbook on Private Law Theory* (Edward Elgar, 2020); LA Fennell, 'Property beyond exclusion' (2019) 61 *William & Mary Law Review* 521 and 'Property as the law of complements' in Dagan and Zipursky (ibid); Under a fragmented approach property law, internal governance becomes more important: see eg GS Alexander, 'Governance Property' (2012) 160 *University of Pennsylvania Law Review* 1853; TW Merrill and HE Smith, 'The Property/Contract Interface' (2001) 101 *Columbia Law Review* 773.

dismissed the contrary arguments, any more than they have considered whether and when private property would be justified compared with common ownership or state ownership, or whether the overall societal distribution of property is justified.

Thus the distributive justice approach has difficulty explaining the justice of bilateral claims in private law and the form of the private property regime (echoing the objections made earlier with respect to contract and negligence). However, just as for contract and negligence, the objections to the distributive justice approach can be overcome if the law is understood under the standpoint limitation, as I discuss below. But, first, as for contract and negligence, the difficulties with a distributive justice approach have contributed to the plausibility and appeal of the corrective justice approach.

The Corrective Justice Approach

According to the 'Lockean labour principle' approach to private property,[9] a thing is unowned until someone brings it into ownership by 'applying labour' to it, for example by taking it into possession or control. An individual has a moral power to acquire a moral right over specific property in this way, which the law should recognise as a legal right through the law of private property. Ownership depends exclusively on the exercise of this moral power, and not on the interests of anyone else, or the public interest, in having the benefit of the thing. In other words, distributive justice is excluded. This approach does account for at least the basic character of private property law: an individual right to the benefit of a specific thing, binding everyone else and so generating bilateral rights and remedies. It explains how private property law can be legitimately constructed 'bottom up' through the common law, and need not be constructed by way of legislation 'top down' as the distributive justice approach requires.[10]

The way the Lockean labour principle should be understood has remained elusive and there is no canonical version. One might think that it is concerned with reward or desert for an investment in return for the public benefit accruing from the investment, but this would imply that it is a matter of distributive justice (as for the private property principle referred to above). It is understood instead as a principle of individual liberty or autonomy that justifies a moral power to secure a right to property independently of any other interests or the public interest. It is said to be based on a right of self-ownership, from which is derived a right to

[9] Or principle of 'justice in acquisition': R Nozick, *Anarchy, State and Utopia* (Blackwell, 1974) 150ff. Derived from J Locke, *Two Treatises on Government*, discussed by J Waldron, *The Right to Private Property* (Oxford University Press, 1990) ch 6. See also Epstein (n 6). See also A Brudner with JM Nadler, *The Unity of the Common Law* (Oxford University Press, 2nd edn 2013) ch 3.

[10] Epstein (n 6) 99.

labour and then a right to the product of labour in the form of property to which labour is applied.[11]

The main objection to the principle is that it does not provide an adequate justification for C to acquire a right with respect to specific property that overrides the interest of anyone else.[12] How can taking possession or control of property have this powerful moral effect? Because it prevails over the interests of everyone else, C's property right limits the state's moral right to override it. The state cannot impose common ownership or public ownership, or curtail rights of ownership in favour of the lesser property rights of others or of the general public, or regulate property use, or impose taxation that depletes the property, beyond what is necessary to protect the property rights acquired under the principle.

The Lockean labour principle approach in its original form attempts to accommodate the objection of unfair preference to C through certain limitations: first, that C can only acquire property insofar as there is 'enough and as good' left over for others to acquire on the same basis; and secondly, that C cannot secure the right to more property than C can actually make use of.[13] These limitations have been as controversial as the principle itself. They seem to reflect a concern for distributive justice, though the principle itself is supposed to be independent of distributive justice, and they prompt the question why, if distributive justice is relevant to this extent, it should not be taken further into account, though this would seem to involve abandoning the Lockean labour principle approach altogether.[14]

Although this approach may be able to explain the basic common law right to specific property binding others and giving rise to a claim to recover property, independent of the distribution of property across society, there are other features of the common law that it has difficulty with. The principle would appear to apply to intangible products of labour such as intellectual property, but intellectual property is not usually recognised at common law (as considered further below). Also, at first blush it may seem that the Lockean labour principle approach can explain only rights of ownership and not lesser property rights, and so might be able to account for the traditional dominant ownership approach of the common law. However, there is a problem that owners should be able to create lesser property rights in whatever way they choose by granting such rights in their property, and this is not what is found in the law under the numerus clausus principle.

Another problem is the 'historic entitlement' or 'unbroken chain' problem.[15] Initial ownership arising under the Lockean labour principle is the right to all the

[11] Waldron (n 9) ch 6.

[12] See generally Murphy (n 3), especially at 462–65; J Waldron, *The Rule of Law and the Measure of Property* (Cambridge University Press, 2012) 26–41; M Chatterjee, 'Lockean Copyright versus Lockean Property' (2010) 12 *Journal of Legal Analysis* 136. See also Murphy and Nagel (n 1) 8–10, 31–37.

[13] Waldron (n 9) ch 6.

[14] On one view, the provisos imply an assumption of equal ownership of natural resources: see M Otsuka, *Libertarianism Without Inequality* (Oxford University Press, 2003); Vallentyne (n 1).

[15] See Waldron (n 12) 32; Nozick (n 9) 150ff; Murphy (n 3). See also E Sherwin, 'Locke and Private Law' in Dagan and Zipursky (eds) (n 8) 182.

benefit of the thing, encompassing a power of voluntary transfer. Ownership in general depends on the valid application of the principle to generate initial ownership, followed by a valid transfer or sequence of valid transfers of ownership. If there was no valid original acquisition, or if there has at any time been a break in the chain – an invalid transfer resulting, for example, from a mistake or misappropriation – the current ownership is morally invalid. A break in the chain is by no means unlikely, but the law ignores the possibility unless a problem comes to light within a very limited period in the recent past. Furthermore, under doctrines such as adverse possession or bona fide purchase the law allows for an owner to lose a property right without having made a voluntary transfer. These rules are understood to be justified in order to protect the interests of others or the public interest in the efficient use of property, but on the Lockean labour principle approach there seems no basis for them.

Finally, to return to a point discussed in chapter five, the Lockean labour principle approach is normally understood not only to explain private property at common law, but also to imply that the legislature should not be free to override individual property rights acquired under the Lockean labour principle any more than the judges should be free to. This means, as pointed out above, that there is no room for compulsory expropriation of property in the public interest, or regulation of use in the public interest, or even taxation, beyond very narrow limits.[16] It is, in other words, the libertarian variant of the corrective justice approach referred to in chapter five. As considered in chapter five, the libertarian approach is not the usual understanding of the corrective justice approach. The usual understanding would appear to be that an approach along the lines of the Lockean labour principle operates with respect to the common law, but at the same time the legislature is not precluded from providing for a different regime in the interests of distributive justice, including the measures just mentioned. This paradoxical feature of the corrective justice approach was considered in chapter five and seems to be an insuperable objection to it.

Distributive Justice Subject to the Standpoint Limitation

The Private Property Principle at Common Law

Distributive justice subject to the standpoint limitation can explain private property in the common law more satisfactorily than either the ordinary distributive justice approach or the corrective justice approach. Take the simple case where C has invested in acquiring or working on some land, not owned by anyone else, which has now come into the hands of D without a valid transfer from C. At common law, in the absence of any prior authority, should C have a right of

[16] Presumably, to the extent necessary for the operation of such a regime: see n 9 above.

ownership of the land binding D? If a legislature were legislating for this situation on the basis of distributive justice, it could construct a property regime that determines what sort of thing can be an object of private property, what property rights can subsist in it, and how such a property right can be acquired, along with provisions for the regulation of property use and for taxation to ensure that the regime overall is distributively just. This cannot be done under the standpoint limitation, that is to say, based on ordinary common knowledge at the time of C's investment in the land. Under the standpoint limitation, it is not possible to determine the contents of a general property regime, or a particular part of a regime. The various elements of a regime are interdependent and have to be determined together, and in part this will be arbitrary and it will involve policy analysis that goes beyond ordinary common knowledge. Common ownership and state ownership are not viable options, because C and others could not do anything in the circumstances to enable the land to be used on either basis. What then is the position at common law, as a matter of distributive justice under the standpoint limitation?

In the circumstances, C has only the choice whether to invest in the land by the application of labour and resources, or not to do so, and the issue is whether, if C does invest, the investment has the effect of giving C a right to the benefit of the land as a result. If the question is put in this way, it does seem right to say that, at least in principle, C should acquire a right to the benefit of the property, since it provides the only feasible basis, under the standpoint limitation, on which it can be used productively, not only for C's benefit but also in the public interest. As a matter of distributive justice under the standpoint limitation, it would seem that the common law should recognise a private property principle, such that when C invests in a thing that is capable of being an object of property C acquires a property right in it. This is the private property principle identified earlier as a component of a distributive justice regime, the effect of the standpoint limitation being to overcome the objections to such a principle identified earlier, that is to say the absence of a full private property regime and the unequal societal distribution of property.

Such a private property principle is like a Lockean labour principle in the sense that it can account for a property right in a specific object of property, and it can justify genuine bilateral rights and remedies, though it is a principle of distributive justice. It follows that, even though it is a matter of distributive justice, private property law can be constructed 'bottom-up', through the decisions of the common law courts, and need not be constructed 'top-down', through legislation.[17] Also, because the rationale is to facilitate the productive use of property in the public interest as well as C's interest, rather than purely to protect C's interest in preference to everyone else's, as under the Lockean labour principle, it makes sense that it should be sufficient for the property merely to have been taken into control or possession by C, even though this may not

[17] See Epstein (n 6).

amount to a substantial investment by C.[18] This approach also makes sense of the limitations associated with the Lockean labour principle mentioned above: that C cannot acquire more property than C can use; and that C cannot acquire property if the effect is to leave inadequate property for others. These limitations can be understood as considerations of distributive justice that it is possible to take into account under the standpoint limitation.

At common law, when C has a claim for restitution of an invalid transfer of property, or a claim for payment for an unauthorised use of property, the principle of interpersonal justice behind the claim is the private property principle understood in this way. Although the principle is a principle of distributive justice, the claim is independent of the societal distribution of property. As considered in the previous chapter, claims to recover invalid money payments, including payments from a bank account, are often said to be claims based on a principle of unjust enrichment but in fact they are claims to recover property. The justifying principle for such claims, which has been at the heart of the controversy over unjust enrichment, is the private property principle.

The Unbroken Chain Problem

The suggested approach avoids the unbroken chain problem mentioned above. The problem arises under the Lockean labour principle approach because the effect of the original acquisition is to give the original owner a right to the benefit of the property that prevails indefinitely over any other interest. The principle operates only once – on first acquisition – with subsequent ownership depending exclusively on a chain of valid transfers. The private property principle on the suggested approach need not operate in this way.

On the suggested approach, on acquisition an owner's property right is a matter of distributive justice subject to the standpoint limitation and can be subject to limitations that are justifiable as a matter of distributive justice on the basis of ordinary common knowledge. On this basis, the property right could be defeasible in certain circumstances. At the same time, the private property principle can operate to protect a new owner in respect of the investment made in the property.[19] Normally the principle should apply only where the new owner has received the property through a voluntary transfer, but it is possible for the private property principle to be applied in the absence of a voluntary transfer, so as to override the

[18] The traditional common law 'first possession' rule need not be understood as a recognition of the Lockean labour principle. Cf CM Rose, 'Possession as the Origin of Property' (1985) 52 *University of Chicago Law Review* 73.

[19] This is not to say that a donee cannot become an owner through a gift, but here the right is derived, in the first instance, from the power of the donee as owner to make a gift. The private property principle can also justify protection independently for the donee once the donee has in some way acted in reliance as owner.

existing ownership without a valid transfer. This is what happens in the case of the doctrines mentioned above. In these types of case, there is a clash between the comparable interests of a possible new right-holder and the existing right-holder in having a property right under the private property principle. It may not be easy to say how the clash should be resolved, but it may be justified in the public interest for the original owner's right to give way in some circumstances.[20]

What can be an Object of Property?

As discussed in the previous chapter, if a property right is the right to the benefit of property, there is no reason why an object of property must be tangible. An intangible thing from which people can derive a benefit through use is capable of being an object of property. The existence of a property right is reflected in the remedies of restitution and licence fee damages. Both intangibles in the nature of intellectual property and intangibles in the nature of rights of payment such as financial instruments and investments are capable of being objects of property.

More particularly, the law recognises as objects of property those things that the law determines should be subject to the operation of the private property principle. To be an object of property, the private property principle must be capable of applying with respect to it. Consequently a thing can be recognised as an object of property if it is well defined and has a stable existence over time, so that one can relate the benefit to be obtained from it to the investment of labour and resources in it.[21] The principle can apply with respect to land and goods, but it can also apply with respect to a contractual right to payment created with a view to its being transferrable, so that it can be held as an investment or realised. Such a contractual right of payment operates as a repository of value created by an investment of money or labour or other resources. Indeed, it is intrinsic to money, whatever its particular form, that it embodies the value of the investment of labour or resources made in acquiring it, and the rationale for protecting it is to protect this investment. Under the private property principle, money in whatever form is necessarily a form of property and should be protected as such.[22] The private property principle can also apply to an intangible in the nature of an idea or invention or information, in the sense that the creator invests in creating the intangible

[20] Reliance is generally regarded as a quite different basis for a claim from the labour principle, ie as a 'counter-principle': see the discussion in Brudner (n 9) 134–43; J Singer, 'The Reliance Interest in Property' (1988) 40 *Stanford Law Review* 611.

[21] In *National Provincial Bank v Ainsworth* [1965] AC 1175 at 1247–48, Lord Wilberforce stated that to be proprietary an interest must be 'definable, identifiable by third parties, capable in its nature of assumption by third parties, and have some degree of permanence and stability'. These criteria make sense with respect to the private property principle but it is not clear whether they make sense under the right of exclusion theory understood in terms of a right against interference or right of control.

[22] Conventionally the claim could take various forms including conversion for coins as goods or a cheque, or common law restitution.

and by way of an intellectual property right receives a right to a defined part of the benefit of the intangible.[23]

Productive investment in a tangible thing such as land or goods is unlikely to be made unless it is an object of property in which a property right will accrue. Only then can someone be confident of having the benefit of the investment. The same is true for a rivalrous intangible such as a right of payment or receivable. However, an intangible in the nature of an idea or invention or information that might be protected through an intellectual property right can be used by any number of people at once. The creator C may be able to use and get a return on the investment made in creating the intangible even if other people are not prevented from using it as well. Giving C an intellectual property right over the intangible increases C's return, but it is impossible to say, on the basis of ordinary common knowledge, what sort of intellectual property regime – for example as to the duration of protection – would be appropriate to achieve a reasonable return for C or a return that is sufficient to support the activity of creation, or whether any intellectual property protection is required at all. This is a matter of policy analysis. For certain types of intangible, no intellectual property protection is available and it does not seem to be necessary. For example, intellectual property protection is not available for new and original steps or moves in sport or dance, or new fashions in clothing.[24]

At common law, the usual rule is that no intellectual property right arises, and intellectual property has generally been recognised only by statute.[25] *Victoria Park Racing & Recreation Grounds Co Ltd v Taylor* held that there was no 'property in a spectacle'.[26] The owners of a racecourse had no property right over the racing as a spectacle and could not stop people who could see the races from outside the ground from reporting the results. The standpoint limitation explains why the common law has not in general recognised intellectual property rights. A principle along the lines of the private property principle has been suggested in a variety of guises, for example the 'sowing and reaping' principle, the 'sweat of the brow' principle, the principle of unfair competition, the principle of misappropriation, or the principle of common law intellectual property, as well as the principle of unjust enrichment.[27] These have all been proposed with a view to achieving the effect of

[23] See further P Jaffey, 'Private Property and Intangibles' [2022] *Conveyancer and Property Lawyer* 47.

[24] See MA Heller and J Salzman, *Mine* (Doubleday, 2021) ch 3.

[25] *Victoria Park Racing & Recreation Grounds Co Ltd v Taylor* [1937] HCA 45. There are possible exceptions such as copyright in unpublished works, passing off and breach of confidence which may be explicable as being originally concerned with protection against personal harm. *International News Service v Associated Press* 248 US 215 (1918) represents a possible exception in the US but appears not to have been influential.

[26] *Victoria Park Racing & Recreation Grounds Co Ltd v Taylor* [1937] HCA 45.

[27] See eg DF Libling, 'The Concept of Property: Property in Intangibles' (1978) 94 *Law Quarterly Review* 103; D Friedmann, 'The Protection of Entitlements via the Law of Restitution – Expectancies and Privacy' (2005) 121 *Law Quarterly Review* 400; RA Epstein, '*International News Service v Associated Press*: Custom and Law as Sources of Property Rights in News' (1992) 78 *Virginia Law Review* 85. The concepts of misappropriation and 'reap where you have sown' were invoked in *INS v Associated Press* 248 US 215, 239 (1918).

a property right to an intangible in the nature of intellectual property at common law, but generally without success.

As mentioned above, the Lockean labour principle approach is said to rely on the concept of self-ownership. The same concept is sometimes said to be the basis for the other liberty rights on the corrective justice approach, such as the moral power to make an agreement and the right against interference with the body. The approach suggested here in terms of distributive justice subject to the standpoint limitation does not rely on the concept of self-ownership, at least in the ordinary sense of ownership that applies in private property law.[28] The right to the person or the body does not arise by application of the private property principle to the person or body as a thing that one can invest in and subsequently obtain the benefit of the investment. Similarly, the right to one's labour, which is understood to be derived from the right of self-ownership and presupposed in the Lockean labour principle approach, is not a right of ownership of labour on the approach suggested above. The right to one's labour is better understood in the common law as the right to determine how one applies one's labour, and is protected in contract by a power to contract for payment for services, and in tort by a right against interference in the exercise of this contractual power. It does not arise from the application of the private property principle to one's labour.[29]

The Property Regime: Types of Property Right

Should the owner of property be able to grant a property right of a sort not hitherto known to the law? This would not override any existing property rights. It would not be open to objection as between grantor and grantee and could bind them personally. However, the numerus clausus principle precludes the creation of a novel form of property right at common law.[30]

The efficiency argument mentioned above supports the dominant ownership model with a limited number of property rights. The opposing progressive property or bundle of rights argument is receptive to a regime with a wider range of property rights. Neither argument is conclusive with respect to a particular property right. There are many possible ways of constructing a regime, and whether a particular property right should be introduced depends on the consequences of introducing the right as part of the regime and is a matter of policy analysis. On

[28] See the discussion in JW Harris, 'Who Owns My Body?' (1996) 16 *Oxford Journal of Legal Studies* 55, 62–65, on 'body ownership rhetoric'.

[29] The theory of unjust enrichment treats the provision of labour as a transfer and payment for it – for example by way of a quantum meruit – as the recovery of a transfer, as if labour were property. This is the standard approach in the restitution textbooks.

[30] See generally as to the numerus clausus principle B Rudden, 'Economic Theory v. Property Law: the Numerus Clausus Problem' in J Bell and J Eekelaar (eds), *Oxford Essays in Jurisprudence*, 3rd series (Oxford University Press, 1987).

the basis of ordinary common knowledge, it is impossible to determine whether a proposed property right ought to be recognised as part of the regime or not. For a purchaser of property or an interest in property, it would be impossible to know whether a new property right might exist or anticipate the introduction of a new property right. Possibly this is why the numerus clausus principle applies at common law. Under the standpoint limitation, a new property right can be recognised only when it has first developed informally, as a customary practice.[31] Here there is good reason to adopt the practice because it is a way of co-ordinating the use of property for the common benefit that the parties ought to know about and defer to, even if a legislature might have reason to override it in the light of other considerations.[32]

The courts did develop the trust, so introducing a distinctive new type of property right. As discussed in the previous chapter, in a trust the beneficiary has a property right in the form of a right to the benefit or some aspect of the benefit of the trust property, but without control, which is with the trustee, the ostensible owner. This was introduced into the law consistently with the standpoint limitation because the beneficiary's property right in the trust property does not adversely affect purchasers. A purchaser of trust property deals with the trustee and is not bound by a beneficiary's property right provided there is no notice of it.

Nuisance

When D uses property in a way that interferes with the use by D's neighbour C of C's property, the law of nuisance determines how the conflict should be resolved.[33] On the conventional analysis of property in terms of rights against interference, nuisance is puzzling because, if a property owner has only a right against interference, any such conflict can be resolved without injustice simply by preventing either or both parties from causing any interference. The problem arises only because both parties have a right to the benefit of their respective properties. By virtue of the right to the benefit of the property, D may be entitled to use D's

[31] This is a standard account of the development of private property rights, derived from David Hume: see Murphy (n 3) 455; Waldron (n 12) 52–60. See also Y Chang and HE Smith, 'The Numerus Clausus Principle, Property, Customs, and the Emergence of New Property Forms' (2015) 100 *Iowa Law Review* 2275.

[32] More generally, configuration of property, that is to say, determining how the benefits of things should be combined for the benefit of individuals and the common good, as discussed in LA Fennell, *Slices & Lumps in Law and Life* (University of Chicago Press, 2019), may emerge by custom but cannot be achieved through adjudication under the standpoint limitation because it has a conventional element. An example is where wells in neighbouring plots place too great a demand on a common water source, leading to overuse. Overuse is damaging to both parties, but a party who abstains may lose out. What is needed is co-ordinated use, by way of 'unitisation', or common ownership, or through quotas, but this cannot be achieved by the common law in adjudication. A similar problem arises with common ownership through overgrazing or overfishing. See Heller and Salzman (n 24), ch 3.

[33] See ch 3.

property in a way that causes some degree of interference with C's use. The question is whether C's or D's use falls within that party's right to benefit, as this is determined by weighing C's and D's rights to the benefit of their respective properties against each other where they ostensibly or prima facie conflict.

A controversial issue is the extent to which the public interest should be taken into account in this weighing exercise to determine the rights of the two parties. On an ordinary distributive justice approach, such as EAL, the issue is how to optimise the benefits of property in the interests of the whole society. The law should take account of all the consequential benefits of C's and D's uses in determining the right balance between the two parties' rights. Where an activity is manufacturing, this might involve establishing what benefit there is to the community from the factory, what the costs to the community are, and whether this location for the factory provides the best balance of costs and benefits (amongst other things). On this understanding, nuisance law is continuous with environmental regulation and planning law.[34] This would seem to make property rights precarious, since they are always liable to be curtailed or lost in order to advance any sort of project that might serve the public interest. There is something in common with the balancing of policy factors in negligence as discussed in chapter four. By contrast, the corrective justice approach would involve comparing the two parties' property rights in isolation and it would exclude the public interest altogether. It is argued that this should mean establishing which party's use is the more fundamental land use.[35] Under the standpoint limitation, the position should depend on what is a fair arrangement amongst property owners on the basis of ordinary common knowledge. This means principally taking into account local and immediate harms and benefits as between neighbours. For example, on this approach whether a wind turbine or a factory is a nuisance depends on the local and immediate harms and benefits and not on national or local policy concerning employment or the environment.[36]

Planning law allows for the co-ordination of activities by the use of zoning. This aims to optimise the use of property by bringing together mutually compatible activities in particular areas to reduce the detrimental effects of conflicting uses, and to enhance the synergistic effects of complementary uses. Courts cannot introduce planning or zoning as part of the law of nuisance under the standpoint limitation. This involves policy analysis, and it involves a co-ordinating scheme that would require adjustment by individuals for it to operate fairly. The closest the courts can get to this is the 'locality rule', according to which the activities that property owners should be expected to tolerate for the purposes of the law of nuisance depend on what is customary in the area. Where this amounts to a local

[34] See D Priel, 'Land Use Priorities and the Law of Nuisance' (2015) 39 *Melbourne University Law Review* 346; M Lee, 'The Public Interest in Private Nuisance: Collectives and Communities in Tort' (2014) 74 *Cambridge Law Journal* 329.

[35] A Beever, *The Law of Private Nuisance* (Hart, 2013).

[36] Cf GC Keating, 'Nuisance as a Strict Liability Wrong' (2011) 4 *Journal of Tort Law*.

convention, arguably it should be respected in the interests of distributive justice as the arrangement for use that the local population have arrived at. Some may regard this rule as unjust,[37] but in any case this seems to be its rationale.

Statutory Regulation and Compulsory Purchase

As discussed earlier in connection with contract and tort, under the standpoint limitation the common law may not be optimal as a matter of distributive justice. Free of the standpoint limitation, the legislature may be able to make law that better advances distributive justice. In contract and tort, statutory reform free of the standpoint limitation governs future interactions, and the law that has developed subject to the standpoint limitation applies with respect to interactions before the statutory reform. For property, however, past interactions – investments in property – generate continuing rights to benefit. This is why property law has a particular association with expectations.[38] Can the legislature simply cancel or curtail such continuing rights to benefit on the ground that they are not consistent with distributive justice free of the standpoint limitation? This may seem to undermine the standpoint limitation altogether, but if instead rights acquired under the standpoint limitation are immune to cancellation or curtailment, the ability of the legislature to promote distributive justice would be severely inhibited.

The issue arises with respect to the power of compulsory purchase for a public purpose by a public authority exercising a statutory power.[39] Where such a power is exercised, C is expropriated but is entitled to be compensated by the authority. Under the Lockean labour principle approach, such a power would seem illegitimate except in very narrow circumstances. It would be justified only where strictly necessary to uphold the system of property rights. The power seems justifiable on the suggested approach, however. It allows the authority to promote distributive justice by expropriation for a public purpose, but it also respects the standpoint limitation by allowing the right to compensation, even if C's right would not have been justified in the first place, free of the standpoint limitation. On the ordinary distributive justice approach, the legislature might be free to override the property right without compensation in such a case.

[37] S Steel, 'The Locality Rule in Private Nuisance' (2017) 76 *Cambridge Law Journal* 145.

[38] As discussed with reference to Bentham by Waldron (n 12) 53–56.

[39] See eg LS Underkuffler-Freund 'Takings and the Nature of Property' (1996) IX *Canadian Journal of Law and Jurisprudence* 161; L Weinar, 'The Concept of Property and the Takings Clause' (1997) 97 *Columbia Law Review* 1923.

11

Legal Reasoning in the Common Law

Introduction

Generally the law as established by precedent is sufficiently settled to be followed and applied without undue difficulty, but sometimes a judge has to exercise moral judgement to decide the law. The common law has been built up through such decisions. They amount to the law's authoritative determination of what justice requires. I have argued that the courts ought to develop the law to give effect to distributive justice subject to the standpoint limitation, and furthermore that this is generally, though not always, what they have done. In addition, I suggest in this chapter that common law legal reasoning constrains the judges to do this. I discuss two theories of the authority of a precedent, which I refer to as the individual rule approach and the holistic approach. I shall suggest that the holistic approach provides a better account of legal reasoning in the common law, and that it imports the standpoint limitation and remedial consistency into the common law.[1]

Law as Binding Rules

On the individual rule approach, a court makes law by authoritatively laying down a binding rule.[2] In adjudication, it either applies a rule previously laid down, or it formulates a new rule to apply. A later court is bound to apply the new rule, where the facts fall under it. The law is the aggregation of the binding rules previously laid down. There always remain gaps, where no rule previously laid down applies and there is no law. The courts make law 'interstitially' by laying down a new rule in a gap.

This straightforward account may appear to follow directly from the very idea of law built up through the authority of precedent, but the way in which legal reasoning operates in the common law differs markedly from what one would

[1] This chapter draws on P Jaffey, 'Authority in the Common Law' (2011) 36 *Journal of Legal Philosophy* 1; 'Two Ways to Understand the Common Law' (2017) 8 *Jurisprudence* 435; and 'Policy and Principle in Private Law' (2020) 11 *Jurisprudence* 387.

[2] J Raz, *The Authority of Law* (Clarendon Press, 1979) 183–84.

expect on this account, as various commentators have pointed out.[3] One problem concerns the concept of the 'ratio decidendi' or ratio or holding of a decision. This is what is authoritative in a decision – the contribution it makes to the law. On the individual rule approach, the ratio is the rule laid down by the court in making the decision.[4] This is difficult to reconcile with the way in which courts identify the ratio. It is often contentious what the ratio is.[5] A judge does not necessarily explicitly state the ratio in the judgment, and even if this is the case, the judge's statement of the ratio is not conclusive. Furthermore, on the individual rule approach the ratio of a case is dependent purely on the decision itself, and it is fixed from the time of the decision, but in practice the ratio of a case may emerge from the interpretation of a body of case law, with the implication that the ratios of different cases may be interdependent and that a ratio may be attributed to a case, as it has come to be understood, rather than simply found in it.

Another problem concerns analogical reasoning. Analogical reasoning is generally thought to be characteristic of the common law, but it is not easy to find a place for it on the individual rule approach. In analogical reasoning, the court compares the facts of the case it has to decide with the facts of a previous case, and if it considers them analogous – in other words, whatever differences there may be between the cases do not justify a different outcome – it decides the new case in the way that the previous one was decided. The rationale for analogical reasoning is contested.[6] Under the individual rule approach, a court respects a precedent by applying the rule it laid down, which does not involve analogical reasoning. Analogical reasoning may appear to have a role where there is a gap in the law, as a method of moral reasoning about the new rule that should be laid down. One might think of it as a way of extending an existing rule by a sort of extension of the authority of the previous decision. However, the court in the previous case weighed up all the considerations that it considered relevant in arriving at the rule it laid down. In effect, the previous court determined the range of cases that it considered analogous in its formulation of the rule. Beyond this, there is no reason for the court now to consider whether the new case is analogous, so far as deference to the authority of the previous decision is concerned. In the absence of binding authority, the new court should exercise its own moral judgement to determine the best rule for the situation.

[3] See eg AWB Simpson, 'The Common Law and Legal Theory' in *Oxford Essays in Jurisprudence, Second Series* (Oxford University Press, 1973); L Alexander and E Sherwin, *Demystifying Legal Reasoning* (Cambridge University Press, 2008) 49; M Martin, *Judging Positivism* (Hart, 2014) 35–36; H Hurd, 'Sovereignty in Silence' (1990) 99 *Yale Law Journal* 945, 947.

[4] Raz, *The Authority of Law* (n 2) 183–84.

[5] See eg W Twining and D Miers, *How to Do Things with Rules* (Cambridge University Press, 5th edn 2010) 306; RM Dworkin, *Taking Rights Seriously* (Duckworth, 1977) 337; F Schauer, 'Precedent' in A Marmor (ed), *The Routledge Companion to the Philosophy of Law* (Routledge, 2015).

[6] Raz, *The Authority of Law* (n 2) ch 10; N MacCormick, *Legal Reasoning and Legal Theory* (Oxford University Press, rev edn 1994) ch 7; GJ Postema, '*A Similibus ad Similia*: Analogical Thinking in Law' in D Edlin (ed), *Common Law Theory* (Cambridge University Press, 2007); MA Eisenberg, *The Nature of the Common Law* (Harvard University Press, 1988).

An alternative rationale is that analogical reasoning is justified as a matter of equivalent treatment. The argument is that, given how the previous case was decided, it would be unfair to the litigants in the current case if the decision were not made in an equivalent way. Thus the court should decide the current case in the equivalent way, even if, in its own independent judgement, it would have decided differently. But it is difficult to see what the value of equivalent treatment is, in itself. The court should aim for a just decision, either as determined by the previous court where the rule laid applies, or otherwise as determined by the current court. Aiming for equivalent treatment between cases, as a separate objective from justice, will merely allow an injustice to be extended more widely.[7]

Thus some proponents of the individual rule approach think that analogical reasoning does not have any genuine role in common law legal reasoning. It can only be understood as a sort of heuristic method that provides a starting point for the court in considering what rule might be appropriate to fill a gap.[8] This sceptical view of analogical reasoning is at odds with the conventional understanding of legal reasoning in the common law, which gives an important role to analogical reasoning.[9]

It is equally difficult to explain the practice of distinguishing under the individual rule approach. Under this practice, if a previous decision has laid down a rule that applies to the facts in a new case, but the court in the new case thinks that these facts are distinguishable from those of the previous case, it can limit the scope of the rule previously laid down to exclude the new case.[10] The implication is that a court can modify a rule previously laid down, simply because it takes a different view of what is just on the facts, and it seems impossible to reconcile this with the individual rule approach, which holds that the rule previously laid down is binding.

Like analogical reasoning and distinguishing, coherence reasoning is widely regarded as a characteristic feature of the common law.[11] There is controversy over how to understand coherence reasoning, but it certainly involves reasoning from a body of cases taken together, and the individual rule approach does not appear to allow for it. On the individual rule approach, rules laid down previously are conclusive and binding as law where they apply, and in developing the law a court is generally confined to gap filling, which it should do according to what is morally best for those circumstances. There is no room for moulding the law in the light of coherence across a body of cases.

[7] Alexander and Sherwin (n 3) 37–39, 66–88.

[8] Alexander and Sherwin (n 3) 86–87; Raz, *The Authority of Law* (n 2) 205–06.

[9] See eg A Burrows, 'In Defence of Unjust Enrichment' (2019) 78 *Cambridge Law Journal* 521.

[10] Raz, *The Authority of Law* (n 2) 183–89; HLA Hart, *The Concept of Law* 3rd edn (Clarendon Press, 2012) 134–35.

[11] See eg Postema (n 6); GJ Postema, 'Law's System: The Necessity of System in Common Law' [2014] *New Zealand Law Review* 69. MacCormick (n 6); A Fell, 'The Concept of Coherence in Australian Private Law' (2018) 41 *Melbourne University Law Review* 1160.

Under the individual rule approach, the law consists exclusively of rules. A rule is laid down in a decision, and a rule is applied to the facts of a case to determine the result. A rule is conclusive where it applies –that is to say, when the facts fall within the ambit of the rule. Where there is a gap, in formulating a new rule to apply the court can weigh up moral principles and other moral considerations. A principle is not conclusive but has weight and is taken into account in a balancing exercise.[12] The law consists only of legal rules, supplemented by moral principles and other moral considerations that are relevant in a gap.[13] There is no place for legal principles. A legal principle has authority or standing in the law derived from previous decisions because it has contributed to the justification of the rule adopted, but it has never been laid down as a rule and is not applied as a rule to determine the outcome of a case. However, there do seem to be legal principles in the common law.[14] The principle of agreement as the basis for contract law would appear to be a legal principle in this sense, and also the principles of negligence and private property as discussed in earlier chapters. Their authority arises not from having been laid down as a rule in a particular case, but from having been relied on explicitly or implicitly as a justifying principle over time in a series of decisions.

A legal principle is the justifying principle behind the body of rules that make up a doctrinal category and its associated cause of action, for example contract or negligence or private property. Where the law is unsettled, the issue in a particular case is whether the facts can be brought under a particular cause of action, and the law develops through the development of the elements of the cause of action. This makes sense if a cause of action is based on a legal principle, and the way in which the law develops depends on how the legal principle is interpreted. However, on the individual rule approach a doctrinal category or cause of action cannot work in this way. If the law consists simply of rules and there are no legal principles, the only way to understand a doctrinal category or cause of action is as a convenient label for a set of rules, and applying such a label cannot be relevant to what rules there are, or how they develop.

On the individual rule approach, the law has a binary character. There is a categorical distinction between pre-existing law in the form of legal rules previously laid down, and new law in the form of new rules devised for a gap, where there is no pre-existing law. In principle, it would seem to be important to be clear about which type of case is in issue, since the two types involve different forms of legal reasoning, but it is difficult to see any such hard and fast distinction in the law. The law may be described as settled or unsettled, but this is understood as a matter of degree rather than a categorical distinction, and furthermore an issue of unsettled law may be resolved not by formulating a new rule but by determining

[12] Dworkin (n 5) 22–28, 71–80.

[13] See generally Alexander and Sherwin (n 3) 88–103.

[14] In favour of legal principles: J Waldron, 'The Need for Legal Principles' (1997) 82 *Iowa Law Review* 857.

that it is governed by a rule previously laid down, once the ratio of the previous case is properly understood.

The declaratory theory of law is at the heart of the common law, and it reflects the fact that the common law does not have a binary character. A court always presents its decision as an application of pre-existing law, however unsettled the law may have been. Under the individual rule approach, the declaratory theory implies that a rule previously laid down is always available in the circumstances – in other words, it assumes a crude version of formalism.[15] On this basis, the declaratory theory has been described as a fairy tale.[16] In reality, the rule applied may be newly devised. It is said that a new rule is treated as part of the pre-existing law by way of a fiction, to avoid conveying the impression that the judges make new rules and apply them retrospectively.[17] On the individual rule approach it would surely be better for the courts to be explicit about when a decision is retrospective and when it is not and, even if retrospectivity is unavoidable, it might be possible sometimes to limit the retrospective effect of a decision to avoid unfairness.

Although the individual rule approach often seems to be assumed, in particular with respect to the authority of precedent (as considered further below), it is very difficult to reconcile it with the usual understanding of legal reasoning in the common law. It cannot explain what are widely taken to be characteristic features of common law legal reasoning – the ratio, analogical reasoning, distinguishing, coherence reasoning, legal principles, doctrinal categories and causes of action, and the declaratory theory of the law. One might infer that legal reasoning should change to be consistent with the individual rule approach, which would involve eliminating these characteristic features, though such a reform would involve a complete transformation of the common law.

The Holistic Approach

On the holistic approach, to arrive at a rule for a decision the court exercises its judgement to construct a body of rules to account for previous cases.[18] This involves coherence reasoning. Whereas coherence reasoning is incompatible with the individual rule approach, it is intrinsic to the holistic approach. In constructing rules that account for previous decisions, the court aims to be consistent across the law with respect to the justification of rules. Coherence reasoning involves looking behind the rules laid down to their justification. Rules that apply

[15] See ch 2.

[16] Lord Reid, 'The Judge as Law Maker' (1972) *Journal of the Society of Public Teachers of Law (New Series)* 22.

[17] *Kleinwort Benson v Lincoln City Council* [1992] 2 AC 349 per Lord Goff.

[18] Versions of the holistic approach have been adopted by eg R Dworkin, *Taking Rights Seriously* (n 5) ch 4 and *Law's Empire* (Fontana, 1986); MS Moore, 'Precedent, Induction, and Ethical Generalisation' in L Goldstein (ed), *Precedent in Law* (Clarendon Press, 1987); EJ Weinrib, *Corrective Justice* (Oxford University Press, 2012) ch 2; Postema, 'Law's System' (n 11).

in different situations are not directly inconsistent with each other, but they may reflect inconsistent judgements with respect to their justification.

On this approach, the rule formulated and applied in a previous case is not necessarily authoritative. Though the decision is conclusive as between the parties, the rule applied to decide the case is provisional so far as the law in general and subsequent courts are concerned.[19] What is binding in effect is the outcome of the case on its facts. This does not mean that a later court always has to start again to construct a body of rules. It can adopt a rule previously applied, or it can qualify or extend it, or it can devise a different rule that is consistent with the outcome in the case. In doing so it may consider different facts in the original judgment to be crucial or characterise them differently, with a view to accounting for other cases at the same time.

This is consistent with the way arguments about the ratio are conducted.[20] The ratio of a case, as the rule for which the case stands, is not fixed at the time of the decision, nor is it independent of other decisions. It becomes settled over time as a settled body of rules develop. This approach also explains 'distinguishing'. A court can distinguish an earlier decision by qualifying the rule, provided that it respects the outcome of the case on the facts. Similarly, a court can extend a rule by way of analogy, as part of the process of constructing a body of rules. Analogical reasoning and distinguishing are incompatible with the individual rule approach as discussed above, but under the holistic approach they are sound forms of reasoning from a previous decision, based on the assumption that the previous decision is correct as to the outcome on the facts, so that the later court should decide consistently with it if it can detect no moral difference. Coherence reasoning also provides a basis on which anomalous decisions – decisions that cannot be reconciled with a coherent account of the case law – can be isolated or overruled. Whereas the holistic approach allows for the law to evolve over time into a more coherent form without arbitrary and unnecessary distinctions in the law, the individual rule approach normally develops by way of gap filling, with increasingly detailed coverage, rather than by evolution. A court can overrule a decision only if the decision seems wrong considered in isolation.

The holistic approach involves the exercise of judgement as to what justice requires on the facts of the case to be decided and other cases, and through coherence reasoning it also implicitly draws on the judgement of other courts on different facts. It allows for 'bottom-up' reasoning through analogy and distinguishing from the facts of cases, and it also allows for 'top-down' reasoning in which the court draws on its judgement of moral principles and theory.

[19] As to the provisional character of common law rules see eg F Schauer, 'Is the Common Law Law?' (1989) 77 *California Law Review* 455 (1989); MA Eisenberg, *The Nature of the Common Law* (Harvard University Press, 1988) 65; SR Perry, 'Judicial Obligation, Precedent, and the Common Law' (1987) 7 *Oxford Journal of Legal Studies* 215.

[20] See Postema, 'Law's System' (n 11).

The holistic approach requires these considerations to be harmonised, at least as an ideal.[21]

The holistic approach allows for a legal principle as the justificatory principle behind a doctrinal category, and it is consistent with the way doctrinal categories and causes of action work and the way the law evolves through the evolution of the conditions for a cause of action. The holistic approach allows for legal principles to bring coherence to a body of case law. For example, Weinrib argues that the rules governing different aspects of the law of negligence should be coherent in the sense that in different contexts they should all reflect the same justification (on Weinrib's approach, corrective justice), for example with respect to the exclusion of policy considerations, the availability of remedies rather than sanctions, and the objective character of the law.[22] It was suggested earlier that the rules governing the various remedies that can be available in contract should be coherent in the sense that they should all reflect a version of the reliance theory, based on a particular understanding of the way in which the principle of agreement is given effect in contract law.[23]

Sometimes essentially the same issue has been resolved in different ways in different bodies of law, and by way of coherence reasoning the different bodies of law can be brought into alignment or assimilated. Important historical examples are the formation of a unified law of contract and a unified law of negligence out of disparate bodies of law. Coherence reasoning can also justify dividing a body of law by differentiating between issues that have been treated together but should in principle be treated separately. For example, I suggested earlier that, as recent developments show, the law of confidentiality, as traditionally understood, conflated the protection of a personal interest in privacy restricting the disclosure of personal information and the protection of a right of ownership of commercial information as property, which should be treated separately.[24]

The holistic approach is also consistent with the absence in the common law of two distinct stages concerned with pre-existing law and new law applied in gaps, as the individual rule approach requires. On the holistic approach, it is impossible to distinguish between pre-existing law and new law to apply in a gap. A decision always involves determining what is required by previous decisions, even though moral judgement may also be required. This is consistent with the declaratory theory of the common law. The judge formulates a rule but the rule is an

[21] They are harmonised through a 'reflective equilibrium'. Dworkin refers to 'theoretical ascent': see R Dworkin, 'In Praise of Theory' in *Justice in Robes* (Harvard University Press, 2008). See also Postema, 'Law's System' (n 11); K Mason, 'Do Top-Down and Bottom-Up Reasoning Ever Meet?' in E Bant and M Harding (eds), *Exploring Private Law* (Cambridge University Press, 2010); M Bryan, 'Justice Callinan's Judgements in Private Law: Story Telling, Legal Coherence and Corrective Justice' (2008) 27 *University of Queensland Law Journal* 29.

[22] EJ Weinrib, 'The Disintegration of Duty' in S Madden (ed), *Exploring Tort Law* (Cambridge University Press, 2005).

[23] See ch 3.

[24] See P Jaffey, 'Private Property and Intangibles' [2022] *Conveyancer and Property Lawyer* 47, as discussed in ch 9.

attempt to capture the law in the light of the cases rather than to make law where there is no law. This also means that decisions are not retrospective, and no fiction is involved in the declaratory theory. It may seem paradoxical that the law can develop by the exercise of moral judgement whilst not being retrospective, but this is the implication of the holistic approach. It is also how corrective justice and Dworkin's interpretative approach are understood.[25]

On the holistic approach, the law cannot be equated with a body of binding rules. The law is more in the nature of a particular authoritative account or version of morality or justice, which is captured for the time being in provisional rules through the holistic approach. The law can equally be expressed in terms of principles and rights, more particularly the bilateral rights of private law.[26]

Comparing the Two Approaches

There is support for both of the two approaches to the common law outlined above in the views of commentators. The holistic approach does seem to do better in accounting for common law legal reasoning as it is conventionally understood,[27] though some commentators doubt whether the broad coherence arguments and abstract theories permitted under the holistic approach are part of standard legal reasoning.[28] Coherence reasoning is liable to be controversial because the rationale for a body of rules may be obscure and contentious. For example, the theory of unjust enrichment holds that various parts of the law that were historically treated separately should be united to form a law of unjust enrichment, on the ground that they are all concerned with the same principle of unjust enrichment. The theory of unjust enrichment is inconsistent with both the analysis of contract law and the analysis of private property suggested in earlier chapters and in my view is misconceived, though it has been very influential in English law.[29] Disagreements of this sort can arise on any approach and the holistic approach would seem to provide the better way of accommodating and resolving them.

The holistic approach, and in particular these aspects of it, may be thought to lead to uncertainty in the law.[30] However, in making a comparison with the individual rule approach, it would be necessary to consider how common gaps in the law are, how predictable law-making in a gap is, how often rules are overruled, and how predictable overruling is. In addition, under the individual rule

[25] See Dworkin (n 5), esp ch 4; A Beever, *Rediscovering the Law of Negligence* (Hart, 2009) 3.

[26] Dworkin, *Taking Rights Seriously* (n 5) 22–28, 71–80; *Justice in Robes* (n 21) 234.

[27] See eg AWB Simpson, 'The Common Law and Legal Theory' in *Oxford Essays in Jurisprudence* Second Series (Oxford University Press, 1973); S Perry, 'Judicial Obligation, Precedent, and the Common Law' (1987) 7 *Oxford Journal of Legal Studies* 215, 234–39; Alexander and Sherwin (n 3) 49.

[28] See eg J Stapleton, *Three Essays on Torts* (Oxford University Press, 2021) 24–25. B Leiter, 'The Theory of Esoteric Law' University of Texas Law, Public Law Research Paper no 121, 3–4.

[29] See chs 3 and 10.

[30] Eg Leiter (n 28).

approach, because of the absence of coherence reasoning and legal principles, one might expect the law to be prone to become unduly complex and obscure.[31] Under the holistic approach, the law can develop into a body of rules that, although technically still provisional, because of cumulative support across the law is actually very stable. Placing undue emphasis on certainty of individual rules in the short term may be counterproductive.[32]

The holistic approach is thought to fall foul of a theoretical objection concerning the nature of authority. The decisions of the courts encapsulate the moral judgements of the judges as the law's authoritative determination of justice. They may not actually be sound, but it is definitive of the internal approach that their authority is accepted. As authoritative decisions they provide direction or guidance as to what justice requires. For an authority to be capable of providing direction or guidance, according to Raz it must be possible for people following the authority to know what it requires without the need for any moral judgement on their part.[33] This is because the authority functions by relieving individual subjects of the need to judge for themselves what justice requires of them in the circumstances, by providing individual subjects with an authoritative determination, which they ought to defer to, on the assumption that the judge is better able to determine what justice requires in the circumstances than the individual subject.[34] This means that the authority's guidance and direction must take the form of a rule. A rule is conclusive with respect to the situations it governs and so removes the need for moral judgement. It is necessary only to establish whether the rule applies in the circumstances.

This argument appears to rule out the holistic approach, under which the law does not consist of authoritative rules, and an exercise of moral judgement may be necessary to ascertain the law.[35] The implication is that if the judges are using the holistic approach, they are under a misconception if they understand it to involve treating precedents as authorities. But can it be right to say that an authority can never operate through the moral judgement of someone following it? Is it not possible that an authority could make decisions that provide genuine guidance even though these decisions can be followed only in a way that involves moral judgement? If S has good reason to think that A makes sound decisions in certain circumstances, and S decides in the same way as A when S judges that the circumstances are morally equivalent, could this not be a rational method for S to improve the chances that S's decisions will also be sound, even though moral judgement on the part of S is required? In any case, the common law seems to

[31] Eg Rudden describes the common law as having an innate 'hostility to abstract order': B Rudden, 'Torticles' (1991–92) 6/7 *Tulane Civil Law Forum* 105.

[32] Cf K Oliphant, 'Against Certainty in Tort Law' in GA Pitel et al (eds), *Tort Law: Challenging Orthodoxy* (Hart, 2013), discussing the incrementalist approach to negligence law, which seeks to establish certainty in the law in the face of uncertainty on underlying issues.

[33] See Raz, *The Authority of Law* (n 2); Raz, *The Morality of Freedom* (Clarendon Press, 1986) ch 3. See also Alexander and Sherwin (n 3) 88–103; Leiter (n 28) 3–4.

[34] Raz, *The Authority of Law* (n 2); Raz, *The Morality of Freedom* (n 33).

[35] Eg J Raz, 'The Relevance of Coherence' (1992) 72 *Boston University Law Review* 273.

follow the holistic approach, and it certainly gives the impression of providing genuine guidance.

Whereas on the individual rule approach a court has the authority to lay down a binding rule, under the holistic approach the authority of the court is to determine a just outcome on the facts. At the same time, it might be better to say that, rather than each court making a decision as a separate authority, as under the individual rule approach, the holistic approach recognises the courts as having collective authority, with the implication that to follow the authority of precedent a court must construct a body of rules that account for previous decisions collectively. On this understanding, analogical and coherence reasoning are not separate from authority, as they are under the individual rule approach (if they can be explained at all), but part of the process of drawing on the authority of previous decisions to establish the law. The advantage of the holistic approach would seem to be that by combining the judgements about justice of previous courts with its own, in the way that the holistic approach allows, the current court is more likely to arrive at a just rule.[36]

The Standpoint Limitation in the Common Law

For present purposes, a crucial feature of the holistic approach is that it imports the standpoint limitation into the law. On the holistic approach, the judge has to consider how to develop the law in a way that takes account of consistency in justification across the case law. Consistency in justification across cases depends on the assumption of the same background knowledge. To make a comparison between two sets of facts in analogical reasoning, it is necessary to assume this. Similarly, more generally, it must be assumed for the purpose of constructing rules to account for a body of decisions in coherence reasoning. Implicitly, there must be an assumption that decisions are justified relative to ordinary common knowledge. Courts cannot take account of expert knowledge or the possibility of introducing new conventions when they compare cases or draw on them collectively. Cases that are equivalent in the light of ordinary common knowledge might appear quite different if they were compared without this limitation. This is why a statutory regime, which is not subject to the standpoint limitation, may employ concepts and distinctions that are foreign to the common law, as is sometimes apparent from statutes that reform private law. It follows that the holistic approach implicitly incorporates the standpoint limitation. This may be why the courts normally adopt the standpoint limitation without referring to it explicitly. One might say that it is part of the adjudicative mindset, as it was put previously.[37] This implicit

[36] The implication is that coherence is not valuable for its own sake but as part of the process of doing justice. It is not necessary to find a separate rationale for coherence, eg 'integrity'. As to the possible such rationales, see Fell (n 11).

[37] See ch 6.

constraint may give rise to the illusion of a distinct type of justice applicable to private law as developed in the common law, as the corrective justice approach claims.

As discussed above, the common law adopts the declaratory theory of law. This is difficult to explain under the individual rule approach, because it implies that there is always an existing rule previously laid down that can be applied. The declaratory theory is consistent with the holistic approach, in the weaker sense that no decision about what the law is can be made free of the influence of previous decisions. Furthermore, under the holistic approach, by virtue of the standpoint limitation the rule applied is intended to reflect what is actually just as between the parties, in the sense of what can actually be morally required of them in the circumstances. The law is an authoritative version of justice in this sense, and in this sense the declaratory theory correctly describes the common law.

By contrast, the individual rule approach does not implicitly assume the standpoint limitation, and if a court recognised the standpoint limitation in laying down a new rule, it would have to do so explicitly as a separate constraint. In fact, commentators who support the individual rule approach have taken the view that judges should adopt the best rule for the circumstances, taking everything into account, which reflects the ordinary distributive justice approach, excluding the standpoint limitation.[38] A court should act just as the legislature should if it were legislating for the same circumstances, but without the requirement normally applicable to the legislature that the rule laid down applies only prospectively. This allows for the court to draw on policy reasoning and policy analysis in making law, as a legislature can do. It means that the new rule may be unfairly retrospective because it could be a rule that it might be impossible to anticipate, or impossible or unfairly burdensome to comply with. Arguably this is the position where the courts have used policy reasoning to determine whether there is a duty of care in negligence.

Under the holistic approach and the standpoint limitation, the difference between case law and statute reflects the different forms of authority of the courts and the legislature. The authority of the courts arises from their competence at determining the law, which may involve moral judgement of the sort that ordinary people also have to make, as to the balance of harms and benefits assessed in the light of ordinary common knowledge. By contrast, the authority of the legislature is based on its democratic legitimacy, and its authority extends to legislating to promote distributive justice in general. Under the individual rule approach, by contrast, without the standpoint limitation the judges are liable to exceed their legitimate authority by legislating in the same way as a legislature, but without democratic legitimacy.

[38] See J Raz, 'Facing Up: A Reply (1989) 12 *Southern California Law Review* 1153; T Endicott, 'Adjudication and the Law' (2007) 27 *Oxford Journal of Legal Studies* 311. According to Raz, the authority of a court arises, as for a legislature, from the fact that it has expert knowledge and is in a position to lay down co-ordinating conventions: see Raz, *The Morality of Freedom* (n 33) 30, 48–50.

In modern times, the common law has increasingly been modified or supplemented or replaced by statute. Some commentators argue that a theory of private law should encompass both case law and statute, and legal reasoning should be able to integrate case law and statute into a single coherent body of law.[39] By contrast, the corrective justice approach aims to account only for the common law. It accepts that statute can legitimately be a matter of distributive justice, whereas it holds that the common law is a matter of corrective justice, and the implication is that the common law cannot be integrated with statute into a coherent body of law.

The extent to which judges can draw on a statute in developing the common law is controversial. It is difficult to see how it can be justified to apply the policy behind a statute beyond the rules it lays down. The legal effect of a statute is surely exhausted by these rules, as for the rule laid down in a case under the individual rule approach. Statute cannot be integrated into the common law using analogical and coherence reasoning in the way that case law on its own can be integrated on the holistic approach. However, it is possible to distinguish between two types of statutory provision, as suggested previously.[40] A statute may be designed free of the standpoint limitation and based on policy reasoning and policy analysis. Judges purporting to draw on the policy of such a statute in developing the common law exercise their own judgement about what the policy is and how to apply it, so that in reality they exercise the authority of the legislature to make law, free of the standpoint limitation, without democratic legitimacy.

Sometimes instead a statute is intended to correct what is deemed to be an error in the common law, rather than going beyond the standpoint limitation to do what the common law cannot do.[41] Such a statute can be integrated into the common law, at least in the sense that the effect of the statute is to substitute for the erroneous case or line of cases and their influence in the law.[42] This broadly reflects Atiyah's suggestion that statute and common law can be integrated where the statute is largely in the province of the common law, and where the statute is a reform of a common law rule regarded as obsolete or unjust.[43] In fact, private law statutes are commonly of this type, for example the Frustrated Contracts Act 1943 and the Law Reform (Contributory Negligence) Act 1945.

[39] See eg Fell (n 11); R Grantham and D Jensen, 'Coherence in the Age of Statutes' (2016) 42 *Monash University Law Review* 360.

[40] See ch 6.

[41] Similarly where the statute consolidates the common law or builds on it in the way that the courts might have done. See PS Atiyah, 'Common Law and Statute Law' (1985) 48 *Modern Law Review* 1; J Beatson, 'Has the Common Law a Future?' (1997) 56 *Cambridge Law Journal* 291; A Burrows, *Thinking About Statutes* (Cambridge University Press, 2018), 'Lecture 2 – The Interaction between Common Law and Statute'. Codification may go beyond consolidation or restatement: see P Giliker, 'Codification, Consolidation, Restatement? How best to systematise the modern law of tort' (2021) 70 *International & Comparative Law Quarterly* 271.

[42] A possible example is the common law construction of exemption clauses following the enactment of the Unfair Contract Terms Act 1977, as considered in *George Michell v Finney Lock Seeds* [1983] 2 AC 803, as discussed by Atiyah (n 41) 23. See also Burrows (n 41) 51–56.

[43] Atiyah (n 41); Beatson (n 41) 311.

Remedial Consistency in the Common Law

Under EAL, although there are bilateral legal rights, they are a device for protecting what are really public rights and duties. C has a power to impose a sanction on D to advance the public interest. This means that there is no room for a requirement of remedial consistency linking primary rights to remedial rights and remedies. A sanction does not represent a version of the primary right.

Under the standpoint limitation, however, there are bilateral moral rights and remedies as between the parties to an interaction, and the requirement of remedial consistency applies, linking the remedial right to the primary right. The holistic approach, by introducing the standpoint limitation, also introduces bilateral rights and the requirement of remedial consistency. By contrast, under the individual rule approach, which need not incorporate the standpoint limitation, one cannot assume that there are bilateral rights or that remedial consistency applies. The individual rule approach is compatible with public rights and duties enforced by sanctions.

12

How to Understand Private Law

The two leading schools of thought in private law are the distributive justice approach and the corrective justice approach. Distributive justice – justice with respect to interests in benefits and harms across society – applies in principle to the interactions governed by private law, such as accidents, transfers of property, and the making and performing of contracts. The standard example of the distributive justice approach is the economic analysis of law. When the legislature legislates with respect to these interactions, in principle it aims to promote distributive justice (as it understands it). However, the law that the legislature makes for interactions is often quite different in character from private law as it has developed at common law, and the distributive justice approach cannot plausibly account for this traditional form of private law.

It is not just that the common law cannot produce the types of scheme that can be created by legislation in pursuit of distributive justice, such as accident compensation funds, allocation of goods and services by public authorities, or the public ownership of resources. In addition, the distributive justice approach cannot provide a plausible account of the characteristic features of traditional private law, in particular its bilateral relations, its use of remedies rather than sanctions, and the way in which private law focuses principally on the particular interaction and its immediate effects on the parties involved and not the wider consequences for others and society. This weakness of the distributive justice approach in accounting for the common law is the basis for a powerful critique in the corrective justice literature. The critique gains support from the way the law has developed where the distributive justice approach has been influential, for example through policy reasoning in negligence. Here, as a result of the focus on public purposes such as the reduction of loss through accidents or the alleviation of hardship caused by accidents, the law appears to have become quite inapt to do justice between the two parties.

Proponents of the corrective justice approach argue that private law should be understood instead exclusively in terms of the basic liberty rights of parties to an interaction, which directly bind other parties to the interaction and exclude other considerations in determining the law. This approach can explain the bilateral relations and remedies of private law and the focus on the interaction and its immediate effects, but it fails to explain certain features of traditional private law. For example, it does not explain why private law does often take account of some considerations that go well beyond the liberty rights of the parties to the interaction, or why private law is often (notwithstanding the orthodox language of private law) not genuinely concerned with wrongdoing.

More importantly, the corrective justice literature has not managed to provide a convincing account of how corrective justice relates to distributive justice. The corrective justice approach is said to apply to interactions, because, so far as the common law is concerned, corrective justice represents the justice of the interaction. This is why, it is said, considerations of distributive justice should be excluded from private law, as it has developed at common law. At the same time, however, it is acknowledged that the legislature is right to draw on distributive justice when it makes provision for the same interaction by statute. This apparent inconsistency is addressed in the literature, but it seems to me to be an insuperable problem for the corrective justice approach.

It is sometimes said that distributive justice is relevant only to the legislature and other institutions, which are responsible for implementing it. However, distributive justice also makes demands directly of individuals, insofar as it is possible for individuals to respond to distributive justice in the circumstances they are in, given what they can be expected to know and do. I have argued that private law is based on distributive justice as it affect individuals with respect to interactions, or, as I propose, distributive justice assessed relative to ordinary common knowledge. When a court develops private law through adjudication, it formulates a rule based on justice in this sense, because it has to apply a rule that represents a just resolution of the dispute between the parties. The courts apply distributive justice from the standpoint of ordinary people, or under the standpoint limitation. Under the standpoint limitation, the courts do not draw on expert knowledge or policy analysis or make law in pursuit of public purposes, and they do not construct regimes designed to achieve social co-ordination. I have argued that this approach produces a body of law that looks very much like traditional private law. In this respect it does better than the corrective justice approach.

On this approach, negligence is not based on a moral duty owed by D to C, and C's correlative right, that D act with due care not to infringe C's right against interference, without regard for the interests of others or the public interest. Nor does negligence have the rationale of advancing public purposes such as reducing accident losses or alleviating hardship or need from accidents by spreading losses. A claim in negligence arises from a fair allocation of the risk of loss as between C and D, assessed relative to ordinary common knowledge at the time of the interaction. Similarly, the justification for enforcing agreements in contract is not simply that a promisor has a power, by making a promise, to undertake a duty to the promisee, which is independent of the public interest or the interests of others. Nor is it that the enforcement of agreements serves the public interest by maintaining the practice of contracting and promoting the exchange of benefits by contract. The justification is the value of the mutually beneficial exchange between the two parties on the agreed terms, considered in isolation from contracting in general. Finally, property rights in the common law are not justified on the basis of a Lockean labour principle that creates a property right in things, such as land and goods or intangibles such as money or inventions, that automatically prevails over the interests of everyone else and the public interest. Nor are they based on a distributive justice regime that governs the distribution across society of rights of control and use of such things. They are based on a private property principle that gives a right to the benefit of a thing to someone who has invested in it, for example by making, acquiring or using it, as a matter of distributive justice but independently of the societal distribution.

On this approach, private law is normally concerned with C's right that D bear the risk of loss under an allocation of risk, or C's right against D (and others) to the benefit of an object of property. These primary rights generally give rise respectively to claims for compensation for loss and claims for restitution of property. They are not rights correlated with duties in the ordinary sense, that is to say they are not primary duty relations but primary liability relations. The basis for C's remedial right or claim relative to the primary right is the requirement of remedial consistency – consistency with respect to the justification for the primary right – not a principle of responsibility for wrongdoing.

I have also argued that the common law employs the holistic approach to precedent and legal reasoning. This is consistent with certain characteristic features of private law, such as doctrinal categories, analogical and coherence reasoning, and the declaratory theory of the common law. Furthermore, the holistic approach imports the standpoint limitation and remedial consistency automatically into the common law.

The legislature can legislate free of the standpoint limitation. It can draw on expert knowledge and policy analysis to promote public purposes and construct co-ordinating schemes to advance distributive justice in ways not open to the common law. It can provide a superior form of private law, or replace private law. One might say that whether and how the legislature should reform or replace private law is the most important question about it. Nevertheless, this is not relevant to the common law development of private law, and it does not detract from the fact that private law as it developed in the common law has, in its own way, a sound basis in justice.

The approach I suggest is a moral theory of private law, that is to say it is about what justice requires, in general terms, as between individuals with respect to interactions in the absence of legislation, and accordingly how the courts ought to develop the common law. I also suggest that ordinary legal reasoning incorporates this approach into the common law, and that, on the whole though not always, this is how the courts have developed the common law, so that for the most part it accounts well for the common law.

INDEX

www.ingramcontent.com/pod-product-compliance
Ingram Content Group UK Ltd.
Pitfield, Milton Keynes, MK11 3LW, UK
UKHW020819290926
15470UKWH00003B/1253

9 781509 953882